"Peterson has composed for us a beau. phonic poem in three movements. As a seasoned Lutheran theologian whose work is a prayer for the unity of a divided church in a world yearning for the spiritual life, she writes a balanced-yet-engaging symphony in an ecumenical and missional key. Under the grand theme of the Holy Spirit as our life giver, companion, and empowerer, the composer joyfully invites us to participate in the transformative work of the Spirit for us, in us, and through us. Bravo! Encore!"

—**Leopoldo A. Sánchez M.**, Center for Hispanic Studies, Concordia Seminary

"Finally! Here is a book that corrects longstanding bilateral lacunae in pneumatology. *The Holy Spirit in the Christian Life* has theological breadth and depth as well as pastoral and practical applications. Not only does it adroitly and incisively address existing theological lacunae in the Reformed and Lutheran traditions regarding pneumatology and provide serious engagement of developing Pentecostal pneumatologies; it is also well-written, making it both instructive and enjoyable. With Peterson's personable style and careful scholarship, this text is a must-read. Definitely recommended!"

—**Tony Richie**, Pentecostal Theological Seminary

"In this wonderful book, Peterson brings together biblical and theological resources on the Holy Spirit. Grounding herself within classic Reformation understandings of the Spirit's person and work, rooted in the Word and sacrament, she also attends to contemporary spiritual expressions—from the Pentecostal and charismatic to those considered 'spiritual but not religious.' I highly recommend this book for use in colleges, seminaries, and congregations and to anyone interested in the work of the Holy Spirit in our time."

—**Lois Malcolm**, Luther Seminary

"An exquisite pneumatological feast. A rare combination of profound theological learning, mature pastoral sensitivity, and keen religio-cultural analysis. Drawing widely from Lutheran resources, in dialogue with emerging Pentecostal theologies of the Spirit, and in consultation with the best of the pneumatological reservoir of ecumenical theology, Peterson establishes her fame as the leading American Lutheran pneumatologist. *The Holy Spirit in the Christian Life* is a must-read not only for mainstream Protestants but also for Pentecostals and charismatics—and everyone who wishes to learn more about a fresh experience of the divine Spirit."

—**Veli-Matti Kärkkäinen**, Fuller Theological Seminary and University of Helsinki

"Peterson's book is a welcome contribution to conversations about the Holy Spirit. She brings her reflections to bear upon our daily engagements with the world. Peterson has done us a service by focusing on God's activity in and through us, speaking of the Spirit's work in and after justification. Her approach helps us to articulate our experiences of the Spirit in trusting ways."

—**Nelson Rivera**, Moravian Theological Seminary

The
HOLY SPIRIT
in the
CHRISTIAN LIFE

THE SPIRIT'S WORK FOR, IN, AND THROUGH US

CHERYL M. PETERSON

Baker Academic
a division of Baker Publishing Group
Grand Rapids, Michigan

© 2024 by Cheryl M. Peterson

Published by Baker Academic
a division of Baker Publishing Group
Grand Rapids, Michigan
BakerAcademic.com

Printed in the United States of America

Library of Congress Cataloging-in-Publication Data
Names: Peterson, Cheryl M., author.
Title: The Holy Spirit in the Christian life : the spirit's work for, in, and through us / Cheryl M. Peterson.
Description: Grand Rapids, Michigan : Baker Academic, a division of Baker Publishing Group, [2024] | Includes bibliographical references and indexes.
Identifiers: LCCN 2023046015 | ISBN 9781540963925 (paperback) | ISBN 9781540967336 (casebound) | ISBN 9781493444557 (ebook) | ISBN 9781493444564 (pdf)
Subjects: LCSH: Holy Spirit. | Christian life.
Classification: LCC BT121.3 .P475 2024 | DDC 231/.3—dc23/eng/20231130
LC record available at https://lccn.loc.gov/2023046015

Baker Publishing Group publications use paper produced from sustainable forestry practices and post-consumer waste whenever possible.

24 25 26 27 28 29 30   7 6 5 4 3 2 1

For my colleagues on the
International Lutheran-Pentecostal Dialogue
(2016–22)

CONTENTS

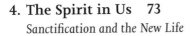

Acknowledgments

In many ways, this book is a natural outgrowth of my first book, a work on ecclesiology starting with the Spirit.[1] I am indebted to my doctoral advisor at Marquette University, D. Lyle Dabney, for initially putting me on this path and for helping me see the significant role that pneumatology can play in moving the church past historic theological impasses.

I want to thank my colleagues in the global communion that is the Lutheran World Federation for continuing to inspire my theological attention to the person and work of the Holy Spirit: from those I met at the 2009 theological seminar in Augsburg, Germany, "Theology in the Life of Lutheran Churches: Transformative Perspectives and Practices Today," to those I met at the 2019 seminar in Addis Ababa, Ethiopia, "I Believe in the Holy Spirit," and everyone in between. In this regard, I want to acknowledge especially those colleagues with whom I was privileged to serve on the first round of the International Lutheran-Pentecostal Dialogue (2016–22): Walter Altmann, Anne Burghardt, Tamás Gáncs, Kaisamari Hintikka, Veli-Matti Kärkkäinen, Dirk Lange, Opoku Onyinah, Jean-Daniel Plüss, Cecil Robeck, Wilfred John Samuel, Sarah Hinlicky Wilson, Gani Wiyono, Yee Tham Wan, Olga Zaprometova, and Johannes Zeiler.

I am deeply grateful for my Pentecostal classmates from my doctoral program at Marquette University, especially for their warm welcome years later into the Society for Pentecostal Studies (SPS), at which I first presented a paper in 2013, and for all the Pentecostal and charismatic scholars I have since encountered through this academic society. They have all enriched my theology in so many

---

1. Cheryl M. Peterson, *Who Is the Church? An Ecclesiology for the Twenty-First Century* (Minneapolis: Fortress, 2013).

significant ways in the past ten years, and I look forward to many more rich conversations in the years to come. Many of the chapters in this book began as paper presentations at SPS annual meetings.

I am particularly grateful to those Pentecostal and Lutheran scholarly colleagues who graciously read individual chapters and offered helpful, critical feedback: Lisa E. Dahill, Andrew K. Gabriel, Lois Malcolm, Leopoldo A. Sánchez M., Joy Schroeder, Christopher A. Stephenson, Lisa P. Stephenson, Steven M. Studebaker, Sarah Hinlicky Wilson, and Johannes Zeiler. I am appreciative of those who attended the 2021 Theologians of Ohio (TheOh) conference for their questions and comments on my presentation of an early version of chapter 2.

I also want to thank all the students at Trinity Lutheran Seminary I had the privilege of teaching over the past eighteen years, whose questions and contributions to class discussions helped me sharpen my thinking about the person and work of the Holy Spirit.

I thank my acquisitions editors at Baker Academic for their enthusiastic support of this project: David Nelson, who brought the proposal to the Baker editorial team, and Anna Gissing, who guided the manuscript through to completion with patience and encouragement. I am grateful to my amazing project editor at Baker, Alex DeMarco, and his team of copyeditors and proofreaders for their careful reading, questions, clarifications, and suggested revisions, all of which significantly improved the final text in many ways. Any remaining errors are my own.

I first conceived this project during a one-year sabbatical in 2012–13, granted by the Trinity Lutheran Seminary board of directors. Much of the work on this book was completed during my subsequent sabbatical (2021–22), for which I offer my thanks to the Capital University board of trustees and the Capital University faculty development committee.

Writing is a solo activity, but I was usually more productive when I had colleagues to write alongside of. My profound thanks to Nita Sweeney and the women of Writeth-On, with whom I spent several weekends over the past several years working on this project; to the W-4 (Wonderful Women Who Write)—Dikiea Elery, Denise Rector, Joy Schroeder, and Rachel Wrenn—whose weekly encouragement helped me get to the finish line; and, most of all, to Joy Schroeder, who for the past ten years was my most faithful writing companion. Our regular parallel writing sessions helped to keep me focused and on task. I remain grateful for her ongoing collegiality and friendship.

As this book came to completion, my husband, Chuck, and I found ourselves in major transitions. We moved to Dubuque, Iowa—I, from Columbus, Ohio, and he, from Pematangsiantar, Indonesia—for new personal and professional opportunities. I was starting as the new academic dean at Wartburg Theological Seminary, and Chuck was beginning a new call as pastor of St. John's Lutheran Church. Above all, I am grateful for his love and support, which has kept me grounded through it all.

Introduction

While Apollos was in Corinth, Paul passed through the interior regions and came to Ephesus, where he found some disciples. He said to them, "Did you receive the Holy Spirit when you became believers?" They replied, "No, we have not even heard that there is a Holy Spirit."

Acts 19:1–2

My theological interest in pneumatology dates to my days as a PhD student at Marquette University. Until then I had not spent a lot of time thinking about the person and work of the Holy Spirit in my pastoral ministry and theological studies. My dissertation director, D. Lyle Dabney (himself a student of Jürgen Moltmann), convinced me that the best methodological approach for writing about ecclesiology was to "start with the Spirit."[1] I subsequently discovered that Lutheran pneumatology was not a rich field in and of itself.[2]

Although trinitarian in framework, Lutheran theology historically has been marked by a strong christological orientation that grounds the "chief article of the faith," justification: human beings are justified by grace, through faith, on account of Christ, apart from works of the law.[3] Lutheran theologians such as Gerhard Forde spent their careers protecting the doctrine of justification from

1. I propose an ecclesiology of the "third article"—that is, I "start with the Holy Spirit," in *Who Is the Church? An Ecclesiology for the Twenty-First Century* (Minneapolis: Fortress, 2013), which is based on the dissertation.

2. To date, the only full-length work on Luther's pneumatology remains Regin Prenter, *Spiritus Creator: Luther's Concept of the Holy Spirit*, trans. John M. Jensen (Philadelphia: Muhlenberg Press, 1953).

3. Augsburg Confession, art. 4, in *The Book of Concord: The Confessions of the Evangelical Lutheran Church*, ed. Robert Kolb and Timothy J. Wengert (Minneapolis: Fortress, 2000), 38–39. The Augsburg Confession will hereafter be cited as CA (this traditional acronym is based on the

xiii

any hint or suggestion of human contribution or interference, keeping the focus solely on what God has done for humanity through the death and resurrection of Jesus Christ. This strong christological focus often left little room for pneumatology, although as Sarah Hinlicky Wilson correctly points out, justification properly belongs in the third article, rather than the second, "being a doctrine primarily about the Spirit and the Spirit's work."[4]

Where the historical documents of the Lutheran churches (the Lutheran Confessions) do refer to the Spirit, it is almost always in relation to the doctrine of justification and related topics. However, there is no one specific article devoted exclusively to the person and work of the Holy Spirit in the Augsburg Confession or its Apology, or in the Smalcald Articles, or in the Formula of Concord (Epitome and Solid Declaration).[5] The most extended treatment of the Holy Spirit in the Lutheran Confessions appears in Luther's Large Catechism, in his explanation of the Third Article of the Apostles' Creed, where he addresses what it means to be "made holy," although even here the main focus is on the Spirit's role in justification. The work of the Spirit is understood primarily in terms of making available to the believer salvation won by Christ on the cross, whereby the Spirit subjectively applies the benefits of Christ to individuals by bringing them to and sustaining them in faith.[6]

In addressing this work of the Spirit, the Lutheran Confessions repeatedly raise two concerns. First, the Holy Spirit itself is a gift that creates both the faith that justifies and the good works that result from justification in the life of the believer. In contrast to their Roman opponents, the Reformers stressed that free will and good works did not contribute to the reception of grace; grace is an unmerited gift that involves no human cooperation in its reception. The underlying concern is the unconditional character of the gift of God's grace: grace is given freely "on account of Christ's sake,"[7] without any human response, work, or preparation; and this grace is received by faith, or trust in the promise of God, which itself is a gift from God. Second, the Holy Spirit does not work

---

Latin title *Confessio Augustana*), and page references to *The Book of Concord* will be supplied with the abbreviation BC.

4. Sarah Hinlicky Wilson, "Dialogue: Spiritless Lutheranism, Fatherless Pentecostalism, and a Proposed Baptismal-Christological Corrective," *Pneuma* 34 (2012): 418.

5. The article that comes closest is CA 5, on the office of preaching, which addresses the means through which the Holy Spirit works. See BC, 40–41. This article is discussed in chap. 6.

6. E.g., Eilert Herms, *Luthers Auslegung des Dritten Artikels* (Tübingen: Mohr Siebeck, 1987); and Jeffrey Mann, "Luther and the Holy Spirit: Why Pneumatology Still Matters," *Currents in Theology and Mission* 34, no. 2 (2007): 111–16.

7. CA 4, in BC, 38.

apart from external means, by which the Reformers meant the Word (especially in the kerygma, or proclamation)[8] and the sacraments of Holy Baptism and the Eucharist. This teaching was emphasized against the so-called enthusiasts such as Andreas von Karlstadt, who insisted that God spoke directly, apart from any mediating human speech or sacraments.[9]

Some contemporary theologians have charged the Reformers with subsuming the Holy Spirit's work under Christology by limiting it to the present application of the past event of the cross and resurrection in the life of the individual believer.[10] The insistence that the Spirit works only through the external means of Word and Sacrament is viewed as unnecessarily restrictive, hierarchical, and even unbiblical. A significant exception among mainline Protestants in this regard is, of course, the Methodists, who are rooted in the Wesleyan tradition with its concern for renewal and transformation, at once both personal and social. Churches with Wesleyan origins historically lay claim to a richer engagement with the work of the Spirit, seen in revival and holiness movements of the nineteenth and early twentieth centuries, which in turn gave shape to one of the major branches of the Pentecostal movement.[11] However, for many mainline Protestants, especially Lutherans in the Northern Hemisphere, pneumatology can still seem like a foreign land yet fully to be explored.[12]

Twentieth-Century Pneumatological Renaissance

Some Protestant theologians began to explore this terrain in the mid- to late twentieth century. This gave rise to a new pneumatological paradigm that began

8. Later Lutherans and Reformed theologians would focus more on the written Scriptures and the Spirit's inspiration of the written Word.

9. See, e.g., Martin Luther, The Smalcald Articles, 3.8.3, in BC, 322. This point is discussed in more detail in chap. 2.

10. D. Lyle Dabney, "Naming the Spirit: Toward a Pneumatology of the Cross," in *Starting with the Spirit*, ed. Stephen Pickard and Gordon Preece (Adelaide: Australian Theological Forum, 2001), 32–33.

11. Major Pentecostal churches with Wesleyan/holiness roots include the Church of God (Cleveland, TN), the Church of God in Christ, and the International Holiness Pentecostal Church. The other two major branches of the Pentecostal movement that originated from the Azusa Street Revival are Finished Work Pentecostals (e.g., Assemblies of God) and Oneness Pentecostals (e.g., United Pentecostal Church). For a brief description of each, see https://www.oikoumene.org /church-families/pentecostal-churches.

12. As we will see, Lutherans in the Southern Hemisphere do not have the same nervousness about the Holy Spirit that many North American and European Lutherans do. From conversations I have had with Lutheran church leaders from the Global South, however, there is still an eagerness for more theological treatments of pneumatology from a specifically Lutheran perspective.

not with the Spirit's work as relating to Christ and the promise of salvation as mediated by the church or the Word but with the Spirit's work in all forms of life—indeed, in creation itself. In this schema, the Spirit is, as Mary Grey puts it, "the depth principle of life—human and non-human," the vitality and energy that is at the source of all life and wholeness.[13]

This renewed theological attention to the Spirit, ironically, can be traced to Karl Barth in two respects. On the one hand, interest in pneumatology correlated with the revival of trinitarian theology that began with Barth. On the other hand, it also emerged in reaction to Barth's theology of the Word, which seemed to have little room for human experience as a source for theology. In the pioneering volume *The Spirit of Life*, Reformed theologian Jürgen Moltmann outlines a robust trinitarian theology of the Spirit.[14] Moltmann takes aim at the false alternative between divine revelation and human experience and explores the Holy Spirit as the giver of life in ways that reach beyond the traditional categories of justification and sanctification—and for that matter, beyond only human flourishing. Moltmann's book heralded a new paradigm for pneumatology in the West that he claimed was beginning to take shape but had not yet fully emerged. Molly Marshall concurs: "Moltmann is right when he adds that we are witnessing a transition from an anthropocentric to a holistic pneumatology, one that embraces the whole of creation and recognizes in the Spirit the symbol of wholeness, relatedness, energy and life."[15] This new paradigm shifts the focus from the individual as the locus of the Spirit's activity and from the Spirit's work specifically in faith and sanctification (often described in terms of "resisting the flesh," where "flesh" is understood in dualistic terms that are body-negative) to the whole cosmos as the locus of the Spirit's activity, an activity that has as its aim the renewal of all creation. To be fair, even as Moltmann broadens the horizon cosmically, he also addresses the traditional questions in Christian theology about the Spirit's work in faith and sanctification. However, in the thirty years since this book was written, the landscape has changed significantly, especially with the emergence of new generations of Pentecostal and charismatic theologians who

13. Mary C. Grey, *Sacred Longings: The Ecological Spirit and Global Culture* (Minneapolis: Fortress, 2004), 109.

14. Jürgen Moltmann, *The Spirit of Life: A Universal Affirmation*, trans. Margaret Kohl (Minneapolis: Fortress, 1992).

15. Molly Marshall, *Joining the Dance: A Theology of the Spirit* (King of Prussia, PA: Judson Press, 2003), 5.

offer fresh perspectives on the person and work of the Spirit in the Christian life.[16]

The Holy Spirit in the Christian Life

The past thirty years have seen a fuller emergence of this paradigm, with several theologians developing and reenvisioning pneumatology in exciting and provocative directions by expanding the work of the Spirit well beyond the realm of redemption in the individual believer and the church. Some examples include social and political liberation,[17] science and evolutionary theory,[18] world religions,[19] trauma theory,[20] and ecology.[21]

Far fewer theological books have been written of late by mainline theologians that examine the person and work of the Holy Spirit in the Christian life in view of the fresh perspectives offered in this paradigm, specifically the renewed focus on the Spirit as the giver of life and agent of transformation. A notable exception is the work of Robert Davis Hughes III, an Anglican theologian. His magnum opus, *Beloved Dust*,[22] examines the transforming work of the Spirit in three movements, or "tides," in the Christian life: conversion, transfiguration, and glorification. While his *Beloved Dust* has been characterized by some as a

16. While Moltmann acknowledges the emergence of these new perspectives in this book, it was not until after the book was published that he directly engaged Pentecostal theology. See, e.g., Jürgen Moltmann, "A Pentecostal Theology of Life," trans. Frank D. Macchia, *Journal of Pentecostal Theology* 4, no. 9 (October 1996): 3–15. This essay followed a special issue of the *Journal of Pentecostal Theology* 2, no. 4 (1994), offering reviews of *Spirit of Life* from Pentecostal theologians from around the globe, to which Moltmann responded. However, the fruit of this dialogue seems not to have gone outside Pentecostal theological circles.

17. Gloria L. Schaab, *Liberating Pneumatologies: Spirit Set Free* (New York: Crossroad, 2021); and Leonardo Boff, *Come, Holy Spirit: Inner Fire, Giver of Life, Comforter of the Poor*, trans. Margaret Wilde (Maryknoll, NY: Orbis Books, 2015).

18. Jan-Olav Henriksen, *Life, Love, and Hope: God and Human Experience* (Grand Rapids: Eerdmans, 2014).

19. Kirsteen Kim, *The Holy Spirit in the World: Global Conversations* (Maryknoll, NY: Orbis Books, 2007); Amos Yong, *Beyond the Impasse: Toward a Pneumatological Theology of Religions* (Grand Rapids: Baker Academic, 2003); Grace Ji-Sun Kim, *The Holy Spirit, Chi, and the Other: A Model of Global and Intercultural Pneumatology* (New York: Palgrave Macmillan, 2011); and Veli-Matti Kärkkäinen, *A Constructive Christian Theology for the Pluralistic World*, vol. 4, *Spirit and Salvation* (Grand Rapids: Eerdmans, 2016).

20. Shelly Rambo, *Spirit and Trauma: A Theology of Remaining* (Louisville: Westminster John Knox, 2010).

21. Mark I. Wallace, *When God Was a Bird: Christianity, Animism, and the Re-enchantment of the World* (New York: Fordham University Press, 2018).

22. Robert Davis Hughes III, *Beloved Dust: Tides of the Spirit in the Christian Life* (New York: Continuum, 2008).

work in spirituality, it is in fact a theological treatment of the Spirit's work in the Christian life (what he calls spiritual theology), with significant attention to the person of the Spirit. Hughes and I share a concern that the Spirit be the subject of this theological exploration. We are both trinitarian in our theological framework and are equally concerned with the Spirit as agent of transformation.

The present work differs in several ways from Hughes's treatment. While I also address the movement of the Spirit in the Christian life, I approach the question more directly, from the framework of pneumatology rather than theological anthropology. Hughes brings a strong focus on the human side of the equation through an engagement with behavioral science and psychology and by delving into questions of moral theology. A second difference relates to how each of us frames the Spirit's movement in the Christian life. As an Anglican, Hughes unsurprisingly does not frame his exploration in terms of Reformation categories or concerns. His three "tides"—conversion, transfiguration, and glorification—reflect his primary theological interlocutors, who are largely Anglican, Roman Catholic, and Orthodox.[23] In addition, while Hughes's work reflects theologically on the transforming work of the Spirit, he does not explicitly engage two key movements in the United States today with that focus, the first of which is the Pentecostal and charismatic movement. Though Hughes is aware of and seemingly appreciative of Pentecostal and charismatic concerns, apart from Veli-Matti Kärkkäinen he does not engage any Pentecostal theologians or explore their concerns or unique contributions, such as Spirit baptism. Neither does Hughes engage the emerging and growing phenomenon of the "spiritual but not religious," those among the "Nones" (those who claim no religious affiliation) who have turned to language of the Spirit to explore personal and social transformation.

More recently, Simeon Zahl, another Anglican, has written an important study of the Holy Spirit and human experience.[24] I directly draw on Zahl's work in chapter 2, especially his claims that experience cannot and should not be excluded in the theological task and that the best way to theologically approach experience is by way of the doctrine of the Holy Spirit. I also resonate with his critique of "pneumatologies of presence" and propose that the personhood of the Spirit provides a more fruitful framework for considering the Spirit's work

23. Notable exceptions include John Wesley, the Anglican founder of the Methodist movement, and Lutheran Robert Jenson, whose later theology is also shaped by Orthodox and Catholic influences.
24. Simeon Zahl, *The Holy Spirit and Christian Experience* (New York: Oxford University Press, 2020).

in the Christian life. Unlike Hughes, Zahl engages key Protestant categories and figures, such as Martin Luther, Philip Melanchthon, and Karl Barth,[25] and his pneumatological reading of Melanchthon's soteriology strongly resonates with my own. Further, the aims for our respective projects very much align. However, we differ methodologically in how we approach the topic. Zahl uses an interdisciplinary method, drawing on affect theory to propose an experiential interpretation of the doctrines of salvation and sanctification. In contrast, I approach the Spirit's work in the Christian life ecumenically, bringing the theological contributions of contemporary Pentecostals into dialogue with Lutheran theology, and I include a third movement central to their theology, that of empowerment for mission. While Zahl recognizes the importance of the worldwide Pentecostal and charismatic movement to Christianity today, this recognition plays more of a background role in his investigation compared to mine. Despite being the fastest-growing expression of Christianity globally (and historically), this movement is rarely engaged by mainline Protestant theologians in the North.

Apart from the recent book *The Holy Spirit and the Reformation Legacy*, I am not aware of any other book-length treatment of the Holy Spirit that brings these two theological streams into critical conversation with each other.[26] For many Lutheran and Reformed theologians, this is most likely due to a general unease about addressing pneumatology apart from the realm of redemption (specifically, justification) and associations of the Spirit with unpredictability (it "blows where it chooses"; John 3:8). They also raise concerns about the Spirit working outside the strictures of the church or the means of grace or Scripture (a concern dating back to the Montanist heresy), fearing that to acknowledge

---

25. Zahl also engages Augustine, neo-Thomism, and Anglican theologians Thomas Torrance and Kathryn Tanner.

26. Mark J. Cartledge and Mark A. Jumper, eds., *The Holy Spirit and the Reformation Legacy* (Eugene, OR: Pickwick, 2020). The book is a collection of papers presented at a conference at Regent University of the same title in 2017; most essays were written by Pentecostal theologians, with a few contributions by Anglican and Presbyterians. None were written by Lutheran theologians. However, it should be noted that Sarah Hinlicky Wilson has written a helpful primer for Lutherans: *A Guide to Pentecostal Movements for Lutherans* (Eugene, OR: Wipf & Stock, 2016). Wilson served as a consultant for the first round of the international dialogue and also for the protodialogue that preceded it, resulting in the publication *Lutherans and Pentecostals in Dialogue* (Strasbourg, France: Institute for Ecumenical Research, 2010). A PDF of the handbook is available at https://ecumenical-institute.org/wp-content/uploads/2022/06/Lutherans-and-Pentecostals-in -Dialogue-Text-FINAL.pdf. In 2016, I edited a theme issue of *Dialog*, "Theology between Wittenberg and Azusa Street," which explored points of connection between these two traditions and to which both Lutheran and Pentecostal theologians contributed (*Dialog* 55, no. 4 [December 2016]).

such operations of the Spirit would be to open the door to emotionalism and revivalism. Lutherans have had their own renewal movements, such as German and Scandinavian Pietism and the charismatic movement, but these have not been without their detractors for some of the same reasons noted above. They too are often met with suspicion and generally ignored by mainline theologians writing on pneumatology today.

My primary reason for writing this book, however, is the need expressed by many mainline Protestant pastors, especially Lutheran, for theological resources regarding the life-giving and transforming work of the Holy Spirit in the Christian life. While one can find Roman Catholic, evangelical, and Pentecostal treatments of the Spirit's work in sanctification and empowerment, these topics are not regularly addressed by mainline Protestant theologians. As a seminary professor, I often make presentations to clergy groups. And from these clergy, I frequently hear a deep hunger for more theological resources consonant with their Reformation heritage that address these topics. Further, ELCA Bishop Leila Ortiz, in her work on "Luthercostals" (that is, Christians who merge Lutheran theology with Pentecostal spirituality and practices), names the lament that many Luthercostals have about the lack of vitality, prayer, and spiritual community in Lutheran congregations.[27]

This concern is also receiving increasing attention at the international level. A Lutheran World Federation consultation, held in 2019 in Addis Ababa, addressed Lutheran identity/identities and took as its starting point the doctrine of the Holy Spirit, specifically Luther's explanation of the Third Article of the Apostles' Creed in his Large Catechism. As part of the consultation, a Pentecostal theologian and an Orthodox theologian (representing two traditions with rich pneumatological engagement) gave papers.[28]

---

27. Leila Ortiz, "A Latina Luthercostal Invitation Into an Ecclesial Estuary," *Dialog* 55, no. 4 (2016): 308–15.

28. These were published in Chad Rimmer and Cheryl M. Peterson, eds., *"We Believe in the Holy Spirit": Global Perspectives on Lutheran Identities* (Leipzig: Evangelische Verlangsanstalt, 2021). The 2019 consultation was the first phrase of a four-year study process on Lutheran identities that concluded with the Thirteenth Assembly of the Lutheran Federation in Krakow, Poland (September 13–19, 2023). See https://www.lutheranworld.org/what-we-do/theology/lutheran-identities, accessed March 25, 2023. Here it seems pertinent to note that Lutherans and classical Pentecostals are in dialogue officially now at the international level. Unlike many other dialogues in which Lutherans have been involved, this one does not include revisiting doctrinal splits and anathemas. Lutherans and Pentecostals historically have been aware of each other's existence. However, apart from the influence of the charismatic renewal among some Lutherans in the 1970s and 1980s and beyond (and the deep influence of charismatic Christianity on Lutherans in many countries in the Southern Hemisphere), they have not really engaged each other's theological

In my previous book, *Who Is the Church?*, I suggested that the church receives its identity and call to participate in God's mission from the Holy Spirit. This is true for the individual Christian as well. This book proposes to explore a theology of the Christian life that starts with the person and work of the Holy Spirit. In what follows, I explore the Holy Spirit as the Lord and giver of life, God's personal presence for us, in us, and through us, as an agent of new life and transformation, through a consideration of three major "movements" in/ of the Christian life in a Protestant schema—justification, sanctification, and calling/mission. In justification, the Holy Spirit works *for* us. In sanctification, the Holy Spirit works *in* us. In our calling into mission, the Holy Spirit works *through* us, empowering us with spiritual gifts for God's calling. The Lutheran tradition historically has been the strongest on the first movement of the Holy Spirit, confused and nervous about the second, and often frightened about the third.

As previously noted, I intend this to be a work of systematic theology, rather than a practical theology of Christian spirituality (though there certainly will be some overlap as I address the role of experience in the Christian life). This book contributes to the field of systematic theology in several ways. It offers a contemporary Lutheran theology of the Spirit for the Christian life and does so through engagement with several significant voices of Pentecostal theology in North America, thus helping to further introduce this movement to Lutheran and other mainline Protestant theologians and leaders.[29] In this way, it is also a work of ecumenical theology. Finally, it is my hope that this work will help Lutheran and other mainline Protestant clergy, seminarians, and church leaders to better understand and engage the doctrine and language of the Spirit in

---

tradition in any concrete or helpful way during their concurrent histories. The first round of the dialogue concluded in 2022 with this report: Dirk G. Lange, Paula Mumia, Jean-Daniel Plüss, and Sarah Hinlicky Wilson, eds., *International Lutheran-Pentecostal 2016–2022 Dialogue Statement: "The Spirit of the Lord Is Upon Me"* (Geneva: LWF, 2023), https://www.lutheranworld.org/resources /publication-spirit-lord-upon-me.

29. Although I refer to both Pentecostal and charismatic movements and spirituality, the theologians I engage with in this work are by and large representatives of classic Pentecostal tradition—i.e., those Pentecostal denominations whose origins can be traced back to the Azusa Street Revival, such as Assemblies of God, Church of God (Cleveland, TN), Church of God in Christ, and so on. This is for a couple reasons. First, this is the family of Pentecostals with whom the Lutheran World Federation is in official dialogue at the international level (through the Pentecostal World Fellowship). Second, I am most familiar with the work of these theologians due to my decade-long participation in the Society for Pentecostal Studies, an "international community of scholars working within the Pentecostal and charismatic traditions." For more information, see the SPS website: https://www.sps-usa.org/.

xxii   Introduction

ways that serve the church's mission as well as the spirituality and vocation of those among whom they serve as leaders.

An Outline of Chapters

In chapter 1, "The Holy Spirit in the United States Today: Contextual Considerations for Fresh Engagement," I explore the claim that we are living in the "age of the Spirit" by addressing two contemporary movements significant for theologically considering the work of the Holy Spirit today. The first is the rise of the "Nones" in the United States, a context that is post-Christendom and increasingly becoming post-Christian. Many of the Nones identify as "spiritual but not religious" and are interested in the possibility of experiencing or knowing the divine, even though they do not wish to join religious institutions. Second, I discuss the emergence and incredible growth of the Pentecostal and charismatic churches and their emphasis on a tangible and transformative experience or encounter with God.

In chapter 2, "The Holy Spirit as Person: Experiencing the Presence of God," I discuss the difficulties that many Protestants have with experience as a source for theology, and I propose, along with Simeon Zahl, that the most helpful way to address experience in Christian theology is by way of pneumatology. Many contemporary theologians have appealed to nonpersonal categories for the Spirit. Instead, I argue for a robust understanding of the Spirit's relational personhood within a trinitarian framework as the basis for our experience of the Spirit as God's personal presence and power. I draw on the Johannine Paraclete tradition (the Spirit as the one who accompanies, our divine companion)[30] and the Nicene Creed's affirmation of the Spirit as the "Lord and giver of life." I also dialogue with contemporary Reformed theologians Jürgen Moltmann and Michael Welker and Pentecostal theologians Andrew Gabriel and Steven Studebaker.

The following three chapters constitute the heart of the book, as they explore the role of the Spirit in the three "movements" of the Christian life. Chapter 3,

---

30. I thank my former student Naomi Morgan for suggesting "companion" as a more personal rendering of "the accompanier," the one who accompanies, when I presented some of this material at an adult forum at a congregation she attended. While a familiar descriptor of the Holy Spirit on evangelical and charismatic websites (see, e.g., https://vineyardusa.org/library/come-holy -spirit-a-constant-companion, accessed May 14, 2023), "companion" is not commonly used by Lutherans and other mainline Protestants to translate the Johannine Paraclete or to otherwise describe the Holy Spirit's ministry. One exception is the Working Preacher post by Lutheran Karoline Lewis, "Resurrection Is Companionship," April 24, 2016, https://www.workingpreacher .org/dear-working-preacher/resurrection-is-companionship.

"The Spirit for Us: Justification and the New Birth," explores the Spirit's effective role in justification—that is, how the Holy Spirit works *for* believers, bringing them into relationship with God through faith, through which they experience God's grace and forgiveness that is "reckoned to [them] as righteousness" in the forensic sense (Rom. 4:3). I bring Lutheran confessional perspectives on this movement of the Spirit into dialogue with Pentecostal perspectives, especially that of Pentecostal theologian Frank Macchia. This chapter also discusses theological ideas such as "regeneration" and "new birth" in these traditions as correlates to effective justification. In the event of being justified by grace through faith, the Christian receives the gift of the Holy Spirit, who simultaneously initiates a new birth in the life of the Christian, one marked by the experience of being forgiven and embraced by God's mercy and love.

In chapter 4, "The Spirit in Us: Sanctification and the New Life," I explore what is probably the most problematic movement of the Spirit for traditions rooted in the Reformation: sanctification, or "being made holy."[31] I offer some historical reflections on the particular Lutheran "allergy" to sanctification (Craig Nessan) and concerns regarding "empirical piety" (Regin Prenter). I argue that a strong pneumatology addresses these concerns and—in dialogue with John Wesley and Wesleyan Pentecostal views, specifically those of Pentecostal theologian Dale Coulter—explore the work of the Spirit *in* believers following justification or conversion, that is, how the Spirit enables believers to live out the gift of forgiveness in relationships with others. I discuss holiness in both its positive and its negative aspects, the biblical fruit of the Spirit, along with various perspectives or models of sanctification, including Luther's idea of "return to baptism" and Wesley's medicinal image of being healed by grace, as well as the Pentecostal claim that one can have "victory" over sin. I propose that the Spirit's work in believers is to transform them to be more productive vessels for God's work in the world.

In chapter 5, "The Spirit through Us: Empowerment for Mission," I explore the work of the Holy Spirit in the individual Christian's calling—that is, how the Spirit works *through* the believer, empowering them to bear witness to and enabling them to participate in and serve the mission of God. Lutherans speak of the origin of Christian vocation (baptism) and its goal (to serve God and the neighbor), but not usually in pneumatological terms. In this chapter, I bring the Pentecostal emphasis on spiritual gifts and the related theological idea of

---

31. The subtitle of Luther's explanation of the Third Article of the Creed in the Small Catechism is "On Being Made Holy." BC, 355.

"baptism in the Holy Spirit" into conversation with the Lutheran theological tradition, exploring ways that Lutherans can affirm the empowerment of the Spirit through various charismata, or spiritual gifts, especially the spiritual gifts of speaking in tongues and prophetic speech, in evangelism and the work of social justice.

Building on the previous discussion, chapter 6, "The Means of the Spirit's Work: Word, Sacraments, and Charisms," explores in more depth the means through which the Spirit works in all three movements: justification, sanctification, and mission. This chapter addresses the Spirit's work in the classic Protestant "means of grace" (Word and sacrament)—including recent Pentecostal and charismatic theological engagement with the sacraments (such as the work by Chris Green and Daniel Tomberlin)—and relates the Spirit's work through these to the Spirit's work through other means, especially worship, speaking in tongues, and laying on of hands for healing.

In the epilogue, I offer some brief thoughts on why Lutherans should be more open to the Spirit's reviving work, some suggestions for what US Lutherans can learn from Pentecostal and charismatic Christians about revival, and criterion for discerning whether the Holy Spirit is at work in a revival.

1

The Holy Spirit in the United States Today

Contextual Considerations for Fresh Engagement

The "age of the Spirit" seems to be upon us. So postulated Phyllis Tickle in her final book. Her use of the phrase clearly invokes the medieval theologian Joachim of Fiore.[1] However, contra Joachim, this age is marked not by increased church attendance and the importance of ecclesiastical institutions and doctrines but by the opposite, and in their place, an emphasis on personal spiritual experience. For Harvey Cox, the emergence of an age of the Spirit globally is marked by "a worldwide outburst of religious energy that belies most secularization theories."[2]

1. Phyllis Tickle with Jon M. Sweeney, *The Age of the Spirit: How the Ghost of an Ancient Controversy Is Shaping the Church* (Grand Rapids: Baker Books, 2014), 115. See also Tickle, *The Great Emergence: How Christianity Is Changing and Why* (Grand Rapids: Baker Books, 2012). Joachim of Fiore was a medieval theologian who divided history into three ages, each corresponding to a person of the Trinity.

2. Harvey G. Cox Jr., "Make Way for the Spirit," in *God's Life in Trinity*, ed. Miroslav Volf and Michael Welker (Minneapolis: Fortress, 2006), 97. See also Cox, *The Future of Faith* (San Francisco: HarperOne, 2010), 1–20. See also Cox, *Fire from Heaven: The Rise of Pentecostal Spirituality and the Reshaping of Religion in the Twenty-First Century* (Reading, MA: Addison-Wesley, 1995). In that earlier book, he wrote, "We may or may not be entering a new age of the Spirit as some more sanguine observers hope. But we are definitely in a period of renewed religious vitality, another 'great awakening,' . . . but this time on a world scale." Cox, *Fire from Heaven*, xvi.

Cox concurs that we are witnessing a displacement of doctrines *about* God with experiences *of* the divine.[3]

In this chapter, I consider two key movements at the heart of the age of the Spirit as important factors for a theological exploration of the person and work of the Holy Spirit in the Christian life in the United States today. For Tickle, both play a key role in the age of the Spirit because each emphasizes direct contact between the seeker or believer and God. The first is the rise of the "spiritual but not religious" phenomenon, and the second is the growth and expansion of Pentecostal and charismatic Christianity. In what follows, I examine how each stresses a tangible and transformative experience or an encounter with God and illustrates (albeit in different ways) the contention that, in the age of the Spirit, *the experience of God* is becoming more important than specific doctrines or concepts about God. Both movements point to the need for Christian theologians to speak more about the Spirit of God, which for Christians is the Holy Spirit.

The Phenomenon of "Spiritual but Not Religious" and the Experience of God

Most Christians recognize that the religious landscape in the United States has undergone significant shifts in recent years. A 2019 Pew Research Center poll found that 65 percent of adult Americans self-identify as Christian, down 12 percent from the previous decade. Not only do fewer people describe themselves as Christian, but for the past few decades the fastest-growing religious identification in the United States has been "none." Those who describe their religious identity as atheist, agnostic, or "nothing in particular" now make up 26 percent of the population, up from 17 percent in 2009.[4] The growth of this group is most evident among younger adults, with four out of ten millennials giving their religious identity as "none."

Unlike in much of Europe, these shifts have not led to an increase in secularization. In the United States, interest in spirituality and belief in the

3. Cox, *Future of Faith*, 20 (emphasis original). See also Harvey G. Cox Jr., "Spirits of Globalization: Pentecostalism and Experimental Spiritualities in a Global Era," in *Spirits of Globalization: The Growth of Pentecostalism and Experiential Spiritualities in a Global Age*, ed. Sturla J. Stålsett (London: SCM, 2006).

4. Pew Research Center, "In U.S., Decline of Christianity Continues at Rapid Pace: An Update on America's Changing Religious Landscape," October 17, 2019, https://www.pewforum.org/2019/10/17/in-u-s-decline-of-christianity-continues-at-rapid-pace.

transcendent remain widespread. A 2017 Pew Research Center survey found that nearly nine out of ten Americans believe in some kind of higher power. However, a "slim majority" (56 percent) profess faith in God as described in the Bible, while an additional 33 percent say they believe in another type of higher power or spiritual force.[5] Among the "Nones," only one-third reject belief in God altogether. According to the 2014 Pew Research Center Religious Landscape Study, nearly half of Nones (49 percent) believe in some kind of deity or higher power with an absolute or fair amount of certainty.[6]

Many of these embrace the designation "spiritual but not religious" (SBNR). While it has been fashionable to make this distinction since the 1990s, the idea has deep roots in nineteenth-century New Thought and Transcendentalism. The phrase itself likely arose among early members of Alcoholics Anonymous.[7] What is new today, however, is an increasing blurring of lines, a recognition of "permeable boundaries," between various religious traditions, including Christian and non-Christian, as well as the adoption of "extra theistic" images not only by the Nones but also by those who affiliate with traditionally theistic religions.[8]

Spiritual and Religious versus Spiritual but Not Religious

According to renowned spirituality scholar Sandra Schneiders, "The term 'spirituality' has undergone an astounding expansion in the last few decades,

5. Dalia Fahmy, "Key Findings about Americans' Belief in God," Pew Research Center, April 25, 2018, https://www.pewresearch.org/fact-tank/2018/04/25/key-findings-about-americans -belief-in-god. The full study can be accessed at https://www.pewforum.org/2018/04/25/when -americans-say-they-believe-in-god-what-do-they-mean. A 2011 Gallup Poll found that 90 percent of US adults believe in God, but it reports that when given the option of saying they believe in a universal spirit or higher power instead of "God," approximately 12 percent choose that option. See Frank Newport, "More Than 9 in 10 Americans Continue to Believe in God," Gallup Poll, June 3, 2011, https://news.gallup.com/poll/147887/americans-continue-believe-god .aspx.

6. Pew Research Center, "2014 Religious Landscape Study," accessed January 29, 2023, http:// www.pewforum.org/religious-landscape-study/belief-in-god.

7. Wade Clark Roof traces "spiritual but not religious" to the 1960s and the disenchantment of baby boomers with organized religion. See Roof, "American Spirituality," *Religion and American Culture* 9, no. 2 (Summer 1999): 133. According to Robert Fuller, "Alcoholics Anonymous . . . is largely responsible for the widespread popularity of the phrase 'spiritual but not religious.'" Fuller, *Spiritual but Not Religious: Understanding Unchurched America* (Oxford: Oxford University Press, 2001), 112.

8. Nancy Ammerman, "Spiritual but Not Religious? Beyond Binary Choices," *Journal for the Scientific Study of Religion* 52, no. 2 (2013): 271. See also Bill Leonard, *A Sense of the Heart: Christian Religious Experience in the United States* (Nashville: Abingdon, 2014), 153.

coming to refer to 'whatever in human experience is alive and intentional, conscious of itself and responsive to others.'"[9] Although religion also includes other elements, such as worship and doctrine, religion by definition includes spirituality and spiritual practices; indeed, religion must be understood to include a spiritual domain.[10]

This unitive view of "religion" and "spirituality" is seen in scholars working within the Society for the Study of Christian Spirituality. Schneiders, one of the founders of the society, points to the inseparability of the domains that are now often treated separately as religion and spirituality. The religion/spirituality distinction can be understood in terms of a body/spirit metaphor. The two *together* are what make up the living tradition: neither body ("religion") nor spirit ("spirituality") can exist in real life apart from the other.[11] Drawing on the history of the term "spirituality," Lutheran Lisa Dahill concurs: "The term 'spirituality' translates the Latin *spiritualitas*, a noun derived in the 5th century from the New Testament adjective *pneumatikos*, or 'spiritual.' Within the Pauline anthropology, flesh and spirit (*sarx* and *pneuma*) do not refer to a body/soul dualism but respectively to life apart from or rooted in the living Spirit of Jesus Christ. Thus the term *spiritualitas* similarly originates as a noun describing the quality or shape of a Christian life formed by the Holy Spirit."[12]

Building on this insight, Dahill defines *Christian* spirituality as "the world-encompassing and life-transforming action of the Holy Spirit of Jesus Christ in the life of a person or community, and her/his/their experience of and response

9. Sandra M. Schneiders, "Spirituality in the Academy," *Theological Studies* 50, no. 4 (1989): 678n11. Schneiders is here quoting Rachel Hosmer, "Current Literature in Christian Spirituality," *Anglican Theological Review* 66 (1984): 425. Schneiders offers her own, more precise definition: "the experience of conscious involvement in the project of life integration through self-transcendence toward the ultimate value one perceives" (Schneiders, "The Study of Christian Spirituality: Contours and Dynamics of a Discipline," in *Minding the Spirit: The Study of Christian Spirituality*, ed. Elizabeth A. Dreyer and Mark S. Burrows [Baltimore: Johns Hopkins University Press, 2005], 5–6). Following Walter Principe, scholars of spirituality generally identify three levels of meaning for the term; this is the first and the one most people mean when they speak about their own "spirituality." See Principe, "Toward Defining Spirituality," in *Exploring Christian Spirituality: An Ecumenical Reader*, ed. Kenneth J. Collins (Grand Rapids: Baker Academic, 2000), 43–60. For an overview of the field of Christian spirituality, see Lisa E. Dahill, "Spirituality: Overview," in *The Encyclopedia of Christianity*, 5 vols., ed. Erwin Fahlbusch et al., vol. 5 (Sh–Z) (Grand Rapids: Eerdmans, 1999–2007), 159–61.

10. Ammerman, "Spiritual but Not Religious?," 276. See also Leonard, *Sense of the Heart*, 154.

11. Sandra M. Schneiders, *Religion and Spirituality: Strangers, Rivals, or Partners?*, Santa Clara Lectures 6, no. 2 (Santa Clara, CA: Santa Clara University, Dept. of Religious Studies, 2000).

12. Lisa E. Dahill, "Spirituality in Lutheran Perspective: Much to Offer, Much to Learn," *Word & World* 18, no. 1 (Winter 1998): 70.

to that action of God."[13] Dahill's focus on transformation is important, since, as F. LeRon Shults and Andrea Hollingsworth rightly point out, "Pneumatological interpretation always occurs in the context of dealing with experiences of transformation."[14]

With this background in mind, it is important to ask what specifically is being rejected by those who say they do not want to be religious. Typically they mean the other elements that come with religion: institutional structures, doctrines, and outward rituals of worship, all of which they see as human created. By "spiritual" they mean an interior experience of the transcendent that they believe is somehow more authentic, personal, or heartfelt; but this, as sociologist Nancy Ammerman notes, is difficult to study sociologically. Further, in her research on this question, Ammerman shows that this binary does not always hold. She writes, "The 'religion' being rejected turns out to be quite unlike the religion being practiced and described by those affiliated with religious institutions. Likewise, the 'spirituality' being endorsed as an alternative is at least as widely practiced by those same religious people drawing a moral boundary against them."[15] Interestingly, Ammerman discovered that most people in her interview sample claimed to be either both or neither.[16]

Other studies, especially those whose interview samples included or focused on persons in twelve-step recovery programs such as Alcoholics Anonymous (AA), found the opposite to be true. Linda Mercadante reports that a full third of her more than one hundred interviewees came to identify themselves as SBNR through their involvement with twelve-step recovery programs.[17] Jennifer Hahn's research findings in her study of the SBNR phenomenon in AA also contrasts with Ammerman's findings, causing Hahn to wonder if perhaps the SBNRs are overrepresented in AA.[18] In spite of these divergences, however, Ammerman and Mercadante agree that the phrase "spiritual but not religious"

13. Dahill, "Spirituality in Lutheran Perspective," 72.
14. F. LeRon Shults and Andrea Hollingsworth, *The Holy Spirit: Guides to Theology* (Grand Rapids: Eerdmans, 2008), 9.
15. Ammerman, "Spiritual but Not Religious?," 275.
16. Ammerman, "Spiritual but Not Religious?," 274. See also David Masci and Michael Lipka, "Americans May Be Getting Less Religious, but Feelings of Spirituality on the Rise," Pew Research Center, January 21, 2016, https://www.pewresearch.org/fact-tank/2016/01/21/americans -spirituality. Masci and Lipka found this to be true both for those who identify as highly religious and for the Nones.
17. Linda Mercadante, "Does Alcoholics Anonymous Help Grow the Spiritual but Not Religious Movement?," *Implicit Religion* 22, no. 2 (2019): 186.
18. Jennifer Lois Hahn, "'God as We Understood Him': Being Spiritual but Not Religious in Alcoholics Anonymous, Past and Present," *Implicit Religion* 22, no. 2 (2019): 109.

tends to be more ideological (Mercadante) or moral and political (Ammerman) than religiously descriptive.[19] Ammerman further asserts a common denominator between the two major types of spirituality she identifies in her study: theistic and extra-theistic. She calls this "ethical spirituality" and states that this is "America's mainstream form of religiosity, with a focus on living one's faith every day and a relative disinterest in doctrinal orthodoxy."[20] In other words, the spirituality of the majority of churchgoers who hold to more traditional views of God and practice their spirituality in religious communities may not be all that different in the end from those who call themselves SBNR.

Jeremiah Carey comes to a similar conclusion in his treatment of the phenomenon of spirituality.[21] He proposes that spirituality is best defined as a particular style of ethical living. However, he grants that all spiritualities—even those not grounded in particular religious traditions—still presuppose some teachings to provide a basis for their moral and ethical foundations.[22] His contention is supported by Mercadante's research into the theology of the SBNRs. She discovered a set of core, though still incipient, theological ideas held by the majority of the SBNRs she interviewed.[23]

Spirituality beyond "Religion"

Mercadante found that many of her interviewees wanted a "re-sacralization of the world"—that is, they wanted to see and experience the sacred in everyday life in ways that are vital and personal. This made her ask whether the SBNR movement is not only a protest against "organized religion" but also a reaction against a secular world that would nullify the spiritual by insisting that science can answer all problems.[24] This includes many mainline churches that, in Mercadante's view, have been influenced by secular modernity to downplay "the awe, respect, and humility we should feel in the presence of God" in their attempt to "be relevant, non-demanding and friendly."[25] She surmises

19. Mercadante, "Does Alcoholics Anonymous Help Grow the Spiritual but not Religious Movement?," 187.

20. Ammerman, "Spiritual but Not Religious?," 272.

21. Jeremiah Carey, "Spiritual, but Not Religious? On the Nature of Spirituality and Its Relation to Religion," *International Journal for Philosophy of Religion* 83 (2018): 261–69.

22. Carey, "Spiritual, but Not Religious?," 268.

23. Linda Mercadante, *Belief without Borders: Inside the Minds of the Spiritual but Not Religious* (New York: Oxford University Press, 2014), 251.

24. Mercadante, *Belief without Borders*, 34.

25. Mercadante, *Belief without Borders*, 251.

this is one reason that many SBNRs stay away from mainline churches.[26] Reggie McNeal speculates that more people are seeking spirituality outside of the church because they find churches to be more secular than the culture that surrounds them. Indeed, he believes that traditional Protestant church culture is not spiritual enough to help people with the questions they are asking about life and God. "The problem is that when people come to church, expecting to find God, they often encounter a religious club holding a meeting where God is conspicuously absent."[27]

According to Diana Butler Bass, whenever a "gulf" opens between people's experience of God and religious institutions' failed attempts to help them process those experiences, the situation becomes ripe for "spiritual revolution, revival or awakening."[28] This spiritual revolution navigates between traditional theism, which posits an "otherworldly" God, and secularism, which posits no need for God. It "enfolds the mundane and the sacred, finding a God who is a 'gracious mystery, ever greater, ever nearer,' through a new awareness of the earth and in the lives of . . . neighbors."[29] Bass sees this revolution occurring within Christianity and outside it; and in her more recent work, she explores various spiritual practices (many that Ammerman would call "extra-theistic"), inviting others to join her in a conversion from "God above us" to "God with us."[30]

The Spiritual in Everyday Life

In her study on the spirituality of Nones, Elizabeth Drescher points to "broader changes in religious and spiritual practices in the United States that

---

26. This is not the case in Pentecostal and charismatic churches such as the Vineyard, but for most SBNRs, their theology is too conservative to be appealing. Mercadante, *Belief without Borders*, 251.

27. Reggie McNeal, *The Present Future: Six Tough Questions for the Church* (San Francisco: Jossey-Bass, 2003), 59.

28. Diana Butler Bass, *Grounded: Finding God in the World—A Spiritual Revolution* (San Francisco: HarperOne, 2015), 21.

29. Bass, *Grounded*, 25–26.

30. Bass, *Grounded*, 277–80. See also Diana Butler Bass, *Christianity after Religion: The End of Church and the Birth of a New Spiritual Awakening* (San Francisco: HarperOne, 2013). As further evidence, she points to the "spiritual experience index" developed by the Public Research Institute, which shows that "65 percent of Americans score in the moderate to 'very high' range of spiritual connection, sense of wonder, inner peace and harmony, and oneness with nature" (Bass, *Grounded*, 20). For more about the spiritual experience index, see Vicky Genia, "The Spiritual Experience Index: A Measure of Spiritual Maturity," *Journal of Religion and Health* 30 (1991): 337–47; and Genia, "The Spiritual Experience Index: Revision and Reformulation," *Review of Religious Research* 38 (1997): 344–61.

institutional religions seem ill equipped to engage."[31] She concludes that "the experience of the spiritual in everyday life"—in interpersonal relationships with friends and family and in practices that integrate body, mind, and spirit—"feels more authentic for many Nones" than the experiences they have had with traditional religious institutions and rituals.[32] Interviewees often found it difficult to explain their spirituality, since they were describing "lived, felt experiences" rather than propositional beliefs; such experiences were "known substantially in sensate and emotional rather than cognitive terms."[33] Further, these experiences did not always require interpretation to be meaningful. Drescher agrees with Talal Asad, who writes, "It is possible for someone to encounter something unpredictably that transforms her, to be gripped through her sense by a force (whether immanent or transcendent) *without having to interpret anything.*"[34]

Drescher's interviewees highlight the transformative significance of their spiritual experiences and encounters. They describe this transformation in terms of individual personal growth and healing but also in communal ways that contribute to the betterment of society through compassionate and ethical actions.[35] Drescher finds that the relational orientation of this spirituality leads many to come together to share the same kind of experiences and practices, even if these are not always interpreted in the same way.[36] The focus, which Drescher highlights, on community and service as integral aspects of SBNR spirituality runs counter to the often-held view that SBNRs and other spiritual seekers are narcissistic navel gazers, those who turn inward, away from the world, as Robert Bellah famously argued in *Habits of the Heart.*[37]

Hahn's research also challenges assumptions that the spirituality of the SBNRs, especially those who are also members of AA, is self-centered and superficial.[38] The "we way" she discovers among AA members in her ethnographic research directly contradicts the individualistic "Sheilaism" of Bellah's

31. Elizabeth Drescher, *Choosing Our Religion: The Spiritual Lives of America's Nones* (New York: Oxford University Press, 2016), 17.

32. Drescher, *Choosing Our Religion*, 44.

33. Drescher, *Choosing Our Religion*, 49.

34. Talal Asad, quoted in Drescher, *Choosing Our Religion*, 49–50 (emphasis original).

35. Drescher, *Choosing Our Religion*, 113.

36. Drescher, *Choosing Our Religion*, 60.

37. Robert Neelly Bellah et al., *Habits of the Heart: Individualism and Commitment in American Life* (Berkeley: University of California Press, 1985). One of the persons interviewed for this book, Sheila Larson, famously described her faith as "Sheilaism, just my own little voice." Bellah et al., *Habits of the Heart*, 220–21.

38. Hahn cites as examples Bellah et al., *Habits of the Heart*, and Mercadante, *Belief without Borders*. Hahn, "God as We Understood Him," 103.

study.[39] Each of the Twelve Steps begins with "We," not "I." The phrase "God as we understood him," while it invites each member to choose their own concept of God, has a unifying effect. Members do not need to agree on a concept of God if they have a concept that works for them. If a member can affirm that there is *something* higher than themselves—even the AA group—then they can "work" the Twelve Steps (spiritual practices based on Christianity that include prayer and service to others) and see their lives transformed. As Ernest Kurtz rightly points out, the Twelve Steps describe, rather than prescribe, a path to recovery. "The Steps do not set rules; they relate experience."[40] According to AA's literature, the sobriety that results from "working the steps" is more than abstinence from alcohol and drugs; it includes living on a spiritual plane. Kurtz reminds his readers that at the heart of AA lies the idea of a "spiritual awakening" or "religious experience."[41] Hahn's research shows that AA members describe spirituality in terms of leading better lives, and service to others is a key component of this.[42]

Other nonaffiliated spiritual seekers are interested in finding meaningful community and making a difference in the world, especially on issues of racial, economic, gender, and ecological justice. For example, although the Black Lives Matter movement did not originate from the historic Black churches, it is incorrect to call it a secular movement because it is grounded in theological principles and spiritual practices and has attracted many SBNRs among its ranks.[43] Civil rights activist and lawyer Michelle Alexander offers another example. Religiously unaffiliated herself, she calls for nothing short of a "spiritual revolution" to address the increasing racial violence in the United States and its history of mass incarceration of African Americans and Latinos. She no longer believes that changing political policies and laws are, in and of themselves,

39. Hahn, "God as We Understood Him," 114. For information on "Sheilaism," see note 38, above. On the paradox of individualism and community in the Twelve Steps, see Ernest Kurtz, "Whatever Happened to Twelve-Step Programs?," accessed January 28, 2023, https://www.preston group.org/aa_docs/kurtz_whatever_happened.pdf, originally published in *The Collected Ernie Kurtz* (1999; repr., Bloomington, IN: iUniverse, 2008), 145–76.

40. Kurtz, "Whatever Happened to Twelve-Step Programs?," 3, 9 (online version).

41. See Kurtz, "Whatever Happened to Twelve-Step Programs?," 23–24 (online version).

42. Hahn, "God as We Understood Him," 111.

43. Alejandra Molina, "Black Lives Matter Is 'a Spiritual Movement,' Says Co-founder Patrisse Cullors," Religious News Service, June 15, 2020, https://religionnews.com/2020/06/15/why-black -lives-matter-is-a-spiritual-movement-says-blm-co-founder-patrisse-cullors. See also Melina Abdullah, "The Role of Spirituality and Prayer in the Black Lives Matter Movement," interview by Jonathan Bastian, June 25, 2020, https://www.kcrw.com/culture/shows/life-examined/religion -slavery-black-lives-matter/black-lives-matter-blm-melina-abdullah-hebab-ferrag-interview.

enough to achieve justice. She writes, "Without a moral or spiritual awakening, we will remain forever trapped in political games fueled by fear, greed and the hunger for power." This is because "at its core, America's journey from slavery to Jim Crow to mass incarceration raises profound *moral and spiritual questions about who we are*, individually and collectively, who we aim to become, and what we are willing to do now."[44]

Summary

From this brief overview of the spirituality of the Nones, and especially of those who consider themselves SBNR, I wish to highlight two key points to keep in mind as I discuss the person and work of the Holy Spirit for the church today. First, while the shifting landscape of spirituality in the United States has not led to a diminishment of belief in God, the primary focus has shifted away from what (and in whom) one believes and toward the difference spirituality can make in one's life. The religiously unaffiliated (and indeed, perhaps also the religiously affiliated!) are interested in a "lived," or everyday, spirituality— a spirituality in which God (or whatever term is used to denote the divine) is present and working in one's life, a power one can rely on for personal guidance and strength. This is especially evident in the spirituality of AA, which Tickle argues is "first in the list of prime movers" in the shifting landscape regarding religion and spirituality in North America in the twentieth century.[45] As we have also seen, it is not only those outside of Christianity who are seeking this "spiritual revolution" (Bass). Many within the church are seeking it as well. And the goal of this pragmatic, everyday spirituality is not only personal, individual growth. Whether through acts of direct service or advocating on behalf of justice, contributing toward the common good is also an essential element of this spirituality.

Second, and related, the discussion above supports Drescher's contention that the categories of "*believing, belonging,* and *behaving*"[46] may not be the most helpful framework from which to examine the spiritual lives of the Nones

---

44. Michelle Alexander, quoted in Richard Beck, "The Spiritual Dimensions of Justice Work," *Experimental Theology*, September 27, 2016, http://experimentaltheology.blogspot.com/2016/09/the-spiritual-dimensions-of-justice-work.html. Alexander originally wrote this as a Facebook post on September 14, 2016.

45. Tickle, *Great Emergence*, 91.

46. Drescher, *Choosing Our Religion*, 14. See also Phyllis Tickle, *Emergence Christianity: What It Is, Where It Is Going, and Why It Matters* (Grand Rapids: Baker Books, 2012), 77, 203–5.

and the SBNRs. She writes, "Rather than expressing itself through traditional modes of *believing, belonging,* and *behaving* that have fueled much recent discussion within religions about how to engage the unaffiliated and to retain current members, this Noneness appeared among the Nones I interviewed in narratives that emphasized experiences of *being* and *becoming*."[47] The key is how spirituality transforms one's life (and, through the living of that life, also transforms one's community and the wider world), not whether one believes or how one belongs or even how one behaves. These are secondary to the transformative experience that is sought—one's "becoming"—which can and does change lives.

The Growth and Expansion of Pentecostal and Charismatic Christianity

The rise of the religiously unaffiliated is perhaps the most significant shift in American spirituality that suggests we are now living in the age of the Spirit. The global situation is another story altogether, with the phrase "age of the Spirit" evoking instead the rise and growing influence of Pentecostal and charismatic Christianity. This is the fastest-growing branch of Christianity today (and historically).[48] Todd M. Johnson notes that "the case for the pentecostal and charismatic renewal as a single interconnected phenomenon can best be made by considering a 'family resemblance' among the various kinds of movements that claim to be either pentecostal or charismatic."[49] Elements in the "family resemblance" include baptism of the Holy Spirit, speaking in tongues and other spiritual gifts, and the overall experiential nature of Pentecostal and charismatic movements. "Renewalist" is a widely adopted term coined by David Barrett to embrace the full breadth of Pentecostal and charismatic Christianity.[50]

According to the *World Christian Encyclopedia,* renewalist Christianity grew from 58 million in 1970 to 635 million in 2020 and currently makes up 25.6 percent of Christians globally, 86 percent of whom are in the southern

47. Drescher, *Choosing Our Religion,* 14.
48. For a helpful article on the challenges involved with measuring the demographics of this movement, see Todd M. Johnson, "Counting Pentecostals Worldwide," *Pneuma* 36 (2014): 265–88.
49. Johnson, "Counting Pentecostals Worldwide," 266.
50. David B. Barrett, George T. Kurian, and Todd M. Johnson, eds., *World Christian Encyclopedia,* 2nd ed. (New York: Oxford University Press, 2001). See also Johnson, "Counting Pentecostals Worldwide."

hemisphere.[51] Based on the data collected by the World Christian Database, the share of Christians globally who can be described as renewalist is expected to grow beyond 30 percent by 2025. While the impact of renewalist Christianity is strongest in the majority world, Christianity in the United States is not immune to its influence. According to the World Christian Database, as of 2010 approximately seventy-six million people in the United States consider themselves renewalists, which is approximately one-third of all US Christians. This makes renewalists the largest demographic of Christians in the United States, ahead of Roman Catholics, who number seventy million, or approximately 30 percent of US Christians.[52]

Harvey Cox's Fire from Heaven

Pentecostalism has not received much attention from non-Pentecostal theologians and scholars of religion. This is likely due to stereotypes, fears, prejudices, and misunderstandings about Pentecostal Christianity. Even so, the lack of attention is striking considering its tremendous growth and influence. There have been some notable exceptions, such as work by Lesslie Newbigin,[53] but since its beginnings in the early twentieth century, more typically the movement has been ignored or dismissed, especially by mainline Protestant theologians.

In 1995, Harvey Cox, an ordained American Baptist minister and professor of religion at Harvard Divinity School, published *Fire from Heaven: The Rise of Pentecostal Spirituality and the Reshaping of Religion in the Twenty-First Century*, one of the first serious treatments of the movement by a non-Pentecostal for

51. Todd M. Johnson and Gina A. Zerlo, *World Christian Encyclopedia*, 3rd ed. (Edinburgh: Edinburgh University Press, 2019), 26. See also Todd M. Johnson and Gina A. Zerlo, eds., *World Christian Database* (Boston: Brill, 2023), https://www.worldchristiandatabase.org.

52. Todd M. Johnson, "The Global Demographics of the Pentecostal and Charismatic Renewal," *Society* 46 (2009): 479–83. Of course, there may be overlap between these categories due to the charismatic movement within Catholicism. Further, the Pew Research Center puts the number of Roman Catholics in the United States closer to seventy-five million, or 24 percent of the US population; either way, the growth of renewalist Christianity cannot be denied. See "The Global Catholic Population," February 13, 2013, Pew Research Center, https://www.pewresearch.org/religion/2013/02/13/the-global-catholic-population/#:~:text=Of%20the%20estimated%2075.4%20million,the%20United%20States%20(30%25).

53. Lesslie Newbigin, *The Household of God: Lectures on the Nature of the Church* (New York: Friendship Press, 1954). Newbigin highlights Pentecostalism as one of three "embodiments" of the church, which stresses that the Christian life is a matter of experiencing the power and presence of God; the other embodiments center around faith (most Protestant traditions) and sacraments (Orthodoxy and Catholicism).

a general audience.[54] I remember reading the book out of curiosity shortly after its publication, since I knew very little at that time about Pentecostals. Cox weaves together a scholarly analysis of the movement with narratives of Pentecostals he met through his research, along with his own personal experiences with Pentecostal worship and activities. He provides a compelling account and assessment of Pentecostalism and its significance for the future of global Christianity.

In contrast to the sixteenth-century Reformation and other movements that center on the dispersal of a new or rediscovered theological insight, the spread of Pentecostalism has been attributed directly to the pouring out of the Holy Spirit upon people "in these last days," as prophesied in Joel 2. Cox attributes Pentecostalism's spread to its ability to speak to the "spiritual emptiness of our time by reaching beyond the levels of creed and ceremony into what might be called 'primal spirituality.'"[55] While appreciating the seriousness with which he approaches the movement, Pentecostal scholars have criticized Cox for sociological and anthropological reductionism and for neglecting the role of the transcendent Holy Spirit in his analysis.[56]

Cox highlights the role of experience as central to Pentecostal spirituality, concluding with some reflections as to its future in the perennial struggle between a fundamentalist impulse and an experientialist impulse, a struggle he finds in all religions. In his discussion of the experientialist impulse, he points to two features we have already seen in the spirituality of the SBNRs and Nones. Experiential spirituality requires more of individuals, who become their own religious authorities, drawing from various traditions what they need or find useful. This "spiritual bricolage" is combined with a pragmatism to develop an everyday spirituality that works for them, to help them live their lives in the here and now.

---

54. It is interesting to note that its publication came thirty years after his groundbreaking first book, *The Secular City: Secularization and Urbanization in Theological Perspective* (New York: Macmillan, 1965). Before Cox's book, Walter J. Hollenweger, a well-known expert on Pentecostalism who served in a Pentecostal mission and was later ordained in the Swiss Reformed Church, authored two significant studies of Pentecostalism: *The Pentecostals: The Charismatic Movement in the Churches* (Minneapolis: Augsburg, 1972); and its sequel, *Pentecostalism: Origins and Developments Worldwide* (Peabody, MA: Hendrickson, 1997).

55. Cox, *Fire from Heaven*, 81. Cox explores this in three aspects: primal speech, primal piety, and primal hope.

56. Nimi Wariboko, "Dialogue: *Fire from Heaven*: Pentecostals in the Secular City," *Pneuma* 33 (2011): 394. To the first point, see Amos Yong, *Discerning the Spirit(s): A Pentecostal-Charismatic Contribution to Christian Theology of Religions* (Sheffield, UK: Sheffield Academic, 2000), 17–20.

At the time, Cox's discovery of Pentecostalism's "persistent accent on personal experience as the *sine qua non* of spirituality and the indispensable touchstone of faith" led him to hope that the movement would find itself "squarely in the experientialist camp," making it "a potent alternative to the authoritarianism and anxious close-mindedness of the fundamentalist temptation."[57] More than twenty-five years later, it would seem that Cox's hopes have been dashed and the fundamentalist wing has won. While Pentecostals and fundamentalists have had an antagonistic history over the charismata, or spiritual gifts, William Menzies notes that "the key ideas of Fundamentalism were readily accepted by Pentecostals."[58] Further, fundamentalism's influence on the movement has been pervasive in the ongoing "culture wars" in the United States, seen most recently in the overwhelming support of Pentecostals and charismatics for Donald Trump. At the same time, many contemporary Pentecostal voices (especially from the Wesleyan stream), including scholars Dale Coulter and Cheryl Bridges Johns, resist the pull toward fundamentalism. As we see in chapter 5, an emerging number of socially progressive and justice-minded Pentecostals reject fundamentalism's political as well as its theological agenda.

Cox points to two factors pertinent to this study that demonstrate the struggle between these two impulses. The first is how Pentecostals define the term "experience," and the second is their conception of the Spirit.[59] Although Pentecostals talk a lot about experience, Cox argues that they need to be much clearer about what they mean by it. Experience is not a monolithic concept in theological discourse (a point to which I will return in the next chapter). Many theological movements and schools, such as feminist theology and liberation theology, make an appeal to experience; however, each one brings a different understanding of how experience should be interpreted and function authoritatively for theology.

Second, although Cox does not highlight the Spirit in his own analysis, he calls on Pentecostals to think more deeply about the Holy Spirit as the object of their experience, the one who they claim "has a purpose not just for them

---

57. Cox, *Fire from Heaven*, 310.

58. See William W. Menzies, "Non-Wesleyan Pentecostalism: A Tradition the Influence of Fundamentalism," *Asian Journal of Pentecostal Studies* 12, no. 2 (2011): 204. John F. MacArthur Jr.'s writings are emblematic of the fundamentalist attack on Pentecostal and charismatic spirituality. See, e.g., MacArthur, *Charismatic Chaos* (Grand Rapids: Zondervan, 1993); and MacArthur, *Strange Fire: The Danger of Offending the Holy Spirit with Counterfeit Worship* (Nashville: Thomas Nelson, 2013).

59. Cox, *Fire from Heaven*, 312.

but for the whole world."[60] Specifically, he is concerned that early Pentecostalism's expectancy and eschatological urgency—with its vision of God's kingdom breaking imminently into the present to bring good news to the poor and marginalized—have given way to various forms of the prosperity gospel.[61] These fears are not unwarranted, but the situation has evolved since his writing. While there continues to be a strong stream of prosperity theology in the movement, an increasing number of Pentecostals are concerned with social justice, tying that concern to the in-breaking kingdom of God.[62] Both of these factors—the definition of experience and the role of the Holy Spirit—have received serious attention by subsequent generations of Pentecostal scholars, as we will see below.

Experience as the "Heartbeat" of Pentecostalism

Contemporary Pentecostal scholars agree with Cox's central contention that Pentecostalism is "the experiential branch of Christianity *par excellence*."[63] Experience is central to Pentecostal identity and theology in a significant and defining way, or as Keith Warrington puts it, experience is the "heartbeat" of the movement and is "intricately woven into Pentecostal identity and praxis."[64] While most Christian denominations and movements are defined primarily by doctrine, polity, and practices, Pentecostalism finds its unity primarily in a common experience of God.[65] Indeed, Pentecostalism can be said to have originated as "an ecumenical movement of people from many denominations

---

60. Cox, *Fire from Heaven*, 316. Most Pentecostals would bristle at this description, arguing that Jesus Christ is the object of their experience and that the Holy Spirit is the one who enables the encounter with Christ.

61. Cox names as a promising exception Hispanic Pentecostal theologian Eldin Villafañe, who sees the genius of Pentecostalism centered not just in an encounter of the Spirit but specifically in an encounter of the *liberating* Spirit. Cox, *Fire from Heaven*, 319.

62. I return to this point in chap. 5.

63. Harvey G. Cox Jr., "Some Personal Reflections on Pentecostalism," *Pneuma* 15, no. 1 (1993): 30.

64. Quoted in Peter D. Neumann, *Pentecostal Experience: An Ecumenical Encounter* (Eugene, OR: Pickwick, 2012), 5.

65. Walter Hollenweger, "From Azusa Street to the Toronto Phenomenon," in *Pentecostal Movements as an Ecumenical Challenge*, vol. 3, ed. Jürgen Moltmann and Karl Josef Kuschel (Maryknoll, NY: Orbis Books, 1996), 7. See also Newbigin on this point: "Its central element is the conviction that the Christin life is a matter of the experienced power and presence of the Holy Spirit today; that neither orthodoxy of doctrine or impeccability of succession can take the place of this" (Newbigin, *Household of God*, 87–88). However, this is not to say that Pentecostals are unconcerned about doctrine. Most Pentecostal denominations have doctrinal statements. E.g., the Assemblies of God lists sixteen fundamental truths (https://ag.org/Beliefs/Statement-of-Fundamental-Truths), and the Church of God (Cleveland, TN) has a declaration of faith (https://churchofgod.org/beliefs/declaration-of-faith/).

who had had an overwhelming experience of the Spirit,"[66] through a "radical openness to God's presence and power."[67] The history of Pentecostalism reveals differences in doctrine and polity that contributed to various splits and the formation of different Pentecostal denominations.[68] Despite this, the centrality of this defining characteristic of the movement remains unchallenged.[69] It is important to note, however, that this experience is grounded in the scriptural narrative itself (in particular, the account of Pentecost in Acts 2:1–21), and further, "a strong reliance on scripture as a path to doctrinal formulations that support and direct the Pentecostal experiences" helps tie together the various streams of Pentecostalism in spite of these splits.[70] Even so, for many Pentecostals, defining this experience has been less important than the experience itself. However, several significant studies have been published in recent years in which Pentecostal scholars vigorously take up Cox's challenge and attempt to define more clearly what they mean by "experience of God" and how this experience functions in their theological method.[71]

When Pentecostals speak about experience, they have a specific kind of experience in mind. While this experience usually includes glossolalia, or speaking in tongues, this is merely one aspect of how Pentecostals understand what it means to experience God's presence. This experience is something that happens

---

66. Allan Heaton Anderson, "Pentecostal Theology as a Global Challenge: Contextual Theological Constructions," in *The Routledge Handbook of Pentecostal Theology*, ed. Wolfgang Vondey (New York: Routledge, 2020), 19.

67. Terry L. Cross, "The Divine-Human Encounter: Toward a Pentecostal Theology of Experience," *Pneuma* 31 (2009): 6.

68. Several key doctrinal issues in the early years focused on how to understand the process of sanctification, the baptismal formula (whether the triune formula or "In Jesus's name"), and tongues as "initial evidence." For historical background on these, see Robert Mapes Anderson, *Vision of the Disinherited: The Making of American Pentecostalism* (Peabody, MA: Hendrickson, 1979), chaps. 9, 10; and Vinson Synan, *The Holiness-Pentecostal Tradition: Charismatic Movements in the Twentieth Century*, 2nd ed. (Grand Rapids: Eerdmans, 1997), 143–66.

69. E.g., a major branch of Pentecostals is non-trinitarian, or "Oneness," who baptize in "the name of Jesus."

70. Wolfgang Vondey, *Pentecostalism: A Guide for the Perplexed* (New York: Bloomsbury T&T Clark, 2013), 71.

71. It needs to be stated that Pentecostal scholars began this work well before the publication of Cox's book. Despite Cox's deep appreciation of Pentecostal spirituality, he makes only brief mention of Pentecostal scholarship. As noted above, he refers to the work of Eldin Villafañe, but he does not refer to Matthew S. Clark and Henry I. Lederle's *What Is Distinctive about Pentecostal Theology?* (Pretoria: University of South Africa, 1983), which has become a standard early treatment of these questions. Steven J. Land's landmark book, *Pentecostal Spirituality: A Passion for the Kingdom* (Sheffield, UK: Sheffield Academic, 1993), warrants a passing citation, but Cox does not engage his main thesis. Land's book originated as a dissertation at Emory under Don Saliers and is still considered a major study of Pentecostal spirituality even by those (e.g., Dale Coulter) who disagree with his typology or method.

to the believer and is interpreted as an actualization of the Spirit's work. In War-rington's words, Pentecostals expect "to touch God and to be touched by him."[72] To better describe this experience, many Pentecostals will use the language of supernatural or divine encounter. For Wolfgang Vondey, it is the "particular set of first-hand experiences surrounding the day of Pentecost, which concentrates on the immediate encounter with God in Christ through the Holy Spirit."[73] In his seminal study on worship, Daniel Albrecht describes the believer's experi-ence with the divine in worship as a "mystical encounter," which is "mediated by the sense of the immediate divine presence."[74] The term "encounter" helps to preserve the transcendence of God.[75] This is important because, for Pentecostals, "the God who is being encountered is a transcendent other, in contrast to God being experienced immanently within common human experience,"[76] which, as we have seen, is more often the case in other experience-based spiritualties, such as those of the Nones and SBNRs. But like the spiritual experience of the SBNRs, the spiritual experience of Pentecostals is one that leads to spiritual transformation. As Terry Cross writes, "Because we have encountered God's presence in the Spirit, we have been transformed."[77]

The emphasis on experience is rooted in the Pentecost event (Acts 2:1–21). Lisa Stephenson explains that Pentecostals often speak of their movement in terms of restoration, specifically a restoration of apostolic power and the expe-riential aspect of faith. It is not uncommon to find Pentecostals criticizing most Christian churches for losing the experiential aspect of faith and for reducing the Holy Spirit to a "subject of theological dogma rather than a burning experience in the personal lives of the believers."[78] If Pentecostalism is truly the restoration of the Pentecost event, then believers today should expect to encounter God in the same supernatural way as the first disciples. The specific experiences or

---

72. Quoted in Neumann, *Pentecostal Experience*, 109.

73. Wolfgang Vondey, *Pentecostal Theology: Living the Full Gospel, Systematic Pentecostal and Charismatic Theology* (New York: Bloomsbury T&T Clark, 2017), 19–20.

74. Daniel E. Albrecht, *Rites in the Spirit: A Ritual Approach to Pentecostal/Charismatic Spiritual-ity* (New York: Bloomsbury T&T Clark, 1999), 239.

75. Pentecostals debate whether this locates Pentecostalism within the broader mystical tra-dition in Christianity. Neumann thinks the term "mystical" can apply to Pentecostals only with qualification; see Neumann, *Pentecostal Experience*, 112–16. See also Daniel Castelo, *Pentecostalism as a Christian Mystical Tradition* (Grand Rapids: Eerdmans, 2017).

76. Peter D. Neumann, "Experience: The Mediated Immediacy of Encounter with the Spirit," in *The Routledge Handbook of Pentecostal Theology*, ed. Wolfgang Vondey (New York: Routledge, 2020), 88.

77. Cross, "Divine-Human Encounter," 6–7.

78. Donald Gee, quoted in Lisa P. Stephenson, "Pentecostalism and Experience: History, Theology, and Practice," *Journal of Pentecostal Theology* 28 (2019): 193.

encounters emphasized by Pentecostals are conversion, or new birth, and Spirit baptism, a subsequent post-conversion experience. Many claim the latter to be *the* Pentecostal experience.[79] These are direct and vivid encounters of God in Christ through the power of the Spirit that transform the believer.[80]

While Pentecostals believe that individual believers experience the Spirit directly, this experience is mediated through communal gatherings, especially worship. Many Pentecostals stress the centrality of the worship service for the encounter with God. First, individual encounters with the Spirit are not in insolation. They occur within and connect to a Christian community. Second, the worship service is the primary place where Pentecostals expect and actively respond to the presence of God in their midst. Albrecht highlights three foundational rites in communal worship that frame Pentecostal spirituality: worship/praise, the pastoral message (sermon), and altar call/response. The worship service itself is an event in which "those who attended have always expected that something will happen, and that it will happen to them."[81] Response can include testimony, another prominent feature of Pentecostal worship, pointing to "the transforming power of the creator" in one's life.[82] A testimony is given for the benefit of others, to "produce encouragement for the listening congregation. The witness may tell an incident in which fear, loss or failure was overcome by appealing to God's promises or submitting to the divine counsel in the Bible."[83]

The Role of Experience in Pentecostal Theology

The expectation of divine encounter is a necessary aspect of Pentecostal identity and theology.[84] As Peter Neumann states, "Whereas other Christian

---

79. Stephenson, "Pentecostalism and Experience," 194.

80. Neumann, *Pentecostal Experience*, 110.

81. Clark and Lederle, *What Is Distinctive about Pentecostal Theology?*, 43.

82. Jean-Daniel Plüss, "Religious Experience in Worship: A Pentecostal Perspective," *PentecoStudies* 2, no. 1 (2003): 10.

83. Plüss, "Religious Experience in Worship," 9. This feature of testimony in worship provides an interesting connection to what is probably the most communal expression of SBNR spirituality: twelve-step recovery meetings, which cannot be described as a worship experience, even though they often begin and end with prayer. In certain twelve-step meetings, however, called "speaker meetings," a member stands up at the podium and gives a "lead," typically between thirty and forty-five minutes long, which is a kind of testimony. They tell, in a general way, what it was like (while they were still drinking), what happened (what made them realize they wanted to stop drinking), and what it is like today (how their life has improved since getting sober and working the twelve steps). God is frequently invoked as the "higher power" who was there when they "hit bottom" and who gives them the power to stay sober, one day at a time.

84. Stephenson, "Pentecostalism and Experience," 194. Also, Dennis G. Jacobsen, *Thinking in the Spirit: Theologies of the Early Pentecostal Movement* (Bloomington: Indiana University Press, 2003), 3.

traditions may emphasize doctrine or formal liturgy as starting points for theological reflection, Pentecostals begin with the assumption of the direct or immediate experience of the Spirit, both personally and communally."[85] In their
1983 (and still frequently quoted) book, *What Is Distinctive about Pentecostal
Theology?*, Matthew S. Clark and Henry I. Lederle highlight the role of experience in their proposal for a Pentecostal hermeneutic to distinguish Pentecostal
theology from fundamentalist influences. Such a hermeneutic will insist on the
"continuity of the mode of God's presence in and among the faithful from the
creation down to this very day."[86] They claim that "the distinctively Pentecostal
experience of the working of the Holy Spirit issues in a distinctively Pentecostal
view of Scripture and approach to Scripture."[87] Their claim has found support
from significant Pentecostal scholarship in recent years.[88]

Experience plays a significant role in Pentecostal theological method, which,
as the following chapter shows, offers a contrast to Reformation traditions such
as Lutheranism. Pentecostals do not all agree on how to relate the Pentecostal
experience to a Pentecostal theological method. Some, like Cross, insist that
it makes a comprehensive difference.[89] Others, such as Coulter, point out that
Christians from non-Pentecostal traditions (e.g., charismatic Lutherans) claim to
encounter God in the same all-encompassing way, including the experience of
what Pentecostals refer to as baptism in the Spirit. This calls into question any
attempt to "forge a distinctive Pentecostal theology" from a specific experience
of God.[90] This is why, in Coulter's view, an experience of the Spirit can help
determine Pentecostalism's theological core, but it cannot be the sole basis for it.

Vondey's narrative approach to Pentecostal theology offers a third alternative.
Vondey uses the Pentecost event in Acts 2 as the "core symbol of Pentecostalism"
to narratively frame Pentecostal theology. For Vondey, Pentecost is a symbol

85. Neumann, "Experience," 84.
86. Mark McLean, quoted in Clark and Lederle, *What Is Distinctive about Pentecostal Theology?*,
28. The book was reprinted by the University of South Africa in 1989 and 1991.
87. Clark and Lederle, *What Is Distinctive about Pentecostal Theology?*, 33.
88. The field of Pentecostal hermeneutics has grown immensely since Clark and Lederle's
initial foray into the topic and cannot be examined in detail here. Significant studies in recent years
include Kenneth J. Archer, *A Pentecostal Hermeneutic: Spirit, Scripture and Community* (Cleveland,
TN: CPT, 2009); L. William Oliverio Jr., *Theological Hermeneutics in the Classical Pentecostal Tradition: A Typological Account* (Leiden: Brill, 2015); and Kenneth J. Archer and L. William Oliverio
Jr., eds., *Constructive Pneumatological Hermeneutics in Pentecostal Christianity* (New York: Palgrave
Macmillan, 2016).
89. Cross, "Divine-Human Encounter."
90. Dale M. Coulter, "What Meaneth This? Pentecostals and Theological Inquiry," *Journal of
Pentecostal Theology* 10, no. 1 (2001): 46.

that points to a "particular experience of God" that, in turn, signals a new in-breaking reality of God's kingdom through the outpouring of the Spirit, which not only defines the Pentecostal experience but also goes beyond it.[91] He places the symbol of Pentecost alongside the "full gospel," which has emerged histori-cally as either a four- or fivefold pattern drawn from the Wesleyan holiness tradition, and into dialogue with foundational ritual practices and experiences for Pentecostals, such as the altar call, tarrying, and Spirit baptism. Regardless of how one approaches the question of theological method, most Pentecostal theologians would agree with Vondey's assertation that "the path of Pentecostal theology proceeds from experience to reflection" and ultimately to praxis.[92]

Conclusion

Tickle was right. We have entered a new age of the Spirit. The SBNR phenom-enon and the rise of Pentecostal and charismatic spirituality offer important contextual considerations for a fresh exploration of pneumatology. There are significant differences, of course, between these two movements. Unlike the SBNRs, Pentecostal Christians do not reject the "God above"; they believe fervently that the God above is present "with us" in palpable, tangible ways that lead to transformation of self and, increasingly, the world. For Pentecostals, the God of the Bible interacts with believers in "tangible, transformative ways that allow God to be encountered, and hence, experienced."[93] Furthermore, spiri-tual experiences are understood to have a specific shape in Pentecostalism—conversion, sanctification, and especially Spirit baptism—each of which will be discussed in more detail in the following chapters.

However, both movements give a central place to spiritual experiences that are transformative for seekers or believers and, through them, for the world. Further, both emphasize the practical and pragmatic aspects of spiritual expe-rience, insisting that spirituality must *work*—that is, be applicable to everyday life and make a difference in the world. As Neumann points out, "Because Pentecostals assume the Spirit is active in the world, the sphere of everyday life and work becomes a testing ground for identifying the activity of the Spirit."[94] Where there is spirit talk today, it is connected to a desire for personal or social

---

91. Vondey, *Pentecostal Theology*, 283.
92. Vondey, *Pentecostal Theology*, 24, 28–30.
93. Neumann, "Experience," 92.
94. Neumann, "Experience," 91.

transformation. According to Vondey, the Pentecostal concept of the "full gospel" is less an explication of theology than it is a narrative of a new way of life. He writes, "Pentecostalism is a form of living fundamentally concerned with the renewing work of God as it emerges from the outpouring of the Holy Spirit on the Day of Pentecost."[95]

Tickle, who highlighted the significance of these two movements in ushering in the age of the Spirit, argues that at the heart of this shift is a question about authority: Who is in charge? For Tickle, this question cannot be fully answered without engaging the Holy Spirit. But who or what is the Holy Spirit? The SBNR phenomenon and the rise of Pentecostalism both point to a need to speak more clearly about the Spirit.[96] While Tickle helpfully narrates the development and diminishment of the doctrine of the Holy Spirit in the West (focusing especially on the introduction of the filioque in the eleventh century, leading to the Great Schism), she does not then outline a constructive theology of the Holy Spirit.

In the following chapters, I attempt to do that from a Lutheran perspective with both movements keenly in mind and in explicit dialogue with one of them: Pentecostalism. A constructive theology of the Holy Spirit for the church today cannot be afraid to speak experientially about the Holy Spirit. It should be able to articulate the Spirit's work in the Christian life in ways that speak to the possibility of transformed existence, not only in the hereafter but also in the present.

95. Vondey, *Pentecostal Theology*, 22, 12.
96. Tickle and Sweeney, *Age of the Spirit*, 19–20.

2

The Holy Spirit as Person

Experiencing the Presence of God

We have seen the importance of spiritual experience in the emerging age of the Spirit, although it manifests in different ways in the Pentecostal/charismatic movement and the SBNR phenomenon. The issue of spiritual experience raises certain questions. For example: What or who is being experienced, and toward what end? For those in the field of spirituality, specifically Christian spirituality, such questions are necessarily explored from the perspective of those having spiritual experiences. As this book is a work of systematic theology, I address these questions from the perspective of pneumatology—that is, as events or actions of the Holy Spirit in the Christian life. While this requires attention to the experience itself, here it is interpreted as an effect of the Spirit's activity, based on our knowledge of the Holy Spirit's personhood from Scripture and tradition.

It is important first to define the personal identity, or personhood, of the Spirit. Christian theology speaks of God in personal terms—as a "Thou," as *someone* we are called into relationship with, rather than as *something* or as an impersonal force. In this sense, one can call God a "person," as Karl Rahner has argued.[1] Christian theology teaches that the one personal God exists in

1. Mark S. M. Scott, "God as Person: Karl Barth and Karl Rahner on Divine and Human Personhood," *Religious Studies and Theology* 25, no. 2 (2006): 161–90.

three "persons": the Father, the Son, and the Holy Spirit.[2] This use of the term "person" comes from patristic trinitarian theology as the English translation of the Latin *persona*, which was used to translate the Greek term *hypostasis*. The latter term was introduced in contrast to the one divine *ousia* (the substance, essence, or being of God), which is shared equally by the three persons of the Trinity. While the Father, Son, and Holy Spirit were said to have the same *ousia*, they each were understood to have a unique *hypostasis/persona*, or person.

Many modern theologians have suggested alternative terms to "person" because the word is misleading in contemporary understanding. Modern thinkers understand the term "person" in psychological rather than metaphysical terms, in contrast to the Greek patristic theologians.[3] Specifically, the term is closely associated with the modern idea of personality as the seat of subjectivity and individual autonomy. For this reason, Robert Jenson has proposed the term "identity" as an alternative. Jenson believes this term is closer to what the Nicene fathers intended, since one cannot identify God except through one or another of God's personal identities.[4]

Others have kept the term "person" but defined it in more relational ways. In his well-known work *Being as Communion*, John Zizioulas posits relationality and communion (*koinonia*) as central to the notion of divine personhood, in terms of both the Godhead and the three hypostases (persons) of the Trinity.[5]

---

2. For the technical discussion of the doctrine of the Trinity in this chapter, I have chosen to use the church's traditional terms for the three persons (Father, Son, and Holy Spirit) and affirm the use of this traditional formulation in the sacrament of Holy Baptism and the historic creeds because it ties us to the church throughout time and space. However, I agree with feminist theologians that our language for God must expand beyond the traditional trinitarian formula (esp. in preaching, testimony, prayers, and hymnody) to include non-male and non-masculine images from the Bible and Christian tradition because God is both inclusive of and beyond human gender categories, per Gen. 1:27. Alternative trinitarian formulas should be measured according to how well they identify God, not only by God's saving acts for us but also by God's internal relations that distinguish the persons from one another and, at the same time, constitute the triune unity. See Barbara K. Lundblad, "Do You See This Woman?," in *Lutheran Women in Ordained Ministry 1970–1995: Reflections and Perspectives*, ed. Gloria E. Bengston (Minneapolis: Augsburg, 1995), 91. For an updated discussion of these issues, see Mary J. Streufert, *Language for God: A Lutheran Perspective* (Minneapolis: Fortress, 2022).

3. Robert W. Jenson, *The Triune Identity: God according to the Gospel* (Philadelphia: Fortress, 1982). The term "identity" is not without problems, as it can be used in a modalistic sense (e.g., I am one person with several identities: daughter, wife, friend, etc.). Others who have proposed alternative language include Karl Barth and Karl Rahner, respectively, "modes of being" and "distinct manners of subsisting."

4. Ted Peters, review of *The Triune Identity: God according to the Gospel*, by Robert W. Jenson, *Currents in Theology and Mission* 12, no. 4 (August 1985): 245.

5. John D. Zizioulas, *Being as Communion: Studies in Personhood and the Church* (Crestwood, NY: St. Vladimir's Seminary Press, 1997).

While a full examination of this issue is beyond the scope of this work, my intention in using the traditional terms "person" and "personhood" is twofold. First, I wish to affirm the church's teaching on the distinction of the three persons within the divine Godhead—that is, that the Holy Spirit is coequal in divinity to the Father and the Son. Second, I wish to affirm the personal and relational nature of the Holy Spirit, along with that of the Father and the Son.[6]

Making the connection between human experiences of the Spirit and the Spirit's distinctive personhood has not always been an easy task for theologians. Concerns raised by some Protestant theologians about the role of experience in theology has led to treatments of the Holy Spirit devoid of any reference to experience. Alternatively, we see the tendency of many contemporary pneumatologies to deemphasize the personhood of the Spirit, speaking of the Spirit in nonpersonal terms, such as "vibration" or "field of force," akin to what Eugene Rogers has called "pneumatologies of presence."[7]

In this chapter, I respond to concerns about experience from a Lutheran perspective, thereby affirming the role of spiritual experience as a resource for thinking theologically about the Spirit. I also show the limitations of so-called pneumatologies of presence and instead affirm the church's catholic teaching on the Holy Spirit's relational personhood within a trinitarian framework. Finally, following the cues of several contemporary theologians, I explore the Holy Spirit as person through an engagement of the narrative of Scripture, especially the New Testament witness. I propose that a robust understanding of the Spirit's relational personhood, within a trinitarian framework and rooted in the biblical narrative, provides a strong theological basis for speaking about *our experiences* of the Spirit as God's personal presence and power, as the giver of life working for, in, and through the Christian life.

The Role of Experience in Reformation Theologies

Although experience historically has played a role in theological inquiry, many Protestants have explicitly excluded or suppressed it as a legitimate dimension

6. In his defense of the traditional terminology, William J. Hill points to its emphasis on relationality and focus on intersubjectivity. By retaining the underlying metaphysical dimension, and by remaining aware of the analogical nature of the term, he argues that anthropomorphism can be avoided with its use. See Hill, *The Three-Personed God: The Trinity as a Mystery of Salvation* (Washington, DC: Catholic University Press, 1988), 255.

7. Eugene F. Rogers Jr., *After the Spirit: A Constructive Pneumatology from Resources outside the Modern West* (Grand Rapids: Eerdmans, 2005), 6.

of theological reflection, due in large part to concerns raised by the twentieth-century Swiss theologian Karl Barth. Much of Protestant theology has viewed experience and subjectivity as "at best ambivalent and at worst catastrophic for theology."[8] In his recent monograph *The Holy Spirit and Christian Experience*, Simeon Zahl addresses these concerns head-on, making two key arguments. First, he argues that experience is unavoidable methodologically and proposes a way to address the role of experience in theology that avoids "common pitfalls" that have troubled Barth and others.[9] Second, he makes an explicit connection between spiritual experience and the Holy Spirit: "When we speak about experience in Christian theology, we are speaking at the same time about the Holy Spirit."[10]

The contextual and theological reasons Zahl raises for attending to the role of experience largely align with my examination in the previous chapter. First, in our late-modern context, the spiritual and intellectual plausibility of Christianity can no longer be taken for granted. There is a growing gap "between theological concepts and people's lived experience." [11] In the United States, one sees this particularly reflected in the phenomenon of the Nones and SBNRs. Zahl points to the "dynamism, creativity, and experiential power of the worldwide Pentecostal and charismatic movements" as another reason for reengaging experience theologically.[12] Finally, he is keen to challenge a common misreading that the doctrine of justification is no more than "a legal fiction" for the Lutheran Reformers, a point I will return to in chapter 3. In short, contemporary theology needs to recover the resources and insights of Christian experience of God and the world, and one way to do this is by paying attention to the doctrine of the Holy Spirit. Indeed, by engaging experience through the work of the Holy Spirit, one can avoid the problems that can arise with a more general appeal to "religious experience."[13]

---

8. Simeon Zahl, *The Holy Spirit and Christian Experience* (New York: Oxford University Press, 2020), 6.

9. Zahl, *Holy Spirit and Christian Experience*, 2.

10. Zahl, *Holy Spirit and Christian Experience*, 3.

11. Zahl, *Holy Spirit and Christian Experience*, 4.

12. Zahl, *Holy Spirit and Christian Experience*, 5. Despite this assertion, Zahl explicitly engages Pentecostal and charismatic theologians only briefly (specifically, Frank Macchia and Amos Yong). He does refer back to this movement in the conclusion. Zahl, *Holy Spirit and Christian Experience*, 241–42.

13. Zahl, *Holy Spirit and Christian Experience*, 6–7. The literature on the scholarly study and critique of the category of religious experience is vast and varied, and well beyond the scope of this study. Zahl reviews some key contributions in *Holy Spirit and Christian Experience*, 50–52. See also Bill Leonard, *A Sense of the Heart: Christian Religious Experience in the United States*

Since the time of the Reformation, there have been anxiety and ambivalence in Protestantism about the "reliability and significance" of Christian religious experience, and that anxiety and ambivalence have led to "one of the most fundamental and enduring debates in Protestant theology from the 1520s to the present."[14] The tension within Luther's writings illustrates this point. On the one hand, Luther appeals to his own general human experience (e.g., his experience of *Anfechtung*, or despair). On the other hand, he seems to insist that no inner experience of God's Spirit can be authentic if it is not mediated through the external means of grace, Word (proclamation) and sacraments, thereby limiting the Spirit's activity.[15] In addition to his debates with Andreas von Karlstadt and other "enthusiasts" who seemed to claim an experience of the Spirit unmediated by the Word, Luther's more pessimistic view of subjective experience is seen in his biblical commentaries, where he admonishes his hearers, "When you no longer accord the Word greater validity than your every feeling, your eyes, your senses, and your heart, you are doomed, and you can no longer be helped. . . . You must judge solely by the Word, regardless of what you feel or see."[16]

However, Luther's primary concern with the enthusiasts is not that they claim to hear the Spirit outside of the Word and sacraments but that they have not tested that inspiration against God's Word—centered in the gospel of justification—and thereby are in danger of confusing God's Spirit with their own.[17] In other words, Luther believes that they have abandoned the criterion of justification and have detached the "good news" from the cross of Christ, making it more about their own (or their followers') glory and power, and in doing so are in danger of preaching a false gospel. To this point, Lutheran charismatic theologian Theodore Jungkuntz explains, "Luther, in spite of his polemic against using 'experience'

(Nashville: Abingdon, 2014); Ann Taves, *Religious Experience Reconsidered: A Building Block to the Study of Religion and Other Special Things* (Princeton: Princeton University Press, 2009); Taves, *Fits, Trances, & Visions: Experiencing Religion and Explaining Experience from Wesley to James* (Princeton: Princeton University Press, 1999); and Caroline Franks Davis, *The Evidential Force of Religious Experience* (Oxford: Clarendon, 1989).

14. Zahl, *Holy Spirit and Christian Experience*, 26, 17.

15. Zahl, *Holy Spirit and Christian Experience*, 20.

16. Martin Luther, "Commentary on 1 Corinthians 7," in *Luther's Works*, American ed., 55 vols. (Philadelphia: Fortress; St. Louis: Concordia, 1955–86), 28:70. *Luther's Works* is hereafter cited as *LW*.

17. See Cheryl M. Peterson, "Rediscovering Pneumatology in the 'Age of the Spirit': A North American Lutheran Contribution," *Dialog* 58, no. 2 (Summer 2019): 102–8. Whether this is a fair assessment of Andreas von Karlstadt and others is debatable, of course, and evaluation of this question is beyond the scope of this book.

as a measuring stick for faith, nevertheless had a very positive evaluation of the place of experience in the life of the Christian."[18] For example, Luther writes, "No one can correctly understand God or His work unless he has received such understanding immediately from the Holy Spirit. But no one can receive it from the Holy Spirit without experiencing, proving, and feeling it."[19] Luther affirms this with his famous Table Talk dictum: "Only experience makes the theologian."[20]

A later, positive evaluation not only of experience in general but also of specifically *spiritual* experience is found in Luther's "Tower Experience of 1519," about which he wrote three decades later. Since the turn of the twentieth century, Luther scholars have debated the actual date, the kind, and the meaning of this "experience" or "insight" (Was it a conversion? A theological breakthrough?)— not to mention why Luther waited three decades to record it.[21] I am interested less in these questions and more in the manner that Luther chose to remember it all those years later. Luther articulates a personal, transformative experience of God's love and power. While meditating and praying on the phrase "the justice of God" in Paul's Letter to the Romans, Luther first affirms his central Reformation insight, that the righteousness by which one lives is itself a gift from God, not something one can or must accomplish on one's own. Then Luther gives an expressive description of how this insight made him feel at the time: "All at once, I felt that I had been born again and entered into paradise itself through open gates. Immediately I saw the whole of Scripture in a different light. . . . I ran through the Scriptures from memory and found that other terms had analogous meanings, e.g., the work of God, that is, what God works in us; the power of God, by which he makes us powerful; the wisdom of God, by which he makes us wise; the strength of God, the salvation of God, the glory of God."[22]

The language Luther uses to describe his experience resonates with contemporary Pentecostals; however, it was his negative assessment of spiritual

---

18. Theodore R. Jungkuntz, "Secularization Theology, Charismatic Renewal, and Luther's Theology of the Cross," *Concordia Theological Monthly* 42, no. 1 (1972): 17. Jungkuntz cites Walther von Loewenich's classic study, *Luther's Theology of the Cross*, trans. Hebert Bouman (Minneapolis: Augsburg, 1976), 86–99.

19. *LW* 21:299, quoted in Jungkuntz, "Secularization Theology," 17–18.

20. *LW* 54:7.

21. For an overview, see Marilyn J. Harran, *Luther on Conversion: The Early Years* (Ithaca, NY: Cornell University Press, 1983), chap. 7. See also W. D. J. Cargill Thompson, "The Problems of Luther's 'Tower Experience' and Its Place in His Intellectual Development," in *Religious Motivation: Biographical and Sociological Problems for the Church Historian*, ed. Derek Baker (Oxford: Basil Blackwell, 1978), 187–211.

22. *LW* 34:337.

experience that made the more lasting impact on Lutheran theology. This was followed by a similar assessment by Karl Barth centuries later.[23] With his rejection of all theologies that take as their starting point anything apart from God's Word addressed to human beings, Barth updates and goes beyond Luther by critiquing any role for human subjectivity in theology. He aims his strong critique at nineteenth-century liberal theologians who often conflated the Holy Spirit with the human spirit.[24] This is not to say that Barth avoids pneumatology; he simply cautions against confusing a turn toward human religious experience with a turn to the Spirit. For Barth, "claims to subjective human experience, whether in terms of feelings or emotions, personal revelations, dispositions, inner intuitions, or any other 'impress of the divine,' and regardless of whether such experience takes a philosophically sophisticated Schleiermachian form or a less complex pietist form, are utterly excluded as a valid starting point in theological reflection."[25] For this reason, Zahl correctly claims that Barth's theology carries "the torch for the Protestant tradition of anti-enthusiasm begun by Luther."[26] This historical backdrop sets up Zahl's argument for a retrieval of experience for Christian theological reflection. I agree with Zahl's proposal to address the theme not with a general category of religious experience but rather "with Christian theology's own internal set of categories"—that is, with pneumatology.[27]

Pneumatologies of Presence

By and large, contemporary theologians do not have the same concerns about including experience in their theological reflection on the Holy Spirit. On the

---

23. Zahl, *Holy Spirit and Christian Experience*, 23–25.

24. Aaron T. Smith examines Barth's reassessment of Schleiermacher at the end of his life as well as Barth's own pneumatology. Aaron T. Smith, *Theology of the Third Article: Karl Barth and the Spirit of the Word* (Minneapolis: Fortress, 2014).

25. Zahl, *Holy Spirit and Christian Experience*, 26–29.

26. Zahl, *Holy Spirit and Christian Experience*, 29. In his later writings, Barth acknowledges that humans can experience God's Word, but he still insists that such experiences cannot play a role in theological method. However, God's Word addresses human beings not in a vacuum but, rather, in a complex array of contextual factors, including one's personal and cultural experiences. Scripture and experience are integrally woven together, as how one reads Scripture is shaped by one's individual and communal experiences as well as by one's wider context. On the one hand, a theologian should bring a certain subjectivity to the theological task, exercising "epistemic humility" when making normative claims on behalf of humanity. On the other hand, to argue for the exclusion of experience from formal theological and dogmatic reflection is "to whitewash the history of the church in the name of modern methodological anxieties." Zahl, *Holy Spirit and Christian Experience*, 37; see also 30–40.

27. Zahl, *Holy Spirit and Christian Experience*, 52.

contrary, many such treatments can be categorized as "pneumatologies of presence."[28] These are often vague in terms of how they define the experience of God's presence, including to whom and to what effect, and in terms of the criteria used for discerning the Spirit's presence. Further, they struggle to affirm fully the personhood of the Spirit. Lack of proper attention to the distinctions between persons of the Trinity often leads to an understanding of the Spirit as simply an *effect* of God's presence and power, or even to modalism.[29] Finally, such treatments can be disconnected from our embodied, everyday existence.[30]

Zahl discusses Geoffrey Lampe's *God as Spirit* (1977) as an example. Lampe reduces the Spirit to the "mode in which Christ becomes present to believers," and he fails to consider the Spirit's own personhood or, for that matter, the distinction between human experience that recognizes God's presence and human experience that does not.[31] The influential monograph by John V. Taylor *The Go-Between God: The Holy Spirit and the Christian Mission* offers another example from the same time period.[32] Taylor defines the Spirit as a force of influence that brings human beings into a new and fresh awareness. Because the effect of this power or force is "always to bring a mere object into a personal relationship with me, to turn an It into a Thou," personal language is often used to understand this force. However, the Spirit is not a "person" but "that power of communion which enables every other reality, and the God who is within and behind all realities, to be present to us."[33]

A more recent example (also one not considered by Zahl) is the hybrid pneumatology of Presbyterian theologian Grace Ji-Sun Kim in *Reimagining Spirit: Wind, Breath, and Vibration*.[34] According to Kim, when we speak of the

28. The term was coined by Eugene Rogers, but the following points are drawn from Zahl, *Holy Spirit and Christian Experience*, 53–68.

29. Zahl, *Holy Spirit and Christian Experience*, 56.

30. This has led Eugene Rogers to call such pneumatologies "boring." Quoted in Zahl, *Holy Spirit and Christian Experience*, 57. See also p. 60, where Zahl speaks about the Spirit's affinity for the material, how the Spirit befriends the body. To this point, see also Cheryl M. Peterson, "Spirit and Body: A Feminist and Lutheran Conversation," in *Transformative Lutheran Theologies: Feminist, Womanist, and Mujerista Perspectives*, ed. Mary J. Streufert (Minneapolis: Fortress, 2010), 153–64.

31. Zahl, *Holy Spirit and Christian Experience*, 58–64. See also John Webster's treatment of Geoffrey Lampe in his article on the difficulty with the Spirit's personhood. Webster, "The Identity of the Holy Spirit: A Problem in Trinitarian Theology," *Themelios* 9, no. 1 (September 1983): 4–7.

32. John V. Taylor, *The Go-Between God: The Holy Spirit and the Christian Mission* (London: SCM, 1972), 16–17. Zahl does not discuss Taylor.

33. Taylor, *Go-Between God*, 16–17, 19.

34. Grace Ji-Sun Kim, *Reimagining Spirit: Wind, Breath, and Vibration* (Eugene, OR: Cascade Books, 2019). This is Kim's fourth book on pneumatology, in which she continues to develop her exploration of the Spirit in light of the Korean concept of Chi. Previous volumes include Kim,

Spirit, we are speaking of the "full presence of God,"[35] further defined in terms of movement,[36] specifically the three movements of light, wind, and vibration. Spirit as light communicates in an intimate way that presence of God within us and is an image of life (in that light brings growth and nourishment) that reveals truth. The image of wind teaches us that the Spirit is ever present in the world, always moving to bring liberation to creation by empowering us to work actively for liberation and justice.[37] The image or movement of the Spirit as vibration— which Kim connects to God's voice (and which, like wind, is connected to the *ruach*, or breath, of God)—also conveys that the Spirit is life-giving, the means by which our world was created and the one who moves us today to work for positive social change.[38] As with light and wind, "this understanding of God as the Spirit that vibrates through the Earth reminds us with great clarity that God has presence on the earth, in ourselves, and in the universe."[39]

Kim's discussion of these images is illuminating and helpful regarding the work of the Holy Spirit, especially in the movement of the Spirit in calling Christians into God's mission. However, by themselves these images do not offer a robust view of God's personhood. Kim implies the personhood of the Spirit in connecting vibration to God's voice, wind to God's breath, and light to Wisdom and Logos, as well as by emphasizing the Spirit's prophetic role. She also acknowledges the traditional Protestant understanding of the Spirit's role in bringing people to faith in Christ, which "gives our lives new direction (the 'new creation' of Scripture), salvation—everything associated with newness of life."[40]

However, she finds the creedal teaching of the Holy Spirit as the Third Person of the Trinity to be "stagnant," and she accuses it of remaining "a white, Eurocentric pneumatology, which has not responded to the challenges and changing contexts throughout religious and social history."[41] On the one hand, she speaks appreciatively of the Cappadocian contribution of the coequality

---

The Holy Spirit, Chi, and the Other: A Model of Global and Intercultural Pneumatology (New York: Palgrave MacMillan, 2011); Kim, *Embracing the Other: The Transformative Spirit of Love* (Grand Rapids: Eerdmans, 2015); and Kim, *The Homebrewed Christianity Guide to the Holy Spirit: Hand-Raisers, Han, and the Holy Ghost* (Minneapolis: Fortress, 2018). Kim is ordained in the Presbyterian Church (USA) but describes her background as a "dynamic mix of Pentecostal, Baptist, Missionary Alliance, and Presbyterian influences." Kim, *Reimagining Spirit*, 78.

35. Kim, *Reimagining Spirit*, 47.
36. Kim, *Reimagining Spirit*, 136.
37. Kim, *Reimagining Spirit*, 65, 73.
38. Kim, *Reimagining Spirit*, 89.
39. Kim, *Reimagining Spirit*, 91, 97.
40. Kim, *Reimagining Spirit*, 58.
41. Kim, *Reimagining Spirit*, 17.

and mutual dependency of the three hypostases of the Trinity for their identities. On the other hand, she criticizes dependency as a Eurocentric idea shaped by Greek philosophy, making it less helpful to non-European communities in understanding the Trinity. More significantly for this study, she is concerned that Western theologians frequently approach the Spirit as an object of study in ways that are disconnected from the materiality and embodiment of our existence. As I hope to show, this need not be the case.

As an alternative to the creedal understanding of the Spirit as "person," Kim proposes the Asian concept of Chi—that is, the vital life force or energy that flows through all living things—and uses it in her work to flesh out a concept of the Spirit as "the life-giving presence of God, felt and experienced by all people in their daily lives."[42] Kim's engagement with Chi to explore the work of the Holy Spirit in the world is an important contribution toward the search for theological common ground between East and West. As Kirsteen Kim (no relation) notes, however, it is less of a contribution toward a full theology of the Holy Spirit, as this would require addressing, among other things, how the Spirit-Chi relates to a traditional trinitarian formulation, including the question of the Spirit's personhood.[43]

Zahl cites Jürgen Moltmann's ground-breaking pneumatology, The Spirit of Life, as another example of a "pneumatology of presence," but this is a somewhat unfair characterization, as Moltmann's contribution is more nuanced.[44] Moltmann does approach the question of the Spirit's personhood in terms of experience (rather than according to a preconceived concept of person), but he does so to avoid the difficulties associated with the concept of person used by Augustine and Aquinas, an individual substance rational in nature.[45] Although in later trinitarian discourse the concept of person would shift to a more relational and perichoretic view, Moltmann notes that this development succeeds only in socializing the Spirit relationally, as the "third in the bond," rather than offering an articulation of the Holy Spirit's unique personhood.

---

42. Kim, Reimagining Spirit, 117.

43. Kirsteen Kim, review of The Holy Spirit, Chi, and the Other: A Model of Global and Intercultural Pneumatology, by Grace Ji-Sun Kim, Pneuma 35 (2013): 113. Kirsteen Kim also critiques Grace Ji-Sun Kim for being too simplistic in her analysis of East and West and colonialism and for promoting Chi as "inherently anti-imperial," as if China were never an imperialistic power. Kirsteen Kim, review of Holy Spirit, Chi, and the Other, 112.

44. Zahl, Holy Spirit and Christian Experience, 56.

45. The influence of sixth-century philosopher Boethius is also noted by Moltmann. See also F. LeRon Shults, "Spirit and Spirituality: Philosophical Trends in Late Modern Pneumatology," Pneuma 30 (2008): 276.

In his pneumatology, Moltmann moves from the activity of the Spirit to the Spirit as actor in the biblical narrative, and then to the Spirit's personhood within the triune Godhead. Drawing on a variety of biblical metaphors for how the Spirit is experienced—including personal images such as Lord and Mother but also a number of impersonal images (e.g., energy, force, fire, wind, light, and water)—Moltmann deduces the Holy Spirit's unique personhood as "the loving, self-communicating, out-fanning and out-pouring presence of the eternal divine life of the triune God."[46] At the same time, he concludes that, based on the biblical narrative, the Holy Spirit is experienced *both* as power *and* as person, not as either one or the other.[47]

The Personhood of the Spirit in the Catholic Tradition

The catholic tradition of the church, reflected in ecumenical creeds, confesses the full deity of the Spirit as a hypostasis (person) of the Trinity, in perfect perichoretic communion with the Father and Son. This doctrinal understanding developed as an outgrowth of the debates over the relationship between the Father and Son that culminated in the Councils of Nicaea (325) and Constantinople (381), and it was codified in the Nicean-Constantinopolitan Creed. The fourth-century Cappadocians (Basil of Caesarea, Gregory of Nyssa, and Gregory of Nazianzus) formulated language that affirmed the full divinity of each while still distinguishing the persons through their relations to one another: the Son is eternally begotten of the Father, and the Spirit eternally proceeds from the Father. In this way, the language of the creed reflects the Cappadocians' important contributions. The bishops did not similarly apply the term used to affirm the deity of the Son (*homoousios*) to the Holy Spirit at the Council of Constantinople. However, the language that was adopted (Lord, giver of life, who with the Father and the Son is worshiped and glorified, who has spoken through the prophets) cannot be interpreted in any other way but as an affirmation of the Spirit's deity, equal to that of the Father and the Son.

---

46. Jürgen Moltmann, *The Spirit of Life: A Universal Affirmation*, trans. Margaret Kohl (Minneapolis: Fortress, 1992), 289. For that matter, Wolfhart Pannenberg's concept of the Spirit as a "field of force" does not fit this category either, since he takes great pains to integrate this concept into a doctrine of the Trinity. See Veli-Matti Kärkkäinen, "The Working of the Spirit of God in Creation and the People of God: The Pneumatology of Wolfhart Pannenberg," *Pneuma* 26, no. 1 (Spring 2004): 17–35.

47. Moltmann, *Spirit of Life*, 288.

Theologians in the past and present have struggled to conceptualize the
Spirit's personal identity in ways analogous to that of the Father and the Son.
To start with, the biblical designations for the Spirit are more impersonal than
the biblical designations for the First and Second Persons of the Trinity. This
has been compounded by the ways theologians, especially in the West, have
categorized the intratrinitarian relationships within the Godhead. A primary
example is how the Thomistic idea that the Spirit is a "bond of love" between
the Father and the Son has contributed to the depersonalization of the Holy
Spirit.[48]

Lutheran theologian Robert Jenson offers a helpful contribution. Jenson's
central theological concern is the identity of God. The triune designation—
Father, Son, and Holy Spirit—provides "a compressed telling of the total narrative by which Scripture identifies God and a personal name for God so speci-
fied in it."[49] For Jenson, relationality is central to God's identity. Following the
Cappadocians, Jenson affirms that God's "being" subsists in the relations of
the three persons (or as he prefers, "identities") within the triune Godhead.[50]
Though distinct from the Father, the Son is "internally related to the Father"
in "a relation necessary to his being God," leading Jenson to claim that "*to be
God is to be related*."[51] Jenson rejects the traditional Augustinian formula in
response to the question "What exactly is the relation by which the Spirit is
an identity other than the Father?," reasoning that if the Spirit is the bond of
love between Father and Son, then the Spirit cannot be a distinct partner in

---

48. Thomas Aquinas, *Summa Theologiae* I.37.1. Thomas builds on the Augustinian idea of the
Spirit as the "one who bonds" and other more active descriptors. See Andrew K. Gabriel, *The Lord
Is the Spirit: The Holy Spirit and the Divine Attributes* (Eugene, OR: Pickwick, 2011), 94. See also
Anthony Keaty, "The Holy Spirit Proceeding as Mutual Love: An Interpretation of Aquinas' *Summa
Theologiae*, I.37," *Angelicum* 77, nos. 3/4 (2000): 533–57.

49. Robert Jenson, *God after God: The God of the Past and the Future as Seen in the Work of Karl
Barth* (New York: Bobbs-Merrill, 1969), 146. Jenson grounds the identity of God in the promise
of the gospel, worked out in the narrative of Scripture, culminating in the death and resurrection
of Jesus Christ. See Jenson, *Story and Promise: A Brief Theology of the Gospel about Jesus* (Philadelphia: Fortress, 1973), 60. A thorough examination and evaluation of Jenson's trinitarian theology
is beyond the scope of this book. It may be worth noting that, for Jenson, God's transcendence
is understood not in terms of radical temporality or timelessness. God's eternity is redefined as
"the unity of Father, Son, and Spirit; the three modes in their temporality are the one God, so that
past, present, and future do not fall apart" (Jenson, *God after God*, 96). To avoid collapsing the
immanent Trinity into the economic Trinity (which would bind God in time), Jenson proposes
that the "immanent" Trinity be understood simply as the eschatological reality of the "economic."
See Jenson, *God after God*, 128.

50. Robert Jenson, *Systematic Theology*, vol. 1, *The Triune God* (New York: Oxford University
Press, 1997), 118–19.

51. Jenson, *God after God*, 85 (emphasis original).

the divine community.[52] If the Father and Son are to be free in their love for each other, then someone must act as liberator. The Spirit is the bond of love between two personal lovers—not as sheer relation but as a true third party, who "in his own intention liberates Father and Son to love each other. The Father begets the Son, but it is the Spirit who presents this Son to his Father as an object of the love that begot him, that is, to be actively loved."[53] For Jenson, the Spirit is personal in that the Spirit is "sheer freedom" and "the Liberator of the Father and the Son."[54]

While promising, Jenson's proposal focuses primarily on the immanent Trinity rather than the economy of salvation, focusing on the relationships between the persons of the Trinity. He does not relate the Spirit's personhood to believers in their experience of God (as, e.g., Luther does when he speaks of the Holy Spirit bringing us to Christ, who in turn reveals to us the heart of the Father, in what Timothy Wengert calls Luther's "reversed Trinity"[55]). Apart from the Spirit's founding role at Pentecost and in church order and worship—that is, charisms for the execution of ecclesial offices and the Spirit's agency (in the *anamenesis*) in the eucharistic celebration—Jenson makes little reference to the Spirit's work in the Christian life and does not apply his narrative method to the economy of salvation.

Too often, discussions of the personhood of the Holy Spirit focus only on the patristic formulations. As important as these are, they focus primarily on the intratrinitarian relations between the persons and not on the character and work of the Spirit in the Christian life. They focus more on the immanent than the economic Trinity. To speak pneumatologically about "spiritual experience," theologians must be able to speak of the Spirit as person in the economy of salvation. As I show, who the Spirit is—immanently and economically—shapes how we understand the work of the Holy Spirit in the Christian life, specifically in the three movements of justification, sanctification, and mission.

Several contemporary theologians have shifted from philosophical to biblical categories to better explore the Spirit's trinitarian personhood in the economy

---

52. Jenson, *Systematic Theology*, 1:148.

53. Jenson, *Systematic Theology*, 1:156.

54. For a detailed and excellent study of Jenson's pneumatology, along with a compelling argument for its capacity to be developed in more economic directions (esp. mission and liberation), see James Daryn Henry, *The Freedom of God: A Study in the Pneumatology of Robert Jenson* (Lanham, MD: Lexington Books / Fortress Academic, 2018).

55. Timothy J. Wengert, *Martin Luther's Catechisms: Forming the Faith* (Minneapolis: Fortress, 2009), 43–47.

of salvation. Instead of starting with metaphors for the Spirit's activity as Moltmann does, I follow Eugene Rogers's suggestion that the best way to approach
the Spirit's identity is through the narrative of Scripture, by giving a "thick
description" of the character of the Spirit and by observing how the Spirit interacts with plot and other characters in the biblical narrative.[56] What does the
biblical narrative teach us about the Spirit as "person," as one who encounters
us in a relationship that justifies, sanctifies, and empowers and directs for our
life's calling (and that of the community into which we are incorporated)? In the
following section, I consider the contributions of several Lutheran, Reformed,
and Pentecostal theologians who reflect on the Spirit's personhood and identity
in view of the scriptural narrative.

The Personhood of the Spirit in View of the Biblical Narrative: Some Contemporary Perspectives

Michael Welker's *God the Spirit* is arguably the second most significant monograph on the Holy Spirit at the end of the twentieth century, after Moltmann's
Spirit of Life.[57] Welker, a Reformed theologian, describes his method as "real-
istic theology" (as opposed to Hegelian or other idealistic totalizing systems),
which begins with a close reading of a variety of biblical traditions, allowing
the theological identity of the Holy Spirit to emerge in all its richness. Beginning with historically early and "relatively unclear" biblical testimonies of
the Spirit in the Old Testament, Welker shows how the action of the Spirit is
experienced initially in unpredictable, unforeseeable, emergent ways, to bring
deliverance and restoration. Welker argues that it is in the life and ministry
of Jesus Christ that the concrete presence of the Spirit is most clearly re-
vealed. The Spirit of Christ delivers, restores, and gives God's people capacity
for justice and mercy, simultaneously giving authority to the powerless and
strengthening those to bear witness and serve the neighbor in a "force field of
love" that breaks down obstacles to communication and relationship.[58] The
outpouring of the Spirit is an action of liberation and of overcoming the world
that calls God's people to a vocation of freedom of life in the world, not to
escape it.

---

56. Rogers, *After the Spirit*, 7. In his work, Rogers limits his observation to the Gospels, specifically the life of Jesus in the Synoptic Gospels.

57. Michael Welker, *God the Spirit*, trans. John F. Hoffmeyer (Minneapolis: Fortress, 1994).

58. Welker, *God the Spirit*, 227.

In his final chapter on the personhood of the Spirit, Welker shifts to philosophy (specifically Hegel) because "person" is not a biblical category. Like Moltmann, he wishes to move beyond metaphysical concepts of the Spirit's personhood and draws out a concept of the Spirit's personhood analogically from the Spirit's activity in the community of God's people. While he affirms that the Spirit is a person, he proposes that the Spirit is a "public person" corresponding to the individual Jesus Christ—that is, a domain of resonance for Christ.[59] Frank Macchia points out that this subordinates the Spirit to the Son and fails to recognize, as traditional trinitarian theology does, the "Spirit as a centre of action distinct from the decisive self-disclosure of God in Jesus Christ."[60]

More helpful for our purposes is Lutheran New Testament scholar Jörg Frey's charting of the development of the Spirit's personhood throughout the unfolding narrative of Scripture.[61] Frey also begins with the impersonal Old Testament images of the Spirit as an empowerment of God's creative activity. He shows an emerging tension in the New Testament between a more dynamic view of the Spirit (as a power) and a more "personal" concept where the Spirit acts, speaks, and teaches (as a "personal" subject).[62] The concept of the Spirit as a "personal" reality is prompted primarily by the correlation of the Spirit with the exalted Christ, though he admits that the biblical picture is still far off from the trinitarian formula of the fourth century. Specifically, he points to Paul, who relates the Spirit's work to that of the exalted Christ, borrowing personal language for the Spirit from his Christology and showing a close connection between them (without identifying them).[63] For Paul, only those manifestations that correspond with Christ's own work can be said to be the Spirit of God.

Frey argues that the personality of the Spirit comes more into focus in Luke-Acts and John's Gospel. In Acts, Luke describes the Spirit at Pentecost using impersonal images (wind, tongues of fire), as a force or phenomenon that empowers the disciples to preach, evangelize, and accomplish signs and wonders. As the narrative unfolds, he begins to depict the Spirit more clearly

59. Welker, God the Spirit, 279–341.

60. Frank D. Macchia, "Discerning the Spirit in Life: A Review of God the Spirit by Michael Welker," Journal of Pentecostal Theology 10 (1997): 12.

61. Jörg Frey, "How Did the Spirit Become a Person?," in The Holy Spirit, Inspiration, and the Cultures of Antiquity, Ekstasis: Religious Experience from Antiquity to the Middle Ages, vol. 5, ed. Jörg Frey and John R. Levison (Berlin: De Gruyter, 2014), 343–71

62. Frey, "How Did the Spirit Become a Person?," 347–49.

63. Frey, "How Did the Spirit Become a Person?," 358.

as a discrete actor rather than as a divine activity. The Spirit appears in several places as an acting subject, directing and guiding the disciples in their mission.[64] The Spirit even intervenes at points in the narrative, weighing in on significant decisions, such as at the Council of Jerusalem, where James speaks of the Holy Spirit as if the Spirit were sitting right there with them at the table: "For it has seemed good to the Holy Spirit and to us" (Acts 15:28).[65]

It is in John's Gospel, however, with the introduction of the Spirit as "Paraclete" (i.e., companion, or "Advocate" in the NRSV), that the Spirit's personal identity emerges most clearly in Scripture. The Spirit's identity and ministry are closely connected to the Son's, especially in the interpretation of the Spirit's ministry in terms of the Logos function, reminding the disciples of the story and the words of Jesus. Everything the Spirit does relates to Jesus, glorifying him and enabling his disciples to continue his work.[66] The Spirit will be with the disciples in Jesus's absence, as "another Advocate" (John 14:16), indwelling them and keeping them in his truth. In this very distinct way, Johannine theology "depicts the Holy Spirit as a divine figure with personal traits" and gives way to a personal understanding of the Spirit, who functions alongside Jesus, focusing on word and truth, "indeed, to a divine person subtly correlated with the Father and Son."[67] Both Welker and Frey show the close connection of the work and personhood of the Spirit to Christ, without identifying the two; however, Frey's fuller survey of the New Testament material, especially his discussion of Luke-Acts and John, articulates the Spirit's distinct personhood more clearly.

More recently, Pentecostal theologians have joined the discussion. Andrew Gabriel echoes Harvey Cox in his acknowledgment that although Pentecostals talk a lot about the Spirit, they focus more on the experience of the Spirit than they do on the doctrine of the Spirit or on questions of the Spirit's personhood. Gabriel takes up the question of the Spirit's personhood toward the development of a genuine Pentecostal pneumatology.[68] For the most part, Pentecostals affirm

---

64. See also William H. Shepherd Jr., *The Narrative Function of the Holy Spirit as a Character in Luke-Acts* (Atlanta: Scholars Press, 1994).

65. See Frey, "How Did the Spirit Become a Person?," 363. For more on the idea of the Spirit as agent of mission in Acts, see Cheryl M. Peterson, *Who Is the Church? An Ecclesiology for the Twenty-First Century* (Minneapolis: Fortress, 2013), chap. 5.

66. Frey, "How Did the Spirit Become a Person?," 367.

67. Frey, "How Did the Spirit Become a Person?," 370–71.

68. Andrew K. Gabriel, "Pneumatology: Eschatological Intensification of the Personal Presence of God," in *The Routledge Handbook of Pentecostal Theology*, ed. Wolfgang Vondey (New York: Routledge, 2020), 206.

the historic Christian doctrine of the Spirit as a divine person.[69] Gabriel's goal
is to explore the divinity of the Spirit from a distinctly Pentecostal perspective,
focusing more on the classical divine attributes (e.g., omnipotence, omnipres-
ence) than on the narrative of Scripture itself. He frames his investigation with
the biblical event of the outpouring of the Spirit at Pentecost, the experience
of which provides the basis for his definition of the personhood of the Spirit.
He writes, "Pentecostals regard and experience the Holy Spirit, poured out
at Pentecost, as the divine person who is experienced as the eschatological
intensification of the presence of God."[70]

Another Pentecostal theologian, Steven M. Studebaker, also begins with
the Pentecost event, arguing for the theological significance of the Pentecostal
experience of the Holy Spirit not only for Pentecostal pneumatology but also
for ecumenical trinitarian theology. His method mines "the biblical narratives
of the Spirit for their Trinitarian yield."[71] The identity of the Holy Spirit has
been largely derivative and its role passive in the history of Christian theology,
especially in the West. However, as Studebaker points out, this is not the case
in the biblical narrative of salvation, where the Spirit plays a prominent role.
His book *From Pentecost to the Triune God: A Pentecostal Trinitarian Theology*
investigates the Spirit's identity within the immanent Trinity through a consideration of the Spirit's role in the economic Trinity.

Studebaker examines the personal narratives of the Spirit in Scripture to
better understand the personal identity of the Spirit. Unlike Frey, Studebaker
is not interested in the development of how the Spirit "became" a person in the
biblical narrative. He takes the church's affirmation of the Spirit as person as
his starting point and, following Rogers, explores what this means by tracing
the Spirit as a character in the biblical story.[72] It is no surprise that the Pentecost event described in Acts 2 takes center stage, considering its importance
in the history of the Pentecostal movement and Pentecostal theology today.
For Studebaker, the entry point for a Pentecostal approach to the Trinity is
the outpouring of the Holy Spirit in the Pentecost event, but the Pentecostal
approach also includes the subsequent fallings of the Spirit on various groups

69. This refers to most Pentecostals who are trinitarian, such as classic Pentecostals like the
Assemblies of God, Church of God, Church of God in Christ, Foursquare Gospel, etc. The one
major exception is the Oneness Pentecostals.

70. Gabriel, "Pneumatology," 206.

71. Steven M. Studebaker, *From Pentecost to the Triune God: A Pentecostal Trinitarian Theology*
(Grand Rapids: Eerdmans, 2012), 3.

72. Studebaker, *From Pentecost to the Triune God*, 5.

of people and their experience of the Spirit (what Pentecostals call "Spirit baptism") throughout the book of Acts. He notes that, in the Pentecost event itself, the Spirit is described not in personal terms but rather by drawing on the Hebrew tradition of using wind to describe the "dynamic and powerful presence of God's Spirit."[73] However, as Frey has also pointed out, "The personal identity of the Spirit emerges from the personal narratives of the Spirit and especially as the Spirit of Pentecost."[74] The Holy Spirit has been poured out on all people—an outpouring that transcends ethnic boundaries—and "is the intrinsic agent and source of human life and redemption," working to bring people into union and fellowship with the triune God.[75]

The event of Pentecost identifies the Spirit not only in the economic work of redemption but also in the immanent fellowship of the Trinity. In his claim that the Spirit is the divine person who fulfills God's triune identity, Studebaker draws a close connection between the economic Trinity and the immanent Trinity without confusing them. The Spirit's work in its economic dimensions bears the properties of the Spirit's identity within the triune Godhead.[76] Studebaker's description of the Holy Spirit as an "an active divine person who consummates the fellowship of the Trinitarian God and plays a co-constitutional role in the formation of the personal identities of the Father and the Son"[77] resonates with Jenson's account of the Spirit's role as freeing the Father for relationship with the Son.[78]

Although they follow different methods and each bring distinctive emphases, these Lutheran, Reformed, and Pentecostal theologians all affirm the identity and personhood of the Spirit through narrative readings of Scripture. The trajectory of Scripture is toward an increasingly personal picture of the Spirit, as one with whom relationship is possible and who acts for, in, and through the people of God.

The Holy Spirit as Person in Luther's Theology

Both SBNRs and Pentecostal and charismatic Christians speak about spiritual experience as transformative in what Christian theologians would call

73. Studebaker, *From Pentecost to the Triune God*, 65.
74. Studebaker, *From Pentecost to the Triune God*, 5.
75. Studebaker, *From Pentecost to the Triune God*, 218–21.
76. Studebaker, *From Pentecost to the Triune God*, 5.
77. Studebaker, *From Pentecost to the Triune God*, 69.
78. Unfortunately, Studebaker does not engage Jenson on this point.

the "economy of salvation"—that is, in the history of God's interaction with the world. We saw that Pentecostals speak of the Holy Spirit in the economy of salvation, and in very personal terms—as one who enables an encounter with God's grace and power, one who indwells and renews. Martin Luther's pneumatology is well-known for its focus on the economic Trinity.[79] Less well known is his emphasis on the Holy Spirit as "God's real, personal presence" in the believer's life. Luther crafted his pneumatology in response to the medieval idea of "created grace," understood as an infusion of a supernatural power or substance into the believer's heart, enabling the believer to love God and to become "righteous," or justified by God.[80] Rejecting this view, Luther defines grace relationally as the personal presence of the Holy Spirit in and with the believer, imparting God's favor and mercy and enabling the believer to respond in love for God and neighbor. As Regin Prenter states, "Luther never doubts that the Spirit is God himself personally and not a mere divine manifestation of power."[81] Following catholic tradition, Luther also rejects modalism, arguing for the distinct personhood of the Holy Spirit. Prenter writes,

> According to Luther the Spirit is God himself. It is nonetheless important to him to distinguish clearly between the personal being of the Spirit and of the Father and of the Son. Only when the Spirit is distinguished clearly from the Father and the Son is it possible to preach Christ's real redeeming presence as *fides Christi*. When the personal being of the Spirit is more or less dissolved in the being of the Father and the Son the relation to Christ becomes possible only as a relation to his historic figure, to the idea of him, or to a power of Christ grasped in a *mystic* experience. That is, the historic Christ remains in the grave. A relation to the risen and living Christ is possible only through the Spirit in a realistic sense and not understood as a mere expression for warm feelings.[82]

---

79. This is not to say Luther was unconcerned with what later became known as the immanent Trinity. See Christine Helmer, "Luther's Theology of Glory," *Neue Zeitschrift für systematische Theologie und Religionsphilosophie* 42, no. 3 (2000): 237–45. See also Helmer, *The Trinity and Martin Luther: A Study on the Relationship between Genre, Language and the Trinity in Luther's Works (1523–1546)* (Mainz: Philipp von Zabern, 1999); and Helmer, *The Trinity and Martin Luther*, rev. ed. (Bellingham, WA: Lexham Press, 2017).

80. Regin Prenter, *Spiritus Creator: Luther's Concept of the Holy Spirit*, trans. John M. Jensen (Philadelphia: Muhlenberg Press, 1953), 19. The idea that habitual grace was something that was created was a commonplace teaching in the twelfth century, as Richard Cross points out. Richard Cross, "Deification in Aquinas: Created or Uncreated?," *Journal of Theological Studies* 69, no. 1 (April 2018): 113.

81. Prenter, *Spiritus Creator*, 176.

82. Prenter, *Spiritus Creator*, 183–84.

In his explanation of the Creed in the Large Catechism, Luther uses strikingly personal language to describe the Spirit's encounter with the believer: "[The Spirit] first leads us into his holy community, placing us in the church's lap, where he preaches to us *and brings us to Christ*."[83]

Conclusion

What does it mean to encounter the Holy Spirit not as an impersonal force or presence in our lives, but rather as the personal presence of God, or as classical trinitarian theology puts, as "person"? Contemporary theological treatments of the Spirit that can be classified as "pneumatologies of presence" (not to mention the SBNR phenomenon) do raise the question: Why *not* simply affirm the Spirit as the presence of God, following Grace Ji-Sun Kim, Lampe, and others? Why insist on the personhood of the Spirit at all? First, to speak of the Spirit only as an effect of God's presence both diminishes the Spirit's distinct personhood and also calls into question the relational capacity of the Spirit to human beings. If we confess the Spirit as God, then it follows that the Holy Spirit is not an impersonal something but *someone*. Further, if the Spirit is the agent of transformation to human beings, individually and communally, this suggests more than an impersonal force or presence; it suggests one who has a will and purpose for our lives, one with whom we can be in relationship and who, through that relationship, can bring transformation and lead us to new life.

Speaking of the Holy Spirit in personal terms makes a difference in how we think theologically about the work of the Spirit in justification, sanctification, and our participation in the mission of God. The scriptural witness is mixed regarding this issue—in that the Spirit is imaged in impersonal as well as personal terms, in the New Testament as well as in the Old Testament. However, as I have shown, the trajectory of the scriptural narrative moves toward an increasingly personal picture of the Spirit, as one with whom relationship is possible and who acts for, in, and through the people of God. The Cappadocian theologians argue that the Spirit is divine because the Old and New Testaments apply all titles of God to the Spirit (except "unbegotten") and because all functions that are attributed to the Holy Spirit are divine functions (creating, renewing,

---

83. Martin Luther, Large Catechism, in *The Book of Concord: The Confessions of the Evangelical Lutheran Church*, ed. Robert Kolb and Timothy J. Wengert (Minneapolis: Fortress, 2000), 435–36 (emphasis added).

making holy).[84] The Holy Spirit is the Lord and the giver of life—God, whom we encounter in a very personal way.[85]

As we have seen, several contemporary theologians have made the shift from philosophical to biblical categories in considering the Spirit's personhood. In the chapters that follow, I draw on their work as I explore the Spirit as the person who encounters us in a relationship that justifies, sanctifies, and empowers us and who also directs our life's calling as we participate in the mission of God. Specifically, I highlight the personal images and character of the Holy Spirit as "Paraclete" in John's Gospel (where the Spirit is the one who accompanies, advocates, guides, and leads into truth) and the agency of the Spirit in the Pauline Epistles and Acts of the Apostles (where the Spirit is the one who gives faith, indwells, and empowers the disciples for lives of holiness and service). The following chapters examine the doctrines of justification, sanctification, and empowerment for mission pneumatologically—that is, from a consideration of the Spirit's role in them as God's personal presence and power. The goal is to provide fresh perspectives on these doctrines, all in continuing conversation with theologians from the Lutheran, Reformed, and Pentecostal traditions.

It is important to note at the outset that classic trinitarian doctrine teaches that the three persons work in perfect harmony in terms of a united will and purpose, which means that the Spirit's agency, will, and character are not divorced from those of the Father and the Son. The persons are distinguished not by their roles (as in modalism) but by their intratrinitarian relationships. However, the biblical narrative (and catechetical treatments, such as Luther's "Explanation of the Creed" in the Small and Large Catechisms) supports what I like to call "starring roles" for each in the economy of salvation. The Son tends to have the starring role in the event of justification, but that does not mean the Spirit has no role or work to do. If we consider justification pneumatologically, and not only christologically, we can flesh out a more vital doctrine that

---

84. See, e.g., Basil of Caesarea, *On the Holy Spirit*, trans. David Anderson (Crestwood, NY: St. Vladimir's Seminary Press, 1997), esp. 73–89.

85. When I first conceived of this book, I included this chapter because I thought I needed to address the person of the Spirit before the work of the Spirit. As I wrote, I came to see that this chapter is more central to the book's argument than I previously expected, not simply because I wish to affirm the catholic church's teaching of the full deity and personhood of the Spirit but because I am convinced that a robust theology of the personhood of the Spirit provides a strong basis for engaging the work of the Holy Spirit in the three movements of justification, sanctification, and mission. As I will show, such a foundation will be helpful in confronting various misunderstandings and concerns that have plagued these doctrines, especially justification and sanctification, throughout church history.

speaks to people looking for spiritual transformation today. By starting with the Spirit relationally—as divine person—one can avoid, for example, some of the problems Luther encountered with his Roman Catholic opponents, who tended to interpret the Spirit in relation to the category of "created grace," something that can be possessed by the believer. This led Luther and Philip Melanchthon to stress the forensic or declarative aspect of justification; however, this is not the whole picture. The Spirit's work is interpreted personally and relationally. The Spirit is the one who leads us to Christ, who opens our ears to hear the good news, giving us the gift of faith to receive the promise. The Spirit is the giver of life who makes Christ "present" to us in faith, from which we receive the gifts of forgiveness of sins and new birth / regeneration, through the Spirit. All of this is received as gift; this is the movement of God acting *for* us in the Spirit, as we are declared righteous and receive the gift of new life by the Spirit.

The Spirit traditionally is accorded the starring role in the movement of sanctification, but historically this doctrine has made some Lutheran and Reformed theologians nervous because of the focus it seems to put on the human subject rather than God. This nervousness is related to medieval ideas about holiness as possessing and growing in infused grace. However, if we conceive of the Spirit not as a substance that we receive to grow in holiness but as God's personal presence received in justification, we can then explore holiness relationally, as growing in relationship with the Holy Spirit, who indwells us as God, a person of the Trinity. Our relationship with the Holy Spirit makes us holy. The Spirit creates in us spiritual impulses that renew us for a life of thankful response to God's gift. Sanctification is the movement of the Spirit in our lives in which we cooperate with the Spirit, whose presence we have received as a gift in the new birth. We can affirm the indwelling of the Spirit in our lives—as God's real, personal presence—in an ongoing encounter with the Spirit as the giver of new life, as the one who transforms us to become more like Christ. This happens in the holy community, the church. The Spirit moves in and around us in community, which is itself rooted in holy things: the Word and sacraments that continually connect us relationally to God. The Spirit is the divine companion who accompanies us as we walk in the new life we have received in justification, in this second movement of the Spirit in our lives, sanctification.

In the Spirit's movement inviting believers to participate in God's mission, the Spirit's role is highlighted, especially by Pentecostals, as the one who empowers Christians for service, evangelism, and ministries of healing, prophecy, and so on. Lutherans also refer to the Spirit's role in terms of our baptismal calling, and more recently in terms of social justice and activism. Pentecostals speak of the Spirit as the necessary "power from on high" (Luke 24:49), or as empowerment itself, to accomplish God's mission in the world. In a similar vein, Lutheran ethicist Cynthia Moe-Lobeda speaks of the Spirit as "moral spiritual-power" needed for facing and engaging the brokenness and evil in the world.[86] What if we considered the Spirit in this movement in the economy of salvation not simply as power or courage but as the empowerer for God's mission? As God, the Spirit cannot be reduced to a power source we can tap into (something we can possess and increase in ourselves); rather, the Spirit is the one who encounters us in relationship and empowers us. The Spirit, as God, relates to God's people relationally. The Spirit is not a substance, or a thing, or an effect that we can possess or control. The Spirit is God's own self: the giver of life, our companion and empowerer. These distinct roles played by the personal Spirit in the drama of salvation are explored in the following three chapters.

86. Cynthia Moe-Lobeda, "The Spirit as Moral-Spiritual Power for Earth-Honoring, Justice-Seeking Ways of Shaping Our Life in Common," in *Planetary Solidarity: Global Women's Voices on Christian Doctrine and Climate Justice*, ed. Grace Ji-Sun Kim and Hilda P. Koster (Minneapolis: Fortress, 2017), 249.

3

The Spirit for Us

Justification and the New Birth

Although theologians pay the most attention to the Holy Spirit's work in sanctification, it is incorrect to say that the Holy Spirit plays no role in the doctrine of justification. While this doctrine centers on the death and resurrection of Jesus Christ—so that we might say the Son plays the "starring role"—redemption is an act of the triune God. While the Second Article of the Apostles' Creed addresses the christological basis for our justification, it is in the Third Article that we read of the benefits received by the believer on account of Christ—that is, forgiveness of sins, resurrection, and life everlasting. In other words, in justification, the Holy Spirit's role is as the giver of life. In justification, the Spirit brings new life to the believer, regenerates and vivifies.[1] This is not the same thing as sanctification, as will become clear.

In this chapter, I explore justification from a pneumatological perspective, bringing classic Reformation theology on this doctrine into dialogue with contemporary critics, including those from the Pentecostal tradition. It is hoped that such a consideration might open fresh insights and pathways for a contemporary theological articulation of justification, not only to address the often-cited

---

1. These are usually distinguished in the *ordo salutis* (order of salvation) of the Lutheran scholastics, but I will argue that according to the Lutheran Confessions, regeneration is best understood as the effective aspect of justification.

impasse between forensic and effective justification but also to speak to the "age of the Spirit" in which we find ourselves today, with its focus on spiritual experience and transformation.[2]

A pneumatological consideration of this doctrine makes it possible to emphasize both aspects of justification in terms of God's acting on behalf of the believer. As the giver of life, the Holy Spirit brings the believer into relationship with God through faith, enabling the believer to trust that God is "for" them on account of Christ. The righteousness that justifies remains in an important way alien to the believer, but it is nonetheless still experienced through faith, as highlighted by the effective aspect of justification. When one is justified by grace through faith, one receives the gift of the Holy Spirit, who, as the giver of life, simultaneously initiates a new birth. Through this regeneration, one is marked by the transforming experience of being forgiven and embraced by God's mercy and love. For a theology that will speak to people today, I propose a fresh consideration of the effective, transformative, and experiential aspect of justification (along with the forensic) as a work of the Holy Spirit.

First, I review the role of the Holy Spirit in justification in the Lutheran tradition. Then I discuss some recent theological proposals that criticize a purely forensic doctrine of justification and reconceive justification specifically in terms of regeneration or new life, and the Spirit as the giver of that new life through Christ. These include proposals from the late Lutheran theologian Gerhard Forde, Reformed theologian Jürgen Moltmann, and Pentecostal theologian Frank Macchia, with whom I bring the Lutheran tradition into dialogue on this question. I conclude with some theological perspectives of the Spirit as God "for us" in the movement of justification.

The Role of the Holy Spirit in Justification in the Lutheran Tradition

Justification as Forensic and Effective

The doctrine of justification was at the heart of Martin Luther's Reformation and continues to be doctrinally central not only for Lutherans but also for

2. Bruce D. Marshall speaks of the "apparent opposition between forensic and transformative accounts of justification" as being "set in stone" and of these two accounts as pointing to "seemingly disparate elements in God's justification of sinful human beings." His proposal draws on the Finnish school of Luther studies, which is discussed below. Marshall, "Justification as Declaration and Deification," *International Journal of Systematic Theology* 4, no. 1 (March 2002): 3.

many other Protestants. Most equate the doctrine with its forensic aspect, so much that it has become synonymous with the doctrine. Forensic justification refers to God's declaration of forgiveness to the sinner on account of Christ, whose righteousness is "reckoned to them" through faith.[3] It guards the passivity of the believer by stressing that justification is completely God's action. God justifies the sinner as a pure gift of God's own grace, a promise that can be received only by faith, or trust. The Reformers' concern here is to protect the doctrine of justification from interpretations that even hint that anything we do contributes toward our justification. Justification is solely God's action, not ours. That is why Lutherans stress that the righteousness that justifies is *alien*, or extrinsic—outside of us.

The alien nature of righteousness in forensic justification has had its share of critics, starting with Roman Catholics who fear that the emphasis on human passivity is in danger of making justification nothing more than "legal fiction." To be declared something one is not, and to remain unchanged after that declaration, does not sound like good news. When I was a graduate student at Marquette University in a course on grace, I remember one of my Catholic professors talking about this and wondering if there was even a "you" that experienced the grace of justification in certain Lutheran versions of the doctrine. It was as if the promise of justification did not actually touch or affect one's life.

While the extrinsic or alien nature of God's act in justifying the sinner remains primary for the Lutheran Reformers, the Lutheran Confessions (collected in the Book of Concord, 1580) treat the doctrine in a much fuller and more nuanced way. For the early Reformers, justification is more than a declaration or "imputation" of God's grace and favor. Finnish scholar Olli-Pekka Vainio writes that for Philip Melanchthon, "Justification is not strictly a forensic act because it also involves an effective and regenerative change by which the unrighteous person becomes righteous."[4] In the longest single essay in the Book of Concord, Apology of the Augsburg Confession (hereafter, AP), article 4, Melanchthon emphasizes the transformative as well as the declarative aspect of God's grace in Jesus Christ through the Holy Spirit. He defines justification as "the making

---

3. Augsburg Confession, art. 4, in *The Book of Concord: The Confessions of the Evangelical Lutheran Church*, ed. Robert Kolb and Timothy J. Wengert (Minneapolis: Fortress, 2000), 38–41. The Augsburg Confession will hereafter be cited as CA, and page references to *The Book of Concord* will be supplied with the abbreviation BC.

4. Olli-Pekka Vainio, *Justification and Participation in Christ: The Development of the Doctrine of Justification from Luther to the Formula of Concord (1580)* (Boston: Brill, 2008), 72.

of a righteous person out of an unrighteous one or as regeneration."[5] The forensic aspect of justification emphasizes that the believer is justified by God's declaration of their righteousness on account of Christ, not by anything they do, including the act of receiving this promise through faith (which is itself a gift from God). The effective aspect of justification connotes that the believer receives not only a declaration of Christ's righteousness but also an experience of it. This gift (as well as the giver of the gift) brings new life to the Christian; it is experiential and transformative.[6]

Justification Considered Pneumatologically

When considering justification pneumatologically, the distinction between forensic and effective justification is less clear. Traditionally in Lutheran theology, the role of the Holy Spirit is articulated in relation to the faith that justifies, the faith by which sinners receive God's promise of grace on account of Christ. In this way, the Spirit's work is seen as an application of the work of Christ to the believer, making the objective work of the cross a subjective experience of the believer through faith, through which the believer experiences the forgiveness of sins.[7] This can be seen in both Luther and Melanchthon, the author of the Augsburg Confession (1530) and the Apology of the Augsburg Confession (1531).

Luther's explanation of the Third Article of the Apostles' Creed reflects his propensity to give the Son the starring role in the narrative of redemption and to identify the office of the Holy Spirit as that of making holy or sanctifying. However, before he unpacks the means by which the Spirit makes us holy (the communion of saints, the forgiveness of sins, the resurrection of the body, and the life everlasting), Luther writes that the Spirit "first leads us into his holy community, placing us in the church's lap, where he preaches to us and brings us to Christ." The Holy Spirit proclaims the gospel to us sinners through the Word and gives us faith to trust in that good news—that is,

---

5. Apology of the Augsburg Confession (hereafter cited as AP), 4.78, in *BC*, 133.

6. Some equate sanctification with effective justification, a move I find problematic for reasons discussed below.

7. D. Lyle Dabney criticizes this as subordinating the work of the Spirit to that of the Son. Dabney, "Naming the Spirit," in *Starting with the Spirit*, ed. Gordon Preece and Stephen Pickard (Adelaide: Australian Theological Forum Press, 2001), 32–33. He is among those who propose we consider the work of the Spirit from the "other side" of the relationship between the Spirit and the Son, in particular the role of the Holy Spirit in Jesus's incarnation, earthly mission, suffering, crucifixion, and resurrection.

knowledge and understanding of the benefits won by Christ. The language here is relational, personal, tender, and familial. The Holy Spirit plays the role both of companion (Paraclete) and of proclaimer. The Holy Spirit, in Luther's words, reveals and proclaims the Word of God to sinners, "through which he illuminates and inflames hearts so that they grasp and accept it, cling to it and persevere in it."[8]

It is interesting to note Luther's use of "heart" language here, offering a contrast to the way many conceive faith as a noetic act of belief. Melanchthon makes a similar distinction between faith as trust in a promise and the one who makes that promise (the faith that justifies) and faith as noetic, as knowledge of something (which even the devil can have). Luther is clear that without the Spirit, we could never know anything about Christ or have faith in him. The treasure of the gospel would remain buried, its blessings not experienced by sinners. Melanchthon makes the same point when he writes that "to obtain such faith, God instituted the office of preaching, giving the gospel and the sacraments. Through these means, [God] gives the Holy Spirit who produces faith, where and when [God] wills, in those who hear the gospel."[9]

The Holy Spirit in Conversion

Later Lutheran scholastic theologians would refer to this particular work of the Holy Spirit, whereby faith is created and experienced, as "conversion." This became one of several stages in the *ordo salutis* (order of salvation), dogmatized and systematized in such a way as to overshadow the more dynamic and personal quality of the Spirit in Luther's pneumatology.[10] Lutheran Pietists would stress the more experiential aspect of conversion as a work of the Holy Spirit, rooting their understanding in Luther's "Preface to the Epistle of St. Paul to the Romans" (1522), in which he describes faith as "a divine work in us which changes us and makes us to be born anew of God, John 1[:12–13]. It kills the

---

8. Martin Luther, Large Catechism, in *BC*, 436. Luther uses "heart" language three times in this section.

9. CA 5, in *BC*, 40. However, his language in the later AP 4 suggests more of a chicken-and-egg relationship between faith and the Holy Spirit, when he writes of faith "receiving" the Holy Spirit. See AP 4.45, 99, 125–29, in *BC*, 127, 137, 140–41.

10. Heinrich Schmid, ed., *The Doctrinal Theology of the Evangelical Lutheran Church*, 3rd ed., trans. Charles A. Hay and Henry E. Jacobs (Minneapolis: Augsburg, 1961), 407–99. By the seventeenth century, Lutheran dogmaticians sought to systematize the teaching of the Lutheran Confessions in their adoption of an *ordo salutis*—i.e., an arrangement of the Holy Spirit's work that begins with "faith and justification," after which follow five "consequences of justifying faith": vocation, illumination, conversion and regeneration, mystical union, and renovation.

old Adam and makes us altogether different [people], in heart and spirit and mind and powers; and it brings with it the Holy Spirit. O it is a living, busy, active, mighty thing, this faith."[11]

Both the scholastics and the Pietists were careful to distinguish the Lutheran position from later Calvinism, which taught that grace is "irresistible." For Lutherans, one cannot say yes to God except through the Holy Spirit, but one can always resist grace and say no. The capacity for faith is given to the sinner by the power of the Spirit, but as C. G. Carlfeldt writes, one "must permit the power of the Spirit to become operative in his life if he is to be converted."[12] For Lutherans, this does not happen by reaching out and grabbing on to the gift God offers you freely in Christ, as some evangelicals teach, usually through the repetition of a prayer in which you invite Jesus into your heart. A former student of mine proposed an image that is more fitting for a Lutheran understanding: that of someone putting headphones on you.[13] By leaving the headphones on, you can assent to listen to and begin to enjoy the music, or you can pull the headphones off if you do not like the music. This is a more passive image than that of grabbing on to something, but it is still participatory. You are the one listening to the music, but you did nothing to get the music to play for you (or even to direct the music into your ears!). This image also connects nicely to the Lutheran teaching that faith is sparked by hearing the gospel being proclaimed.[14]

11. Martin Luther, "Preface to the Epistle of St. Paul to the Romans" (1522), in *Luther's Works,* American ed., 55 vols. (Philadelphia: Fortress; St. Louis: Concordia, 1955–86), 35:370. *Luther's Works* is hereafter cited as *LW*.

12. C. G. Carlfeldt, "The Work of the Holy Spirit," in *What Lutherans Are Thinking: A Symposium on Lutheran Faith and Life,* ed. E. C. Fendt (Columbus, OH: Wartburg Press, 1947), 228.

13. The Rev. Jon Weaver, who currently serves as pastor of Bethel Lutheran Church in Bath, Ohio, shared this image during my 2008 course on the Lutheran Confessions at Trinity Lutheran Seminary.

14. CA 5, in *BC*, 40–41; and AP 4.74, in *BC*, 132. Stephen H. Webb recognizes that the emphasis in Christian theology on the Word as both spoken and heard could easily be used to discriminate against deaf people. He argues that this need not be the case due to the structural similarities between sign language and spoken language. As he notes, "When St. Paul argued that Christians receive God's grace through hearing, he meant that literally, but we know today that the deaf can receive the good news through their other senses as well. While the history of Christianity cannot be told outside the history of sound, preaching can take place in complete silence. Hearing is the gift from God that makes faith possible, whether it is a matter of listening to voices or looking at hands." Further, he appeals to Augustine's argument that "God does not need the physical apparatus of vocalization in order to speak. Nor does God need sound in order to hear, since the Bible clearly states that God hears the mute (1 Macc. 10:18–19). God can speak without air or vibration because the Holy Spirit is God's breath, a divine wind that carries sound even where there is no air. For us, the good news about the divine speech is that it creates the conditions for its own reception." Stephen H. Webb, *The Divine Voice: Christian Proclamation and the Theology of Sound* (Grand Rapids: Brazos, 2004), 51–54.

The language of conversion has mostly been abandoned by Lutherans in recent years, perhaps due to its connection to evangelical Protestant programs of evangelism that stress a more active role for the sinner in accepting the gospel.[15] Pentecostal theologian Frank Macchia acknowledges the "ambiguity of conversion" in his own tradition, noting that it can become a "dividing line between true and false forms of Christian faith that can sound narrow, judgmental and elitist."[16] The preoccupation with conversion has also led to the intentional manipulation of people's emotions in worship services and other messaging. This was a key reason the "mourner's bench" and other "new measures" of revivals like the Second Great Awakening were controversial among many Lutherans and Reformed.[17]

It is not surprising, then, that Lutheran theologians such as Eilert Herms reach for other terms to describe this aspect of the Spirit's work in justification, such as "revelation." Herms defines the Spirit's work as representing the past and future acts of God to the believer.[18] Without the Spirit, the redeeming work of the incarnate Son of God on the cross would remain hidden and unknown, and therefore lost. The Holy Spirit works externally, through the preaching of the Word, and internally, in the human heart, to bring this revelation to each person. This revelation brings an existential transformation to the believer and a new eschatological standing before God.[19] In other words, through the Spirit, believers can experience self-certainty about their redemption.[20] Herms

15. E.g., "Four Spiritual Laws," the Basic Series, created by Cru (formerly known as Campus Crusade for Christ), Campus Ministry Today, accessed February 2, 2023, https://campusministry.org/docs/tools/FourSpiritualLaws.pdf.

16. Frank D. Macchia, "Towards Individual and Communal Renewal: Reflections on Luke's Theology of Conversion," *Ex Auditu* 25 (2009): 93. Interesting, Macchia credits the Reformers with delivering people from the medieval Catholic preoccupation with penance and conversion by shifting the focus to God's victory over sin and death by the cross and resurrection of Jesus Christ, only to have the preoccupation return with Pietism and subsequent revivals, including Pentecostalism.

17. See Frank L. Seilhamer, "The New Measure Movement among Lutherans," *Lutheran Quarterly* 12, no. 2 (May 1960): 121–43; John E. Groh, "Revivalism among Lutherans in America in the 1840s," *Concordia Historical Institute Quarterly* 43, no. 1 (February 1970): 29–43; and Todd W. Nicol, "Lutheran Revivalism: A Request for a Reappraisal," *Lutheran Historical Conference* 12 (1988): 97–117.

18. Jared Wicks points out that the concept of "revelation" became theologically important only after Luther's time, suggesting this category may not be the most appropriate to Luther's own context and concerns. See Wicks, "Holy Spirit—Church—Sanctification: Insights from Luther's Instructions on the Faith," *Pro Ecclesia* 2, no. 2 (Spring 1993): 156n29.

19. Eilert Herms, *Luthers Auslegung des Dritten Artikels* (Tübingen: Mohr Siebeck, 1987), 65, 100.

20. Herms, *Luthers Auslegung*, 74.

also interprets forgiveness of sins as a revelatory experience, as "nothing other than recreated existence in light of the appearance of the truth of the gospel."[21] Herms's interpretation is more individualistic and less relational than Luther's own language suggests, as Luther includes a communal aspect not only in the event of proclamation but also in the living out of the gift of forgiveness of sins.[22]

The first work of the Spirit in justification is to bring the believer to faith (conversion), which is where many Lutheran theologians stop. For example, Jeffrey Mann argues that Luther sees only one proper work of the Holy Spirit, which is to enable the sinner to believe in the promise of the gospel.[23] "Faith is not a good work undertaken by the believer, but something done for us and within us by the Spirit of God."[24] The Spirit enables the believer to "appropriate the saving message of the gospel."[25] The blessings of the gospel are twofold, according to Luther: through the grace or favor of God, the sinner receives a new status before God as justified, and through the gift of God, the sinner receives "an internal change, through faith, which assists the person in overcoming sin."[26] Mann goes on to describe this as sanctification, but he and many other Lutheran theologians fail to acknowledge the role of the Spirit in regeneration, as an aspect of God's justifying work distinct from sanctification.[27]

The Danish Lutheran theologian Regin Prenter titled his classic treatment of Luther's pneumatology *Spiritus Creator* because, for Luther, the proper work of the Spirit is to create life from death, to regenerate. Prenter points out that Luther never doubts that the Spirit is God personally and not merely a presence or manifestation of power.[28] Luther speaks of the indwelling of the Holy Spirit in the human heart not as the transcendent cause of a supernatural nature in human

21. Herms, *Luthers Auslegung*, 96. The translation is mine. The original German reads, "nach nichts anderes als eben die durch das Heiligungswirken des Geistes geschaffene Existenz im Lichte der erschienenen Wahrheit des Evangeliums."

22. On this point, see Cheryl M. Peterson, *Who Is the Church? An Ecclesiology for the Twenty-First Century* (Minneapolis: Fortress, 2013), chap. 6.

23. Jeffrey K. Mann, "Luther and the Holy Spirit: Why Pneumatology Still Matters," *Currents in Theology and Mission* 34, no. 2 (April 2007): 111.

24. Mann, "Luther and the Holy Spirit," 111. He cites Luther's "Preface to the Epistle of St. Paul to the Romans" as well as Luther's "Explanation of the Third Article of the Creed" in the Large Catechism.

25. Mann, "Luther and the Holy Spirit," 112.

26. Mann, "Luther and the Holy Spirit," 112.

27. As noted, this is likely because many confuse regeneration with renewal or sanctification, which is in part attributed to the strong distinction that the authors of the Formula of Concord make in their response to Andreas Osiander. More on this below.

28. Regin Prenter, *Spiritus Creator: Luther's Concept of the Holy Spirit*, trans. John M. Jensen (Philadelphia: Muhlenberg Press, 1953), 176.

beings that produces infused grace, as did the medieval scholastics, but as the real presence of God. The Holy Spirit is God as present in human experience, in the groaning of those who are anxious and caught in the grip of death and hell, to bring new life and the power of Christ's resurrection. This is more than a psychological or existential experience, though it includes such experience.[29]

The Holy Spirit in Regeneration

Lutheran theology sees justification as God's act for the sinner, in Christ through the power of the Holy Spirit. In justification, the Holy Spirit does two things: bring the sinner to faith (conversion) and give the sinner new life (regeneration). Carlfeldt puts it simply: "When a sinner is justified by the grace of God, a new life principle is implanted in that individual by God." In brief, this person receives a "new spiritual life"[30] because salvation means life, not simply a new status or standing before God. This is a gift of God bestowed through the Spirit. "We say, therefore, that the Holy Spirit is the efficient cause of regeneration, and that it is [the Spirit] who works this miracle in the heart of the individual concerned. This act of the Spirit is instantaneous in character and is not, like sanctification, an extended process that is to cover the entire period of life."[31] The Holy Spirit moves the sinner from the realm of death into the realm of life.

It is common for Lutherans to overlook this aspect of the Spirit's work in justification, but it is a central theme not only in Luther's theology, as Prenter shows, but also in the Lutheran Confessions. Melanchthon emphasizes that the work of the Spirit includes regeneration and rebirth. Sometimes he even uses these terms interchangeably for justification.[32] He defines this regeneration through faith as a "work of the Holy Spirit that frees us from death and makes alive terrified minds."[33] Melanchthon emphatically denies that the "bestowing of the Holy Spirit were without any effect."[34] Vainio points out that in Apology of the Augsburg Confession 4, "Several affectual concepts (consolation, joy, peace, tranquility) are used to describe vivification."[35] Melanchthon denies that these affections are causal factors of one's righteousness before God because

29. Prenter, *Spiritus Creator*, 19.
30. Carlfeldt, "Work of the Holy Spirit," 232.
31. Carlfeldt, "Work of the Holy Spirit," 233.
32. AP 4.68, in *BC*, 131.
33. AP 4.115–16, in *BC*, 139.
34. AP 4.63, in *BC*, 131.
35. Vainio, *Justification and Participation in Christ*, 73.

this would mean some human effect is required for one to be justified. Yet this vivification is a work of the Holy Spirit in the sinner.[36]

Vainio also surveys several other key sixteenth-century Lutheran Reformers on this topic, showing that the only one who held a purely forensic notion of justification was Matthias Flacius Illyricus. The others all spoke of regeneration as an aspect of the Spirit's work in justification, including Nikolaus Selnecker, one of the authors of the Formula of Concord (1577).[37] The Formula of Concord also affirms that justifying faith brings an actual change to the sinner; it is more than a declaration. The Holy Spirit effects faith conversion and renews and sanctifies.[38]

In addressing Andreas Osiander's teachings on justification, the authors of the Formula clarify the relationship between justification, regeneration, and sanctification in a way that Melanchthon does not in AP. As we have seen, in AP 4 Melanchthon often uses the term "rebirth" interchangeably with "justification," in the sense of being forgiven and adopted by God. However, the word "regeneration" is also sometimes used to name the renewal that follows justification, or sanctification. In other words, the terms "regeneration" and "rebirth" are used in the confessions to include both the forgiveness of sins and the resultant renewal, or sanctification, that the Holy Spirit effects in those who are justified by faith.

To be justified means to be pronounced righteous, with a clear forensic focus. "The Holy Spirit conveys these benefits to us in the promise of the holy gospel," which they define as being pronounced free of all sin and accepted as children of God, heirs of eternal life.[39] These gifts are received by faith, itself a gift from God. They go on to explain, "Since the word *regeneratio* (rebirth) is sometimes used for the word *iustificatio* (justification), it is necessary to explain this term in its true sense, so that renewal, which results from justification by faith, will not be confused with justification by faith, but that in their narrow sense the two are distinguished from each other."[40] The renewal of life always follows justification; it cannot be mingled with it, lest we believe that our good works contribute to our justification.[41] This is an important distinction that protects the

---

36. See AP 4.115–16 for Melanchthon's references to peace and tranquility; 4.81 and 4.85 for his references to consolation; and 4.100 for his references to peace and joy (BC, 139, 133, 135, 137).

37. Vainio, *Justification and Participation in Christ*, 196.

38. Solid Declaration of the Formula of Concord (hereafter cited as SD), 3.41, in BC, 569.

39. Solid Declaration, Formula of Concord (hereafter cited as SD FC), 3.10–11, in BC, 564.

40. SD FC, 3.18, in BC, 565.

41. "Likewise, too, although renewal and sanctification are a blessing of our mediator Christ and a work of the Holy Spirit, they do not belong in the article or in the treatment of justification

doctrine of justification from works righteousness and Pelagianism. However, a further distinction should also be made in Lutheran theology, based on the proceeding analysis—that is, the distinction between "rebirth" (which happens simultaneously with justification) and "renewal" (a process that is also called "sanctification" and involves the believer's cooperation with the Holy Spirit). We are reborn by the Holy Spirit in justification, but in sanctification and renewal our justified and reborn new selves cooperate with that same Spirit, producing fruit and good works.

Although it does not receive the same attention as bringing the believer to faith, regeneration or rebirth is an important aspect of a Lutheran understanding of the Spirit's work in justification. As God's act in the sinner, justification is both effective and forensic. Therefore, we can say that, for Lutherans, the Spirit is the giver of life in the event of justification. As God "for us," the Spirit brings the sinner to faith (conversion), through which the sinner receives God's grace and the gift of forgiveness of sins. The God who is for us also brings regeneration and rebirth, through the indwelling of the Spirit. Before we can experience God "in us" through sanctification, we first experience God "for us" in justification as both conversion and rebirth, neither of which depends on anything we do.

Although theologians often speak of the indwelling of the Holy Spirit as gift, this can lead to thinking of the Spirit as a *thing* rather than as a *person* of the Trinity. As the giver of life, the Spirit is received not as some*thing* but as some-*one* with whom we are brought into relationship, someone who is self-giving, indwelling us to bring new life. There are gifts that result from that relationship and encounter, such as the affections of joy and consolation.

The Lutheran tradition, however, continues to receive criticism for what is perceived to be a narrow, forensic understanding of justification, one that does not have the power to speak to those who desire such a spiritual encounter with God. In his groundbreaking book *The Spirit of Life*, Jürgen Moltmann brings this critique and proposes that justification includes regeneration. More recently, Frank Macchia has charged the doctrine of forensic justification with being "pneumatologically barren"[42] and has proposed equating justification with the indwelling/reception of the Holy Spirit, which he also calls "new creation." The

---

before God but rather result from it since, because of our corrupted flesh, they are never fully pure and perfect in this life." SD FC, 3.28, in *BC*, 566.

42. Frank D. Macchia, "Justification through New Creation: The Holy Spirit and the Doctrine by Which the Church Stands or Falls," *Theology Today* 58, no. 2 (July 2001): 207. He develops this idea more fully in his 2010 monograph, *Justified in the Spirit*, discussed in detail below.

Spirit is not just declaring the sinner's situation "new"; the Spirit is making it new through new birth. Both situate the doctrine of justification pneumatologically and eschatologically as well. Before discussing their contributions, I first evaluate a more contemporary proposal from within the Lutheran tradition to view justification as a work of the Spirit, that of Gerhard Forde.

Reconceiving Justification Pneumatologically: Some Contemporary Examples

Gerhard Forde

To those familiar with the theology of Gerhard Forde, his inclusion here may seem strange because he is hardly known for his pneumatology. He has never written an article on the Holy Spirit, much less a book. Where he does mention the Holy Spirit, however, it is always in reference to the new birth that is an aspect of the sinner's justification. His theology of justification is rooted in the event of the cross, the place where God's wrath and hiddenness end and the reality of God's eschatological future is introduced.[43] For there to be a resurrection future, there must first be a divine negation, a death. The "happy exchange" (Luther) or "great reversal" (Forde) "spells not only the death of Jesus but also the death of the sinner. Jesus' death is not a substitution for our death; it *is* our death."[44] The death of the old self, bound by the law, is necessary for new life in the Spirit to begin.[45]

Lutheran theologian Mark Mattes argues that, in reclaiming the eschatological nature of God's work of re-creation, Forde brings an experiential dimension to the doctrine of justification that had been neglected in the forensic theory.[46] For Forde, justification is an eschatological act in which the Spirit kills and brings to life through the proclamation of the law and gospel.[47] Forde writes,

43. Gerhard O. Forde, "The Work of Christ," in *Christian Dogmatics*, vol. 2, ed. Carl E. Braaten and Robert W. Jenson (Philadelphia: Fortress, 1984), 71–72. *Christian Dogmatics*, vol. 2, is hereafter cited as CD 2. Portions of this section first appeared in Cheryl M. Peterson, "The Question of the Church in North American Lutheranism: Toward an Ecclesiology of the Third Article" (PhD diss., Marquette University, 2004), https://www.proquest.com/dissertations-theses/question-church-north-american-lutheranism-toward/docview/305177045/se-2.
44. Forde, "Work of Christ," 58.
45. Forde, "Work of Christ," 51.
46. Mark C. Mattes, "Gerhard Forde on Re-envisioning Theology," *Lutheran Quarterly* 13, no. 4 (1999): 374–75.
47. Proclamation happens not only in the sermon but also through the announcement of the forgiveness of sins "for you" during the absolution and in the promise "given for you" in the

"The divine pronouncement of justification for Jesus' sake *is* the death and the new life. To believe the message of justification *is* to die and be raised to newness of life."[48] Forde does not adopt the language of "conversion" for this (no doubt for reasons related to the concerns noted above) but, along with Luther, adopts the Pauline metaphor of "death-life," which he proposes as a complement to the more traditional forensic, or legal, metaphor that dominates much Reformation-heritage theology.[49] By itself, death-life language can easily slip into mysticism and moralism. But if it is restored alongside the forensic image in theological discourse, the "explosive character" of the Reformers' message can reemerge.[50] In justification, the subject is not repaired but "made new" through the action of God, the resurrection of Christ.[51]

Forde shows that, for Luther, Paul's spirit/letter distinction in 1 Corinthians 3:6 refers to two kinds of preaching and hearing (law and gospel) instead of to two meanings in the text (allegorical and literal). This moves Luther "toward an understanding of the Word as active, as doing something to us."[52] In other words, the Spirit is not some inner level of meaning reached by the interpreter, as was common in medieval theology, but the Spirit of God, the one who "comes precisely in and through the letter, the text, the proclamation of it, to kill and to make alive."[53] The Spirit first works through the letter, or the law, to confront ("kill") sinners with the fact that they are lost and can do nothing about their situation. The proper work of the Spirit is to give life through the gospel, offering the possibility of "an entirely new dimension of life; it is a word which is full of promise, which makes all of life blossom with the good news."[54]

Lord's Supper. In the practice of the Lutheran churches, this "given for you" is repeated to each communicant as they come to receive the wine and bread. Gerhard O. Forde, *Theology Is for Proclamation* (Minneapolis: Fortress, 1990), 1–2.

48. Gerhard O. Forde, "The Christian Life," in CD 2:410.

49. Forde states that the forensic model ultimately does not know how to incorporate *sola fide* into its schema because it is a legal metaphor. "We set up the whole matter as a legal process, the process of becoming 'just' according to the law, making progress, doing good, and then at the last moment we suddenly turn and say it is impossible by that route to become just and that one is justified *by faith alone—sola*—and the *sola* means apart from works, love, or merit. One sets up the scheme and then destroys it by saying we get it all by faith anyway." Gerhard O. Forde, *Justification by Faith: A Matter of Death and Life* (1982; repr., Ramsey, NJ: Sigler, 1991), 9.

50. Forde, *Justification by Faith*, 4.

51. Forde, *Justification by Faith*, 18.

52. Forde, "Work of Christ," 79.

53. Gerhard O. Forde, "Law and Gospel in Luther's Hermeneutic," *Interpretation* 37 (1983): 247.

54. Gerhard O. Forde, "Law and Gospel as the Methodological Principle of Theology," in *Theological Perspectives: A Discussion of Contemporary Issues in Lutheran Theology*, ed. E. D. Farwell et al. (Decorah, IA: Luther College Press, 1967), 63.

However, the new life is experienced passively as a promise that is given by God. Because rebirth is an eschatological event, one can live only in anticipation of this reality by faith and hope. As Forde puts it, as one is reborn in faith by the Holy Spirit, "one will see how much one is a sinner and will be until the end. One will see that one is not yet a 'Christian.' One will see precisely that one has no particular advantages over those who are not yet reborn. One will see one's solidarity with the rest of the human race and wait in hope until the end."[55] By faith, believers are given the end and the goal of existence and can begin to believe in the goodness of being God's creatures, waiting "for the time being" for God's kingdom to come.

Although Forde does affirm the Spirit as the giver of life, it remains unclear what aspects of this new life the Christian actually experiences through justification in the present tense, in spite of Mattes's assertion. While the Spirit brings new life, the experience of new life in Forde's thinking seems wholly relegated to the future, not something that transforms the present (other than existentially, the experience of a new awareness). This is why Forde says sanctification is nothing more than "getting used to justification."[56] Even with Forde's language of new life and rebirth, the experience of being justified seems to exist as a promise for the future rather than as a present reality. He describes the rebirth in existential terms: believers are given a new perspective on their present in the light of their promised future. It is unclear if anything, even the forgiveness of sins, is experienced in the here and now. Not only is this a departure from Luther and Melanchthon's theology of regeneration; it is also woefully inadequate to speak to those seeking an encounter with God in this age of the Spirit.

Jürgen Moltmann

In *The Spirit of Life*, Jürgen Moltmann argues that regeneration is an aspect of justification and not a "second grace" that complements the grace received in justification.[57] He claims that apart from Pietism, most Protestant theology has neglected this connection. The idea is biblical, finding its central New Tes-

---

55. Forde, "Christian Life," 450.

56. Gerhard O. Forde, "The Lutheran View," in *Christian Spirituality: Five Views of Sanctification*, ed. Donald L. Alexander (Downers Grove, IL: InterVarsity, 1988), 13.

57. Jürgen Moltmann, *The Spirit of Life: A Universal Affirmation*, trans. Margaret Kohl (Minneapolis: Fortress, 1992). In this work, Moltmann offers a several-pronged critique of forensic justification. His criticism that the doctrine is overly focused on the sinner, rather than the sinned against, received the bulk of attention from other theologians.

tament text in Titus, which frames rebirth in terms of baptism. Interestingly, Titus is also the Scripture cited by Luther in his explanation of baptism in the Small Catechism.[58] As Moltmann writes, "In these texts [i.e., in the Bible] the interpretation of regeneration or rebirth as new creation is christologically based, pneumatologically accomplished and eschatologically orientated."[59] The "medium" of regeneration is the Holy Spirit, who has been poured out in order to make the risen Christ present in the lives of believers and the in-breaking reign of God. Moltmann argues that justification must be reconceived to include this experience of the Spirit.

While Lutherans speak of "effective" justification in terms of the experience of the forgiveness of sins, Moltmann argues that this is a "backward-looking act" and emphasizes instead the "forward-looking act of justification"—specifically, "the new creation of life, the awakening of love, the rebirth to a living hope."[60] However, this is not correct. As we have seen, the Lutheran Confessions speak not only of "forgiveness of sins" but also of life and salvation, "for where there is forgiveness of sins, there is also life and salvation."[61] What Moltmann fails to acknowledge here is the relational aspect of forgiveness, that forgiveness brings new life and an experience of one's restored relationship with God. It is more than the "blotting out" of one's "record." Forgiveness—real and experienced forgiveness—leads into the future and opens up the forgiven sinner to peace, joy, consolation, and an awakening into a new reality as God's beloved child. Moltmann's description of this experience of rebirth, as being "possessed by the Spirit of the resurrection in the present," is striking.[62]

However, Moltmann goes on to make a distinction that ultimately is unhelpful and confusing. He writes, "In the event in which the believers are born again to become children of God and heirs, the efficacies of Christ and the Holy Spirit interpenetrate. If we call this event justification, we are describing the operation of Christ. If we call it sanctification, we are describing the operation of the Holy Spirit."[63] From a Lutheran theological perspective, this is a problematic way to frame the distinction between these two doctrines. As we have seen, the Holy Spirit has a role to play in justification, not just sanctification; and as I will argue in the following chapter, Christ also has a role to play in sanctification.

58. Martin Luther, "The Sacrament of Holy Baptism," 9–10, Small Catechism, in BC, 359.
59. Moltmann, Spirit of Life, 147.
60. Moltmann, Spirit of Life, 149.
61. Martin Luther, "The Sacrament of the Altar," 5–6, Small Catechism, in BC, 362.
62. Moltmann, Spirit of Life, 152–53.
63. Moltmann, Spirit of Life, 153.

The difference between justification and sanctification has to do not with the agency of the persons of the Trinity but with the agency of the justified sinner. In justification, the believer receives the gift of life, salvation, and the forgiveness of sins because of Christ and through the Holy Spirit, the giver of life who brings the believer to faith (a faith that receives these benefits) and who unites the believer with Christ. In sanctification, the believer works with the indwelling Holy Spirit to walk in the way of the new life they have received as a gift in justification. In other words, believers cooperate with the Spirit in their sanctification, a process that involves growth, but justification/regeneration is an unconditional gift that believers receive without any effort of their own. Even faith, which receives the promise of new life, is a gift enabled by the Holy Spirit. As we have seen, regeneration is distinct from sanctification; it is not a process but a pure gift.

Moltmann's description of how people experience the promised "rebirth to life" echoes the kind of experiences highlighted not only by Pentecostal and charismatic Christians but also by spiritual seekers outside of Christianity, such as those who claim to be SBNR. Such experiences include rapturous joy, affirmation of life, peace/shalom. Christians call these experiences of rebirth "experiences of the Holy Spirit," in which they experience God's immanent presence in their hearts that leads to a "transcendent depth."[64] Here again, however, Moltmann wishes to identify or merge rebirth with the process of sanctification, pointing to the growth in faith and new life in this experience of renewal. I argue instead that regeneration is the foundation for the renewal that follows with the sanctified life. First, we are reborn in the Spirit. Once reborn, we learn how to walk in the Spirit, something each Christian does, assisted by the Spirit, who accompanies us (i.e., the Paraclete).

Moltmann's attention to how to speak of the Spirit in regeneration reflects the tension between impersonal and personal images noted in the previous chapter. On the one hand, if new life is experienced and lived "in" the Spirit, then the Spirit cannot be the object of the experience of rebirth; rather, the Spirit is the "medium and space for it," "the broad place in which we have experiences."[65] On the other hand, the description of this experience as rebirth suggests a singular, personal image for the Holy Spirit: that of "mother." The image was used by the Syrian fathers, Julian of Norwich, and the founder of

---

64. Moltmann, *Spirit of Life*, 155.
65. Moltmann, *Spirit of Life*, 157.

the Moravians, Count Nikolaus von Zinzendorf, who "spoke of the motherly ministry of the Spirit."[66]

Frank Macchia

Frank Macchia approvingly points to Moltmann as a recent example of a Protestant theologian who views justification as a transformative reality occurring in the Spirit.[67] Macchia initially takes on forensic justification in a pair of articles written shortly after the signing of the Joint Declaration on the Doctrine of Justification by the Roman Catholic Church and the Lutheran World Federation (October 31, 1999), which he criticizes for not giving the Holy Spirit its due, in spite of affirming the trinitarian foundation for the doctrine. While acknowledging that Luther himself does not hold to a static view of justification that excludes transformation, Macchia raises an important question when he asks, "Where is the Holy Spirit in this forensic model of justification, the Spirit who serves as the agent by which God makes things right for, and with, fallen creation?"[68] He subsequently published *Justified in the Spirit: Creation, Redemption, and the Triune God* (2010), which lays out his own constructive theology of justification and redemption from a trinitarian and pneumatological framework.[69] Taking cues from Moltmann, he expands the doctrine to include all creation, as an eschatological event of new creation, and to include those sinned against as well as sinners. Macchia supports his argument biblically, showing a "fluidity" in the New Testament theological description of salvation in Luke, John, Paul, and James. He shows that William Seymour, whose ministry initiated the Azusa Street Revival, and other early Pentecostals articulated justification in terms of regeneration and the experience of a new and empowered life in the Spirit, and not in the legal categories of the sixteenth-century Reformers.[70] More

---

66. Moltmann, *Spirit of Life*, 159. Nancy Victorin-Vangerud has explored the maternal face of the Spirit in *Raging Hearth: Spirit in the Household of God* (Nashville: Chalice, 2000).

67. Frank D. Macchia, *Justified in the Spirit: Creation, Redemption, and the Triune God* (Grand Rapids: Eerdmans, 2010), 71.

68. Macchia, "Justification through New Creation," 205. See also Frank Macchia, "Justification and the Spirit: A Pentecostal Reflection on the Doctrine by Which the Church Stands or Falls," *Pneuma* 22, no. 1 (2000): 3–21.

69. This is the most fully developed presentation of this argument, which also appears in chap. 2 of Macchia's earlier book, *Baptized in the Spirit: A Global Pentecostal Theology* (Grand Rapids: Zondervan, 2006), esp. 129–40, and has continued to develop in subsequent works. See, e.g., Macchia, *Jesus the Spirit Baptizer: Christology in Light of Pentecost* (Grand Rapids: Eerdmans, 2018), esp. part 3, "Christ's Crucifixion, Resurrection, and Self-Impartation."

70. Macchia, *Justified in the Spirit*, 82.

recently, contemporary Pentecostal theologians such as Veli-Matti Kärkkäinen, Amos Yong, and Steven Studebaker have emphasized the role of the Spirit in salvation as a transformative event.[71]

Defining justification in terms of right relationship with God, Macchia argues that from a pneumatological perspective, this involves the self-giving of the triune God "that is manifested in new birth, witness, and resurrection."[72] Although he recognizes that Luther accepted a "connection" between the event of being justified as "judged righteous" and the inherent change in the believer, he concludes that Luther, and most Protestants, have kept the Holy Spirit "at arm's length" in the substance of justification, as the giver of faith but not the giver of life.[73] He writes, "The Spirit in this story is, at best, reduced to the instrumental function of communicating the declaration of freedom to the criminal's soul or inspiring trust in the judge (or the advocate)."[74] As we saw in chapter 1, the Pentecostal experience is "concentrated on the enjoyment of the divine presence within an intimate communion with God."[75] In other words, God's justification of the sinner is not only something declared to the sinner. "It is felt in the divine presence or embrace."[76] Macchia proposes the way to correct this narrow understanding is through an understanding of Spirit baptism as the indwelling Spirit of God in the believer. He notes, "The Spirit as link between legal and transformative is significant, since the Spirit functions both as advocate and vivifier."[77]

Macchia applauds the attempt by Luther and other Protestants who called for a return to a more theocentric (rather than anthropocentric) understanding of the divine-human relationship, focusing on what God has done for us rather than on our cooperation with God's grace. In this way, the Reformers liberated justification from its "medieval anthropological preoccupation with the dynamics of penance and conversion."[78] Macchia agrees that justification is not something we earn or cooperate with to receive; it is pure gift. We are declared and made righteous by God's action, not our own. However, he is critical of the theological

71. Kärkkäinen will be discussed below; see also Amos Yong, *The Spirit Poured Out on All Flesh: Pentecostalism and the Possibility of Global Theology* (Grand Rapids: Baker Academic, 2005), chap. 2; and Steven M. Studebaker, *The Spirit of Atonement: Pentecostal Contributions and Challenges to the Christian Traditions* (New York: T&T Clark, 2021).
72. Macchia, *Justified in the Spirit*, 3.
73. Macchia, *Justified in the Spirit*, 63. He gives as an example LW 27:277.
74. Macchia, *Justified in the Spirit*, 5.
75. Macchia, *Justified in the Spirit*, 79.
76. Macchia, *Justified in the Spirit*, 80.
77. Macchia, *Justified in the Spirit*, 11.
78. Macchia, *Justified in the Spirit*, 38.

grounding of this understanding, "an extrinsic notion of justifying righteousness construed as a legal or quasi-legal transaction."[79] Justification cannot be limited to a declaration of divine favor, or even the promise of the forgiveness of sins. Macchia views justification as a much fuller reality, "pneumatological in substance, consisting of pardon, the victory of life over death, divine witness and vindication, and participation in the divine koinonia."[80] As we have seen, the Reformers did not teach that justification is simply a forensic reality; it also brings regeneration. While not a condition for justification, regeneration is an aspect of the Holy Spirit's acting "for us" in justification. Lutherans can agree with Macchia that justification does more than pardon sinners or promise them a new future; it creates a new relational and eschatological reality with God through Christ and in the Spirit.

While Macchia affirms the Spirit's role as bringing the sinner into a right relationship with Christ (and thereby with the Father), he insists that this cannot be limited to the "cognitive function of faith."[81] Although this is a common way to think of "faith," it is not the view of Luther and Melanchthon. Both emphasize faith as an experience of the heart, not of the head, defining it in terms of "trust" rather than "belief." Even so, the focus on the Spirit's role in faith has too often neglected what Macchia calls "the very heart and soul of justification: the gift of the Spirit in embracing sinners and taking them up into the life and *koinonia* enjoyed by the Spirit with the Father and the Son,"[82] a *koinonia* in which we are invited to participate.[83] This embrace happens through the Spirit's indwelling, which results in not only the forgiveness of sins but also "the eschatological fullness of life in resurrection and glorification."[84] While the Finnish school of Luther studies has shown that Luther's view of justification includes a "real-ontic" union with Christ, through faith, a clear role for the Holy Spirit has not been addressed until very recently.[85]

79. Macchia, *Justified in the Spirit*, 39.
80. Macchia, *Justified in the Spirit*, 13.
81. Macchia, *Justified in the Spirit*, 39.
82. Macchia, *Justified in the Spirit*, 39; see also 47–48.
83. The language of participation is used in a phenomenological, not ontological, way here. In the Orthodox understanding of "theosis," participation in the triune God is interpreted through a Platonic philosophical frame, which is not how I intend to use the term.
84. Macchia, *Justified in the Spirit*, 12.
85. Veli-Matti Kärkkäinen, *One with God: Salvation as Deification and Justification* (Collegeville, MN: Liturgical Press, 2004), 37. Since Macchia's book was published, Miikka Ruokanen has addressed this lacuna in *Trinitarian Grace in Martin Luther's "The Bondage of the Will"* (New York: Oxford University Press, 2021). I will discuss his contributions below. See also Harald Hegstad, "United with Christ in the Spirit: The Pneumatological Dimension of the Doctrine of Justification," *Dialog* 60, no. 1 (March 2021): 79–85.

Kärkkäinen, who identifies as both Pentecostal and Lutheran, has also, like Macchia, called for a revised understanding of the Lutheran doctrine of justification in pneumatological terms, though his argument builds more explicitly on the contribution of the Finnish school. He points to the recent work of Miikka Ruokanen, who shows (similar to Prenter) that Luther's theology of grace and justification are conceived in pneumatological terms, drawing on Augustine's understanding of the personal presence of the triune God through the Holy Spirit. With this pneumatological grounding, "Ruokanen argues that . . . Luther can completely refute all the synergistic tendencies implied by the *facere quod in se est* [do what lies within you] axiom of the Nominalists. For Luther, pneumatology represents divine initiative, 'God's monergism,' distinct from and in contrast to any notion of the natural capacities of the human will."[86] The Holy Spirit, as the Spirit of Christ, encounters human beings, creating a union between them and the triune God.[87] Grace is the personal presence of the Holy Spirit in the believer. Luther's classic use of pneumatological language avoids the problems caused by using ontological language, offering a crucial modification to the Finnish school of Luther studies.[88]

Even so, Macchia's claim that Protestant theology historically has failed to address the Spirit's role as the giver of life in regeneration and renewal is important for Lutherans to hear. Even with the work of theologians such as Prenter and Ruokanen, the role of the Holy Spirit remains muted in Lutheran theology. Whether Lutheran theology lacks the pneumatological resources to speak of justification in a fuller way is debatable; I believe it is enriched through an engagement of perspectives offered by Pentecostal theologians. Specifically, Macchia's constructive proposal, which equates justification with the indwelling of the Spirit, warrants further consideration for those Lutherans who would

86. Veli-Matti Kärkkäinen, *One with God*, 64, citing Ruokanen's dissertation.

87. Kärkkäinen, *One with God*, 64. Here it seems pertinent to acknowledge the recent work of Candace L. Kohli, which examines how "Luther used justification to parse a changing relation between the Holy Spirit and the human person and, then, how this new way of thinking about the Spirit-human relation made it possible for Luther to reexamine the impact of justification on human intellectual and volitional powers." Candace L. Kohli, "Grasping at the Human as Human: The Human Person after Justification, according to Martin Luther's Pneumatological Lens," in Mary Ann Hinsdale and Stephen Okey, eds., *T&T Clark Handbook of Theological Anthropology* (London: T&T Clark, 2021), 184. See also Candace L. Kohli, "Help for Moral Good: The Spirit, the Law, and Human Agency in Martin Luther's Antinomian Disputations (1537–40)" (PhD diss., Northwestern University, 2019), https://arch.library.northwestern.edu/concern/generic_works/4q77fr419?locale=en.

88. See Ruokanen, *Trinitarian Grace*, where he further develops this argument in Luther's theology.

like to see a more fulsome role for the Spirit as the one who indwells to bring rebirth and regeneration.[89]

A Lutheran Engagement with Macchia

The idea itself of the Spirit indwelling the believer as an aspect of justification is not contrary to Lutheran teaching, as I have shown. Even Martin Chemnitz, one of the authors of the Formula of Concord, taught that when one is justified, one receives the forgiveness of sins and the indwelling of the Holy Spirit as a result, using the word "vivifying" to describe this event.[90] However, Chemnitz and later Lutherans likely did not emphasize this language because of its Osiandrian connotations.[91] Andreas Osiander's views on justification were rejected by the authors of the Formula of Concord (article 3) because of his christological speculation that it is only Christ's divine nature that justifies sinners, that justification occurs as a result of the indwelling of Christ's divine nature in the sinner (a speculation that led to charges of Nestorianism). Melanchthon criticizes Osiander's teaching and insists on the importance of the alien or extrinsic nature of the righteousness that justifies. Vainio writes, "Even if the salvation is realized *in nobis* (and it needs to be), the sinner always turns his or her eyes *extra nos*, to the person of Christ, and it is in Christ's perfect obedience that he has been made manifest as both man and God."[92] While the sinner receives Christ's righteousness, by faith, through the Holy Spirit, for Melanchthon there is no disagreement regarding God's presence in the believer's heart. Vainio writes, "When a person is forgiven through faith in Christ, God simultaneously makes the heart of the believer [God's] dwelling place. This indwelling is felt as consolation (*trost*), which frees one from the fear of God's judgment (*angst*). The Gospel simultaneously offers both the favor (*gratia*), meaning forgiveness of sins, and the gift (*donum*), meaning divine presence."[93]

---

89. Macchia's emphasis on eschatology is also most welcome. While largely absent in the Lutheran Confessions (with the exception of Luther's Large Catechism), this emphasis is central for key Lutheran theologians of the late twentieth century, including Gerhard Forde, Robert Jenson, and Carl Braaten.

90. Vainio, *Justification and Participation in Christ*, 156.

91. Vainio, *Justification and Participation in Christ*, 173.

92. Olli-Pekka Vainio, "Luther and Theosis: A Response to the Critics of Finnish Luther Research," *Pro Ecclesia* 24, no. 4 (Fall 2015): 467.

93. Vainio, *Justification and Participation in Christ*, 82.

At times, Macchia's description of the Spirit's indwelling as "possessing divine essence" echoes Osiander, and he even hints that Osiander may not have been altogether wrong in his proposal.[94] More common is his assertion that the indwelling of the Spirit is at "the source, substance and fulfillment" of the gift of justifying righteousness.[95] He wants to express as close a relationship as possible between justification and the indwelling Spirit who brings rebirth and new creation. He insists that justification is not "an event detached from us" but that it "brings life, the very life of the Spirit."[96] Citing John Calvin's assertion that God is the "fountain of righteousness" in which we participate by faith on account of Christ, Macchia asks, What else could this fountain be other than the Holy Spirit?[97]

It is important to hear Macchia's challenge to the Lutheran tradition with regard to what he calls the "substance," or core, of justification: a relationship with the triune God made possible by the indwelling of the Holy Spirit who brings faith and new life. While Lutherans affirm the relational nature of justification, too often we define its substance in negative terms. But if the Spirit is the giver of life, what is it that we truly receive? Justification cannot simply be the absence of something, a pardon for sins committed. Lutherans should learn to recognize what we receive in justification as more than God's favor, or even forgiveness, for in justification we are truly united with Christ through the power of the Spirit of God acting for us, bringing new life.

Macchia affirms justifying faith as "a gift of the Spirit entered into through new birth."[98] He describes faith in relational terms, as a yielding, an obedient self-offering in response to the Spirit's embrace, not unlike the image of accepting the music from the headphones discussed above.[99] His view that faith involves the totality of our being and transcends our human capacities is very much in line with the teaching of the Lutheran Confessions. Ultimately, he describes faith as participation in Christ, an understanding shared by the Finnish school of Luther studies.

While Macchia recognizes the role of faith, he is critical of the Reformers' preference for faith (over love) as that which in the human being receives justification.[100] Macchia would prefer to speak of justification "by love" because

94. Macchia, *Justified in the Spirit*, 55–59.
95. Macchia, *Justified in the Spirit*, 217.
96. Macchia, *Justified in the Spirit*, 218.
97. Macchia, *Justified in the Spirit*, 65, citing John Calvin, *Institutes of the Christian Religion* 3.11.8.
98. Macchia, *Justified in the Spirit*, 237.
99. Macchia, *Justified in the Spirit*, 221.
100. Macchia, *Justified in the Spirit*, 236–37.

love is the highest expression of the Spirit's indwelling for Pentecostals and the primary fruit of the Spirit's indwelling (not speaking in tongues!).[101] John Wesley, whose theology influenced the stream of Pentecostals with roots in the Holiness movement, taught that sanctification and "Christian perfection" are measured in love, not purity or moral uprightness, as is often thought.[102] Lutherans will affirm this with regard to the second and third "movements" (sanctification and mission). However, the problem with saying that we are "justified by love" is that, as Melanchthon pointedly states, "we never love as much as we should."[103] We can always love more. Faith, in the Lutheran confessional understanding, is an either/or; you are able to trust, or you are not. Love is something that can always grow and deepen. If we are justified by love, then we will always be wondering if we love enough to be justified.

Macchia's most innovative contribution in *Justified by the Spirit* is his framing of justification by the Spirit's indwelling with the Pentecostal doctrine of Spirit baptism, which he dubs the "crown jewel" of Pentecostal theology. As we will see in chapter 5, for Pentecostals, Spirit baptism historically has related more to empowerment for mission than to soteriology.[104] However, Macchia states that "Pentecostals have emphasized both intimate communion and empowered witness" with regard to the indwelling of the Spirit.[105] Macchia is critical of the tendency of Pentecostals (and others) to speak of justification, sanctification, and Spirit baptism as separate and distinct movements or stages in a person's life in the Spirit because all three originate in the Spirit's indwelling in the believer.[106] The Spirit is not doing three things. The Spirit is doing one thing: indwelling

101. Macchia, *Justified in the Spirit*, 89–90.
102. For Wesley, one who is gradually being sanctified will, "as the Apostle expresses it, 'Go on to perfection.' But what is perfection? The word has various senses: here it means perfect love. It is love excluding sin; love filling the heart, taking up the whole capacity of the soul. It is love 'rejoicing evermore, praying without ceasing, in everything giving thanks.'" John Wesley, "The Scripture Way of Salvation (1765)," in *John Wesley's Sermons: An Anthology*, ed. Albert C. Outler and Richard P. Heitzenrater (Nashville: Abingdon, 1991), 374.
103. As Melanchthon writes, "If faith receives the forgiveness of sins on account of love, the forgiveness of sins will always be uncertain because we never love as much as we should." AP 4.110, in *BC*, 139.
104. While this is true historically and still held by many Pentecostal theologians, Macchia is not the only Pentecostal who thinks that this is limiting and could even be disastrous. Studebaker argues that this is a subordination of the Holy Spirit in theological terms and asks whether the outpouring of the Spirit on the day of Pentecost can really be for the purpose of showcasing a subsequent experience of grace that is unnecessary for salvation. Personal correspondence with Steven Studebaker, May 3, 2022. See also Studebaker, *Spirit of Atonement*.
105. Macchia, *Justified in the Spirit*, 75–76.
106. Macchia, *Justified in the Spirit*, 77, 86.

the sinner. This leads Macchia to state, "Justification in the context of Spirit baptism pardons the sinners by embracing, cleansing, and renewing them with the divine indwelling and then continuing to embrace the ambiguous faith and witness that arise in response, regarding them by grace as corresponding to the faithfulness of Christ."[107] While justification is not based on this inner renewal and transformation, it still involves these.

The Lutheran Reformers made a distinction between—but did not separate— the Spirit's work in justification and the Spirit's work in sanctification. When Macchia says that the Reformers "removed all human transformation and the consequent cooperation with divine grace" from the "realm of justification," he is partially correct.[108] The "consequent cooperation with divine grace" is the movement of the Spirit that flows from the regeneration of the believer in justification—that is, sanctification, which involves human cooperation with the Spirit for the believer to live out the new life received in justification. I find it helpful to distinguish the Spirit's role in the three movements because of the possible misunderstanding regarding the role of the sinner, who is passive in the first movement (justification) and active in the other two movements (sanctification and calling/mission). The importance of protecting justification from human cooperation requires this. Although Macchia affirms this point, it is not crucial for Pentecostal theology in the way it is for Lutheran theology. This may be because most Pentecostals are more Arminian and therefore, in- tentionally or unintentionally, less concerned with the works-righteousness problem. This is not to say they support works righteousness; rather, they see the framing of the problem in the Protestant Reformation as historically conditioned and not something that needs to continue as the starting point of soteriological reflection.[109]

Conclusion: The Spirit as the Giver of Life in the Movement of Justification

I have proposed that a fresh way to consider the role of the Holy Spirit in justi- fication is as the giver of life. This highlights the regenerating work of the Spirit, along with the Spirit's work in conversion. Justification includes having not only

107. Macchia, *Justified in the Spirit*, 216.
108. Macchia, *Justified in the Spirit*, 45.
109. I thank Steven Studebaker for this insight. Personal correspondence with Studebaker, May 3, 2022.

a new "standing" before God (in the forensic sense) but also an experience of God's grace relationally, through the indwelling of the Spirit as God for us, as the one who loves us unconditionally. The Spirit gives us the capacity to trust in God's love and favor for us and also enjoins us to rest in this love. This is important for Lutherans and Reformed theologians to address because, as we have seen, the context today calls for an articulation of salvation that includes spiritual experience and transformation. As long as we are clear that our experience of regeneration does not precede or lead to God's justifying grace, this aspect of the doctrine can be affirmed by Lutherans, especially within a pneumatological framework.

The Holy Spirit is the giver of life who brings us into relationship with the triune God, through whom we receive new eschatological life in the Spirit, through faith that unites us to Christ, who reveals to us the heart of the Father. We experience the new life God has "for us"—regeneration—through the Holy Spirit. The experience includes forgiveness of sins, life (regeneration), and salvation—gifts we receive through no effort of our own. A new relational reality is created by the Holy Spirit in justification. We experience this newness of life through the gifts of forgiveness, consolation, and joy—by being cleansed and freed/liberated from sin. This regeneration is "for us" because we are still sinners. We are not yet transformed. We have simply been reborn and are new. This gift of new life is received through faith; it is not something we achieve or work for or contribute to on our own, any more than a new baby contributes to their own birth. In this way, one can move beyond the "forensic" emphasis in Protestant theology that protects the passivity of the believer and say that justification is also regeneration.

While this idea—of the Holy Spirit as the giver of life / new birth—frequently is treated under sanctification, I have argued that it is more appropriate to treat it under justification because new birth is a gift, something that happens to us. Sanctification is the resulting process of learning to walk in the gift of new life we have been given. Sanctification involves our cooperation with the Spirit, who now dwells in us, creating spiritual impulses and enabling us to love God, and our neighbors, in return.

At the same time, I agree with Macchia that we need to think more holistically about the Spirit's work in the Christian's life. For Lutherans, the foundational movement of the Spirit remains justification, but I agree that the language of "stages" can be problematic, especially when considering the second two movements of the Spirit as discussed in this work. We can affirm the unified action of the Spirit who indwells the believer while distinguishing the Spirit's distinctive role in each movement.

My construction of this, as laid out in the chapters of this book, distinguishes the Spirit's roles thus:

- justification as the Spirit "for us," as the giver of life, leading to the Spirit's dwelling in (and regenerating) sinners through faith;
- sanctification as the Spirit "in us," as the Paraclete (accompanier or companion), whereby we cooperate with the Spirit who indwells us so that we might walk in the new life we have received, led by the Spirit who indwells us, bearing the fruit of the Spirit and growing in love of God and neighbor;
- participation in God's mission as the Spirit "through us," as the empowerer, which in some ways is simply an expansion of sanctification—that is, of how the Spirit empowers us for the broader mission of God in the world as we share God's love with others through witnessing, serving others, and working for justice.

4

The Spirit in Us

Sanctification and the New Life

Lutheran treatments of sanctification are not easily found, and when Zondervan published their *Five Views on Sanctification,*[1] the Lutheran view was conspicuously absent.[2] The doctrine of sanctification, of "being made holy," is the most problematic movement of the Spirit for Lutherans. There are a few reasons for this. Readers will recall that we have already discussed "being made holy" in our discussion of justification. In one sense, this phrase can refer to both movements of justification and sanctification. As Martin Luther explains in the Large Catechism, the Spirit is the one who makes us holy in justification by giving us the Holy Spirit and the new birth, which we receive through faith—which is itself a gift of the Spirit "for us," one that inflames our hearts and enables us to cling to the promise of God's grace in Christ. This sometimes is called "positional" (as compared to "possessional") holiness. Positional holiness is a holiness that

---

1. Melvin E. Dieter et al., *Five Views on Sanctification* (Grand Rapids: Zondervan, 1996).

2. Regarding this omission, David Scaer, a Lutheran Church–Missouri Synod theologian, writes, "Perhaps it was rather that Lutherans are not considered Protestants—for which we can be grateful. Or perhaps, even better, Lutherans do not have a distinctive contribution to make to the understanding of sanctification so far as other Christians are concerned." Scaer, "Sanctification in the Lutheran Confessions," *Concordia Theological Quarterly* 53, no. 3 (July 1989): 172.

is ours by virtue of our relationship with the Holy Spirit.[3] Luther further states that the Holy Spirit who *has made* us holy "still makes us holy," and he goes on to refer to other aspects of the Spirit's work in this regard, including spiritual fruit and our living into what he calls "the full forgiveness of sins."[4]

In this chapter, I argue that in the movement of sanctification the Holy Spirit's work continues *in* us so that we can live out the new life and live into the holiness that we have received from God. This addresses the Lutheran concern that talk of sanctification not collapse into moralism or works righteousness.[5] The Spirit's sanctifying work does not add anything to justification, in terms of our acceptance and adoption by God, or make us more holy. In sanctification, believers are invited to cooperate with the indwelling Spirit to resist sin and grow in love of God and neighbor, to live "holy lives" by allowing God's holiness to shine through us.

Pentecostals have had their own historic debates over how best to understand holiness in the order of salvation, but overall they agree that sanctification involves some process of growth and maturity in the Christian life.[6] This is due in part to the significant influence of the Holiness movement of the nineteenth century on Pentecostalism. The Holiness movement emerged in the late nineteenth century out of a concern with, and emphasis on, holy living, defined in terms of empirical piety or outward behaviors.[7] One of the major streams of Pentecostalism grew out of the Holiness movement, but other branches of Pentecostalism, including those with Reformed influences, also have emphasized holy living. An overly strong focus on external behavior, combined with an emphasis on the negative rather than the positive aspects of holiness (i.e., more of a focus on eradicating sin than on growing in love), has led to this doctrine

3. See, e.g., Carl E. Braaten, *The Principles of Lutheran Theology* (Philadelphia: Fortress, 1983), 56–57.

4. Martin Luther, Large Catechism, in *The Book of Concord: The Confessions of the Evangelical Lutheran Church*, ed. Robert Kolb and Timothy J. Wengert (Minneapolis: Fortress, 2000), 435, 438. *The Book of Concord* will hereafter be cited as *BC*.

5. See, e.g., Scaer, "Sanctification in the Lutheran Confessions," 165–81.

6. Specifically, I refer here to the internal debate between "finished work" and Wesleyan Pentecostals on whether sanctification occurs as a "crisis moment" or is more of a process. Many contemporary Pentecostal theologians are seeking a common ground between these two historic positions. For a full historical examination of the positions in this debate and a proposal for a new vision, see J. Benjiman Wiles, *Becoming Like Jesus: Toward a Pentecostal Theology of Sanctification* (Cleveland, TN: CPT, 2021).

7. See Donald W. Dayton, *Theological Roots of Pentecostalism* (Peabody, MA: Hendrickson, 1987), in which he argues that Pentecostalism grew out of Methodism and nineteenth-century holiness revivals. See also Barry L. Callen, ed., *The Holy River of God: Currents and Contributions of the Wesleyan Holiness Stream of Christianity* (Glendora, CA: Aldersgate, 2016).

falling out of use among many contemporary Pentecostal theologians.[8] Chris Green is among those who challenge Pentecostals on their tendency to understand holiness "primarily in individualistic, interiorist, and performative terms."[9] A growing number of Pentecostal theologians are offering fresh and more positive treatments of holiness based on biblical teaching (love, fruit of the Spirit).

Historically, Lutherans have been suspicious of any talk of "holiness" because of its association with moral or spiritual achievement, fearing this would lead people to put trust in their own good works. Further, if one is "made holy"— that is, receives the Holy Spirit as gift and giver of life—in justification and baptism, whereby one is adopted into God's family and has one's sins forgiven, then speaking of "being made holy" as *a process* will lead to confusion, at best, and to works righteousness, at worst. This has led some Lutheran theologians, such as Gerhard Forde, to argue that sanctification adds nothing to justification and that if a descriptor is needed, one might simply say that sanctification is nothing more than getting used to being justified. In one sense, Forde is correct in that sanctification adds nothing to one's justification; however, as I will show, it is more than getting used to being justified.

As we saw in the previous chapter, the rebirth received in justification is a gift. Some theologians use the terms "rebirth" and "regeneration" interchangeably with "sanctification." However, I have proposed distinguishing them based on the role of human cooperation. In the event of justification and regeneration, the believer does not cooperate; the believer receives what God the Holy Spirit gives. In sanctification, the believer cooperates with the Holy Spirit in the process of living out the gift of new life, or as St. Paul puts it, being led by the Spirit, or walking in the Spirit. This also suggests considering sanctification relationally, as a movement of the Holy Spirit (as the giver of life) in our lives of faith, as the Spirit "in us." The goal is not to achieve the gift of new life but to experience it and allow this new life to change and transform us for the sake of God's world.

In other words, if one considers this question pneumatologically, it is possible to affirm holiness as something we receive in justification *and* as something we participate in, or cooperate with, in sanctification. Holiness is both

---

8. See, e.g., Lee Roy Martin, introduction to *A Future for Holiness: Pentecostal Explorations*, ed. Lee Roy Martin (Cleveland, TN: CPT, 2013), 1–5; and Yee Tham Wan, "Bridging the Gap between Holiness and Morality," *Asian Journal of Pentecostal Studies* 4, no. 2 (2001): 153–80.

9. Chris E. W. Green, "'Not I, but Christ': Holiness, Conscience, and the (Im)possibility of Community," in *Future for Holiness*, ed. Martin, 128.

positional and progressive. We are justified by faith and made "holy" in that God has adopted and claimed us, and we have received the Spirit in our lives in a new and powerful way. Because we are simultaneously saint (holy) and sinner, the Spirit continues to "make us holy" not only through the daily gift of God's forgiveness but also through the ongoing presence of the giver of life, the Holy Spirit, who enables us to resist sin's power and walk in the new life we have been given. Luther states in the Large Catechism that the Spirit continues to "make us holy" through daily forgiveness of sins, the fruit of the Spirit, the gifts of the Spirit, and the "holy community" (the church). The Spirit leads us in the new life we have received, accompanying us, as the Paraclete, on this journey of transformation. The Holy Spirit's work continues in us as we live out the new life, the holiness that we have received from God. The goal is not to become more holy; rather, it is for the indwelling Spirit now working in our hearts to be more fully expressed in love of God and neighbor.

In this chapter, I explore the sanctifying work of the Spirit in the believer by bringing the Lutheran perspective into dialogue with Wesleyan and Pentecostal views. First, I briefly return to Forde and Jürgen Moltmann, both of whom highlight the role of the Spirit as the agent of rebirth, to consider how they relate sanctification to regeneration. I follow this with my own retrieval of sanctification in the theology of the Lutheran Confessions and that of John Wesley, who is often considered the theologian of sanctification par excellence and whose teachings have had a significant impact on Pentecostalism. We will see that both in the Lutheran Confessions and in Wesley, holiness is defined primarily in terms of love—that is, in terms of how the Spirit enables us to love and produces the growth of other spiritual "fruit" in us.

I then explore the contribution of Pentecostal historian and theologian Dale Coulter, who offers a fresh and positive theology of holiness grounded in his Wesleyan tradition (Church of God, Cleveland, TN). Coulter and other recent voices reflect a shift away from viewing holiness in negative terms to understanding it in positive terms and, correspondingly, from a moralistic focus on avoiding sin to a focus on growing in the fruit of the Spirit, especially love.[10]

Finally, I engage Coulter's contribution from a Lutheran perspective, concluding with some reflections on the role of the Spirit as Paraclete, the one who accompanies us as we live out the gift of new life we receive from the Spirit

10. Others who offer similar perspectives include Pentecostal theologian Amos Yong and charismatic Wesleyan theologians Daniel Castelo and Chris Green, both of whom were raised in Pentecostal denominations.

in justification, as we "walk in the Spirit," and what this might look like in our daily lives and interpersonal relationships. Here I return to Luther, especially his commentaries on Galatians, his sermons on John's Gospel, and his explanation in the Large Catechism of the Third Article of the Apostles' Creed. The goal of sanctification as a movement of the Spirit that results from the new birth is not to increase holiness; it is, rather, to powerfully experience the holiness—that is, the new life—we have received through the Spirit's personal presence "in us." As we are transformed by the Spirit, we can become more productive vessels for God's work in the world "through us." In the next chapter, I expand this to include the Spirit's work in God's mission in the world, as the Spirit empowers us to work for justice, sharing the love of God beyond our immediate social circles, to all in need. The Holy Spirit is envisioned as our accompanier, or companion, and our empowerer—as the one working *through* us to accomplish God's work in the world.

Lutheran and Reformed Views on Sanctification

In the previous chapter, I noted that Forde and Moltmann—a Lutheran theologian and a Reformed theologian, respectively—both articulate the doctrine of justification in terms of new birth, as an event of the Holy Spirit. However, the similarities end there, as their views on sanctification could not be further apart. As already noted, Forde argues that sanctification does not add anything to justification; he takes it to be included in justification since it is an eschatological and "total state" experienced through faith. The Spirit brings the new birth, the new state of being justified, which he describes in eschatological terms as being "born again into the world God created"—that is, viewing one's life from the perspective of eschatological faith, to becoming a true member of the human race.[11]

This leads to Forde's infamous assertion that sanctification is nothing other than "the art of getting used to justification. . . . It is the justified life."[12] For Forde, sanctification is not defined in terms of ethics and moral progress.[13] It

11. Gerhard O. Forde, "The Christian Life," in *Christian Dogmatics*, vol. 2, ed. Carl E. Braaten and Robert W. Jenson (Philadelphia: Fortress, 1984), 453. *Christian Dogmatics*, vol. 2, is hereafter cited as CD 2.
12. Gerhard O. Forde, "The Lutheran View," in *Christian Spirituality: Five Views of Sanctification*, ed. Donald L. Alexander (Downers Grove, IL: InterVarsity, 1988), 13.
13. Gerhard O. Forde, *Justification by Faith: A Matter of Death and Life* (1982; repr., Ramsey, NJ: Sigler, 1991), 52.

is unfortunate that he develops this argument in negative and anthropological terms, focusing primarily on the uselessness of the law as a moral guide for sanctified living rather than on the work of the Holy Spirit as the one who frees (and empowers) us for this new life.[14] Forde acknowledges that Luther occasionally spoke of progress in the Christian's life but argues that "what [Luther] had in mind was not our movement toward the goal, but the goal's movement in on us. . . . The 'progress' is the coming of the kingdom of God among us."[15] Further, Luther's teaching that we are simultaneously sinful and justified "would seem to militate against any talk of 'progress' in sanctification."[16] The idea of sanctification as a moral progression through the expulsion of sin is, according to Forde, the exact opposite of what Luther taught. What happens is not the removal of sin from the believer's life but a continual process of dying to sin and being raised to new life. This movement is cyclical and repetitive, not a linear path to moral improvement or progress. Forde's views have shaped much contemporary Lutheran thinking on sanctification and have contributed to an ongoing "allergy" to the Spirit.[17]

Forde's language here suggests that he identifies sanctification with regeneration, the declaring/making holy that happens in justification, and not with the life that emerges from this gift—that is, with what Christians *do* with the gift of new life. Forde is correct that our actions do not bring God closer to us; they do not, in that regard, make us *more* holy. He correctly challenges notions of sanctification consisting of linear, moral improvement, which can lead to moralism and works righteousness. At the same time, this does not mean there is no movement whatsoever. The Christian does not simply sit around "getting used to" being justified. The cyclical daily movement from death to life does not leave us in the same place as we started; this is no *Groundhog Day* spirituality. The Holy Spirit is a dynamic personal presence in our lives. The new life that we receive in justification is not a static reality; it is dynamic because of the presence of the Holy Spirit in our lives, accompanying us as we walk in this gift.

---

14. Gerhard O. Forde, "*Lex Semper Accusat?* Nineteenth-Century Roots of Our Current Dilemma," *Dialog* 9, no. 4 (Fall 1970): 265–74.

15. Forde, "Christian Life," 435. See also Forde, *Justification by Faith*, 51; and Forde, "Forensic Justification and the Christian Life: Triumph or Tragedy?," in *A More Radical Gospel: Essays on Eschatology, Authority, Atonement, and Ecumenism*, ed. Mark C. Mattes and Steven D. Paulson (Grand Rapids: Eerdmans, 2004), 126.

16. Forde, "Forensic Justification and the Christian Life," 121.

17. Lutheran theologian Craig L. Nessan addresses this allergy in his article "Allergic to the Spirit No More: Rethinking Pneumatology," *Currents in Theology and Mission* 21, no. 3 (June 1994): 183–96.

Moltmann also does not distinguish sanctification from rebirth in the Christian life, but his blending or blurring of the two is different than Forde's, and his vision for sanctification goes beyond the justified sinner to incorporate all living things. Simply put, for Moltmann, sanctification involves rediscovering the sanctity of life. The "ethic of the reverence of life" requires renunciation of all violence toward any living creature, or being, and the search for the "harmonies and accords of life."[18] The foundation for holiness and sanctification is the Holy Spirit. The Holy Spirit is the agent of sanctification, by which God sets us apart and enables us to participate in the new life we have received as gift. Moltmann states that sanctification as gift (what I have been calling "regeneration") leads to sanctification as charge—that is, "keeping holy what God has already made holy." For the justified sinner, this involves an invitation to discipleship of Jesus and "coming to life in God's Spirit."[19]

Moltmann goes on to explore the "holy life" in several biblical images, including the fruit of the Spirit, the "well of life" as source, and the image of light (which Grace Ji-Sun Kim also highlights, as noted in chap. 2, above). All three show the "emanation of energies flowing from God to human beings." While human beings cannot make or achieve this life on their own, they can "let it be, let it come and clear away hindrances."[20] He does not explicitly speak of sin here—but of course, theologically speaking, sin is the major hindrance to experiencing the new life of the Spirit. Moltmann defines the Holy Spirit ultimately as the power of life, who flows into our life, bringing the new birth and allowing us to experience the new life and vitality we have received from God.

Like Forde, Moltmann rejects moralistic definitions, but for a different reason: because these restrict and reduce life. To fully experience the new life unfolding in us, we need space to stretch our limbs, as it were. Moltmann ends his reflection on this by proposing the Holy Spirit as "our transcendent space for living."[21] Unlike Forde, Moltmann describes the experience of new life as "gift" and "charge" in pneumatological terms, and he affirms human cooperation with the Spirit in removing obstacles to the Spirit's work and responding in discipleship to the Spirit's invitation.

18. Jürgen Moltmann, *The Spirit of Life: A Universal Affirmation*, trans. Margaret Kohl (Minneapolis: Fortress, 1992), 172–73.

19. Moltmann, *Spirit of Life*, 175.

20. Moltmann, *Spirit of Life*, 176–77.

21. Moltmann, *Spirit of Life*, 179.

Interestingly, he begins his treatment with a comparison of Luther and Wesley on the topic. He correctly notes that, for Luther, justification addresses our relationship to God, and sanctification is the way we live out that new relationship. He criticizes Luther for not having a stronger emphasis on the new life in the Spirit and daily resurrection, due to Luther's focus on how each of us is *simul iustus et peccator* (at once justified and a sinner) and thus in need of continual forgiveness. In *The Spirit of Life*, while Moltmann is clearly aware and appreciative of the significance of Pentecostalism, he does not engage any Pentecostal scholars. In the next section, I offer my own comparison of Luther and the Lutheran Confessions with Wesley on this question before engaging the work of Dale Coulter, whose work on sanctification is well regarded in Pentecostal circles.[22]

Regeneration and Sanctification in John Wesley and the Lutheran Confessions[23]

Theologically, Lutherans have been largely concerned with justification and Wesleyans with sanctification. Each has been, at least in part if not wholly, suspicious of what the other has taught. Wesley feared that the Lutheran emphasis on the forensic nature of justification led to antinomianism. If the "justified sinner" can just go on sinning as before, there seems to be no change in the sinner whereby the Spirit enables them to love God and neighbor through following the commandments. Wesley even chides Luther on being ignorant of sanctification.[24] On the other hand, Lutherans fear that putting so much emphasis on the process of sanctification may negate or at least obscure the sufficiency of Christ for the believer's salvation, leading the believer to trust in their own works for salvation.

For Wesley, the redeemed life includes sanctification along with justification, which is a view shared by many Pentecostal theologians, such as Frank

22. In addition to Coulter's more popular theological treatment of the topic, *Holiness: The Beauty of Perfection* (Lanham, MD: Seymour Press, 2021), he also contributed the chapter "Sanctification: Becoming an Icon of the Spirit through Holy Love" to the *Routledge Handbook of Pentecostal Theology*, ed. Wolfgang Vondey (New York: Routledge, 2020), 237–46. He is currently working on a major book on the doctrine of salvation through the lens of holiness.

23. The following two sections have been revised from Cheryl M. Peterson, "A Lutheran Engagement with Wesley on the Work of the Spirit," in *The Holy Spirit and the Christian Life: Historical, Interdisciplinary, and Renewal Perspectives*, ed. Wolfgang Vondey (New York: Palgrave Macmillan, 2014), 93–108. Re-presented with permission of Palgrave MacMillan.

24. John Wesley, "On God's Vineyard," in *John Wesley*, ed. Albert C. Outler (New York: Oxford University Press, 1964), 107.

Macchia. With Luther, Wesley affirms that justification is the article on which the church stands or falls.[25] He follows Luther in teaching that justification is by grace alone, on account of Christ alone, and through faith alone. Justification is wholly a gift from God. One does not need to be sanctified, or holy, to receive it. Far from obedience or holiness preceding justification, according to Wesley we can love God only because God first loves us and forgives us.[26] The Christian life begins only at justification. But as important as this doctrine is, it does not, for Wesley, exhaust the fullness of salvation biblically. Regeneration (or new birth) occurs simultaneously with justification, taking away the power of sin in our lives and beginning the process of sanctification, as a work of the Holy Spirit.[27]

Wesleyan theologian Randy Maddox writes that the new birth is "the instantaneous restoration of our responsive participation in God," whereas sanctification proper consists in "the resulting gradual therapeutic transformation of our lives."[28] Once regenerated, the believer cooperates with the Holy Spirit in the process of sanctification.[29] Sanctification is the immediate fruit of justification, a distinct gift from God through which the believer is enabled to live as God intends (in perfect love and obedience), the process by which "such a love of God and [others] as produces all inward and outward holiness" is realized in the believer.[30] Or to put it another way, justification is what God does for us, and sanctification is what God does in us by the Spirit.[31]

Wesley highlights the role of the Holy Spirit in sanctification. In a striking description of the relationship between faith and love in the sanctified life, Wesley writes that the Holy Spirit is "breathed into the new-born soul; and the same breath which comes from, returns to God. As it is continually received by faith, so it is continually rendered back by love."[32] This offers an interesting point of connection to the Lutheran tradition. While sanctification includes love, it is grounded not in *our* loving actions but always in *God's* love for us, which we

25. Wesley does affirm Luther's teaching on justification. See John Wesley, "The Lord Is Our Righteousness," in *John Wesley's Sermons: An Anthology*, ed. Albert C. Outler and Richard P. Heitzenrater (Nashville: Abingdon, 1991), 383; hereafter cited as *Sermons*.

26. John Wesley, "Justification by Faith," in *Sermons*, 116.

27. John Wesley, "The Great Privilege of Those That Are Born of God," in *Sermons*, 184.

28. Randy L. Maddox, *Responsible Grace: John Wesley's Practical Theology* (Nashville: Kingswood Books, 1994), 145.

29. John Wesley, "On Working Out Our Own Salvation," in *Sermons*, 485–92.

30. Maddox, *Responsible Grace*, 174.

31. Wesley, "Justification by Faith," 114.

32. Wesley, "Great Privilege," 186. See also Maddox, *Responsible Grace*, 156.

receive through faith and cooperate with (though Lutherans would add—and stress—"encumbered with great weakness"[33]) by repentance and good works. Only good works that "spring out of a true and living faith" are good in the sight of God.[34] We cannot love God or neighbor until we have received God's love and justification by faith.[35] Lutherans and Wesleyans can agree on this point: we can love only because God first loves us; God's love for us precedes and grounds our love for God and the neighbor.

Although the Holy Spirit initiates, Wesley emphasizes human cooperation with the Spirit in the process of sanctification. The believer is obligated to work with God's grace in the growth of holiness.[36] However, Wesley takes great pains to stress that this activity is possible only because of the presence of the Holy Spirit at work in our hearts and in our lives. If we are capable of any "work," it is solely because "God works in us."[37] Maddox states, "Wesley was convinced that, while we *can* not attain holiness (and wholeness) apart from God's grace, God *will* not effect holiness apart from our responsive participation."[38]

As we have seen, Lutherans find it important to distinguish justification from sanctification so that no human works (including the cooperation of the human will before justification) are "mixed" into justification, lest one think that human cooperation is required for justification.[39] However, this can lead to antinomianism, or the idea that good works should be avoided.[40] The Formula of Concord (1577) addresses this distorted teaching in response to a controversy over the statement that good works are "necessary" for salvation. While one is justified through "faith alone,"[41] love necessarily follows faith as a work of the Holy Spirit.[42] Good works always follow faith and, in this sense, are necessary.[43]

33. Epitome, Formula of Concord (hereafter cited as Ep. FC), 4.13, in BC, 499.
34. Wesley, "Justification by Faith," 117.
35. Wesley, "Justification by Faith," 117.
36. Kenneth J. Collins, *The Scripture Way of Salvation: The Heart of John Wesley's Theology* (Nashville: Abingdon, 1997), 154.
37. Wesley, "On Working Out Our Own Salvation," 491.
38. Maddox, *Responsible Grace*, 148. Wesleyan David Shipley views human cooperation primarily in terms of "providing no opposition to the divine initiative, by concurring passively in the work of the Holy Spirit. The dynamic of the Holy Spirit strengthens man's will so that he is able to accept the offer of and co-operate with the work of salvation." Quoted in Lycurgus M. Starkey Jr., *The Work of the Holy Spirit: A Study in Wesleyan Theology* (Nashville: Abingdon, 1962), 120–21.
39. Solid Declaration, Formula of Concord (hereafter cited as SD FC), 3.35, 37, in BC, 568.
40. Maddox, *Responsible Grace*, 150.
41. Apology of the Augsburg Confession (hereafter cited as AP) 4.84, in BC, 134.
42. AP 4.151, in BC, 143. See also Philip Watson, "Wesley and Luther on Perfection," *Ecumenical Review* 15, no. 3 (1963): 299.
43. E.g., "The justified necessarily produce good works or fruits." BC, 171.370A.

As Luther writes in the Smalcald Articles, "Love is a fruit that certainly and necessarily results from true faith."[44] Philip Melanchthon states, "Because faith truly brings the Holy Spirit and produces new life in our hearts, it must also produce spiritual impulses in our hearts," enabling us to love our neighbors.[45] The Holy Spirit brings about not only regeneration (in justification) but also this process of subsequent renewal: "The Holy Spirit effects new birth and the inner reception of another heart, mind, and disposition. He opens the mind and the heart so that they understand Scripture and are attentive to the Word. . . . He is a Spirit 'of rebirth and renewal' (Titus 3:[5]). He takes away our hard and stony hearts and replaces them with new, soft hearts of flesh, that we may walk in his commands (Ezek. 11:[19], et al.)."[46]

While there can be no human cooperation in justification and rebirth, the Lutheran Reformers affirmed a place for such cooperation in the process of renewal or sanctification. As the Formula of Concord states, "God makes willing people out of rebellious and unwilling people through the drawing power of the Holy Spirit, and how after this conversion of the human being the reborn will is not idle in the daily practice of repentance but cooperates in all the works of the Holy Spirit that he accomplishes through us."[47] This cooperation is not like that of two horses pulling a wagon together. Instead, after the Holy Spirit begins in us the work of regeneration and renewal, "it is certain that on the basis of [the Holy Spirit's] power we can and should be cooperating with him, though still in great weakness. This occurs not on the basis of our fleshly, natural powers but on the basis of the new powers and gifts which the Holy Spirit initiated in us in conversion, as St. Paul specifically and earnestly admonished, that 'as we work together with' the Holy Spirit 'we urge you not to accept the grace of God in vain' [2 Cor. 6:1]."[48] The authors of the Formula of Concord emphasize, "This is to be understood in no other way than that the converted do good to the extent that God rules, leads, and guides them with his Holy Spirit. If God would withdraw his gracious hand from such people, they could not for one moment remain obedient to God."[49] We are admonished "not to let God's grace have no effect in us, but to exercise ourselves diligently in considering what a

44. Martin Luther, Smalcald Articles, in *BC*, 566.27. Lutherans also teach that only those "good works" done out of faith and by the power of the Holy Spirit are truly "good" before God.
45. AP 4.125, in *BC*, 140.
46. SD FC, 2.26, in *BC*, 549.
47. SD FC, 2.88, in *BC*, 561. See also Starkey, *Work of the Holy Spirit*, 120.
48. SD FC, 2.65–66, in *BC*, 556–57.
49. SD FC, 2.65–66, in *BC*, 556–57.

grievous sin it is to impede and resist the working of the Holy Spirit."[50] This teaching is also found in Luther, who had strong words for anyone who took his teaching on justification as an excuse not to live a life of obedience and love.[51]

Danish Lutheran theologian Regin Prenter contends that Lutherans can affirm both a "passive" and an "active" holiness as long as the "chief article," the doctrine of justification, is not contradicted.[52] Righteousness belongs to Christ and only to the Christian relationally through faith; however, the righteousness of Christ enables the believer to receive holiness from God, that quality of spiritual life given in the new birth that grows and ripens.[53] Prenter goes on to say that this passive sanctity—the mark of which is the cross—is the beginning of "active holiness," a new life (Gal. 5:6).[54] Passive sanctity or rebirth is completely God's gift to us, while active holiness, or sanctification, is the work of the Holy Spirit in our hearts and lives, with which our human will cooperates, even weakly, in love toward God and our neighbors.

Luther's most famous description of this active holiness of "faith working by love" is in his "Preface to the Epistle of St. Paul to the Romans" (which warmed Wesley's heart). The activity of "faith working by love" is holy because it is the work of the Holy Spirit. There is, then, for Luther, such a thing as "active holiness," a truly holy life lived by the Christian, which has both an interior (Godward) and an exterior (humanward) dimension. Prenter cautions, "The holiness of this active life is no holiness at all if it is separated from the passive sanctity of faith in Jesus Christ."[55] The believer "as he stands in the process of sanctification is both passive and active; he is crucified with Christ and he rises with Him to live a new life."[56]

The Process of Sanctification, "Christian Perfection," and Sin

While Wesleyans and Lutherans affirm that the believer is "made holy" by the work of the Holy Spirit and that the goal of the Christian life is perfect holiness,

---

50. SD FC, 2.72, in *BC*, 558.

51. See Martin Luther, "On the Councils and the Church," in *Luther's Works*, American ed., 55 vols. (Philadelphia: Fortress; St. Louis: Concordia, 1955–86), 41:113–14. *Luther's Works* is hereafter cited as *LW*.

52. Regin Prenter, "Holiness in the Lutheran Tradition," in *Man's Concern with Holiness*, ed. Marina Chavchavadze (London: Hodder & Stoughton, 1970), 123.

53. Prenter, "Holiness," 124.

54. Prenter, "Holiness," 135.

55. Prenter, "Holiness," 141.

56. Prenter, "Holiness," 144.

they differ in how they understand the process of "growing" or "progressing" in holiness as well as on how much of this holiness or perfection is possible in this life. Wesley believes that there could come a point in the Christian's earthly life where they are "entirely sanctified" and made "perfect."[57] It is important to note, however, that by "Christian perfection" or "entire sanctification" Wesley does not mean perfect knowledge; freedom from ignorance, error, or infirmity; or freedom from temptation.[58] Positively, it means "perfect love"—that is, allowing love to so rule in one's heart that one thinks only of God and the good of the neighbor. Negatively, it means the ability not to commit habitual sin, to willfully sin, or to act on sinful desires. It also includes freedom from evil thoughts and sinful desires.

Because believers can always grow in holiness of heart and life (i.e., one can always love more), Wesley explains that perfection is best understood as a quality of life that one lives out daily, as one still needs to daily advance in the knowledge of and love of Christ.[59] In other words, for Wesley, Christian perfection is "relative," not absolute; [60] it is dynamic and relational. As Maddox states, it is the promise that "God's loving grace for us and working in us can transform our lives to the point where our own love for God and others becomes a 'natural' response."[61]

This is not a concept found in Lutheran theology, and yet the idea of "perfection" does appear in two places in the Lutheran Confessions. In his Large Catechism, Luther speaks of perfection in the absolute sense: as the eschatological reality in which justified sinners, now only "halfway pure and holy," become "perfectly pure and holy people, full of integrity and righteousness, completely freed from sin, death, and all misfortune, living in new, immortal, and glorified bodies."[62] This is the work of the Holy Spirit, who will "perfect our holiness and will eternally preserve it in us."[63] Because Luther equates perfection with complete sinlessness, he denies the possibility of perfection in this life.[64] Some

---

57. The Wesley brothers disagreed on this point: Whereas Charles believed that perfection happened at death for all Christians, John believed that, while this was true for many (or even most) Christians, some could experience "Christian perfection" yet in this life. See Maddox, *Responsible Grace*, 186.

58. See John Wesley, "Christian Perfection," in *Sermons*, 70–84.

59. Wesley, "Christian Perfection," 73.

60. Watson, "Wesley and Luther on Perfection," 301.

61. Maddox, *Responsible Grace*, 188.

62. Martin Luther, "The Creed," 57–58, Large Catechism, in *BC*, 438.

63. Luther, "Creed," 59, Large Catechism, in *BC*, 439.

64. In the Augsburg Confession, the Anabaptists are condemned for teaching that "some may attain such perfection in this life that they cannot sin." Augsburg Confession, art. 22, §8, in *BC*, 45. The Augsburg Confession will hereafter be cited as CA.

scholars attribute the difference between Luther and Wesley to their respective definitions of perfection: Wesley's Greek notion of perfection, with its more dynamic connotations, as compared to the more static Latin concept, which Luther and the Reformers likely had in mind.[65]

The second reference to perfection is found in the Augsburg Confession (1530). Melanchthon contrasts the Lutheran view with that of the medieval Catholics, on the one hand, who taught that monks are in a state of perfection because they are celibate and live as mendicants, and that of the Anabaptists, on the other hand, who taught instead that "evangelical perfection" came from abandoning civic responsibilities. Perfection here is understood not as an eschatological state of pure and sinless existence but as a way of life that is pleasing to God. For the Reformers, "perfection" is located not in externalities, in lifestyles that take one "out" of the world, but in "fearing God earnestly with the whole heart, having confidence in God's grace because of Christ, expecting help from God in all afflictions, and diligently doing good in our various callings."[66] In this sense, perfection is, in the first place, a state of the heart, not of one's station in life or choice of dress. While this perfection is rooted in fear of God and in faith (rather than love; though as we have seen, love cannot be separated from faith), it comes closer to what Wesley means by Christian perfection than to the eschatological state of sinlessness presumed elsewhere in the Lutheran Confessions.

If this second Lutheran view of "evangelical perfection" is considered alongside Wesley's view of "Christian perfection," we are still left with this question: What is the relationship between sin and holiness in the process of sanctification? For Wesley, as we have seen, the process of sanctification is part of the "way" of salvation. The fullness of salvation includes salvation from both the guilt and the power of sin, "through Christ formed in [one's] heart."[67] The Holy Spirit frees believers from the power of sin that keeps them in bondage and "sheds the love of God abroad in their hearts, and the love of all [hu]mankind; thereby purifying their hearts from the love of the world, from the lust of the flesh, the lust of the eye and the pride of life."[68] Lutherans affirm that following justification and rebirth, the believer is sanctified by the Holy Spirit, who rules

65. Watson, "Wesley and Luther on Perfection," 301.
66. "Confessing Our Faith Together: A Proposal for Full Communion between the Evangelical Lutheran Church in America and the United Methodist Church" (Chicago: Evangelical Lutheran Church in America, 2008), 7, paraphrasing CA 27.49, in BC, 88.
67. John Wesley, "Salvation by Faith," in Sermons, 41, 44.
68. John Wesley, "The Spirit of Bondage and of Adoption," in Sermons, 140–41.

in the heart and enables the believer to die to the power of sin and live in love toward God and others.

Wesley's views on the question of the residual presence of sin in the Christian's life evolved during his lifetime.[69] His mature position acknowledges that although the power of sin is broken in justification and regeneration, the believer continues to struggle with the remains of sin until they are "entirely sanctified." Wesley recognizes that the view that sin is completely absent from regenerated believers contradicts the Word of God and the experience of ordinary Christians.[70] However, the sin that remains in the believer is constantly under attack by the Holy Spirit.

While Wesley describes sanctification as a gradual process of spiritual progress, it is not one without struggle.[71] Although we receive the new birth the moment we are justified, we are sanctified only in part. We are not yet wholly purified, for "the flesh, the evil nature, still remains (though subdued) and wars against the spirit. So much more let us use all the diligence in 'fighting the good fight of faith.'"[72] Those who are "entirely sanctified" are not *incapable* of sin; they are so ruled by the love of God that *not sinning* becomes a more natural way of life for them.

The process of sanctification, then, always moves forward toward the goal of Christian perfection (which also serves as the impetus for believers' cooperation with their sanctification). Reflecting Wesley's dynamic understanding, perfection is at the same time something achievable and something that can be lost. If one is not going forward, then one will go backward. There is, as Kenneth J. Collins says, "no standing still."[73] This leads the mature Wesley to acknowledge that it is possible for one who has been entirely sanctified to fall again into sin.[74]

The view of sanctification as the progressive journey in responsive cooperation with the Holy Spirit is characteristic of Wesley's theology in a way that it has not been for most Lutherans. Further, Wesley's distinctive idea of "entire sanctification" likely strikes most Lutherans as overly optimistic, if not outright delusional.[75] However, some of the ideas underlying Wesley's schema also can

---

69. Maddox, *Responsible Grace*, 163.

70. John Wesley, "The Repentance of Believers," in *Sermons*, 415; and John Wesley, "On Sin in Believers," in *Sermons*, 363.

71. Therefore, repentance has an essential place in the Christian life. Maddox, *Responsible Grace*, 165–66.

72. Wesley, "On Sin in Believers," 369.

73. Collins, *Scripture Way of Salvation*, 155.

74. Maddox, *Responsible Grace*, 183.

75. Maddox, *Responsible Grace*, 190.

be found in Lutheran theology, in ways that may surprise some Wesleyans and Pentecostals. For example, Lutherans affirm the distinction Wesley makes between "the sin that rules" and "the sin that is ruled."[76] The faith that justifies is not an "idle thought"; it "frees us from death, produces new life in our hearts, and is a work of the Holy Spirit." Therefore, it does not coexist with mortal sin, but "as long as it is present, it brings forth good fruit."[77]

The Lutheran axiom that the Christian is *simul iustus et peccator* does not teach that although the Christian is forgiven, sin continues to *rule* in the Christian's heart. In justification, sin is not just forgiven; its power is also broken. While the "pervasiveness of sin" may be a distinctive teaching in Lutheran theology, so is the pervasiveness of the Holy Spirit to battle the "sin that remains."[78] In the Smalcald Articles, Luther writes, "The Holy Spirit does not allow sin to rule and gain the upper hand so that it is brought to completion, but the Spirit controls and resists so that sin is not able to do whatever it wants. However, when sin does whatever it wants, then the Holy Spirit and faith are not there."[79]

Both Luther and Wesley refer to the "sin that remains" in reference to the spirit/flesh distinction in St. Paul's Epistles and as that which can be cleansed through repentance and the work of the Holy Spirit. Luther writes, "This repentance endures among Christians until death because it struggles with the sin that remains in the flesh throughout life. As St. Paul bears witness in Romans 7[:23], he wars with the law in his members, etc.—not by using his own powers but with the gift of the Holy Spirit which follows from the forgiveness of sins. This same gift daily cleanses and sweeps away the sins that remain and works to make people truly pure and holy."[80] Wesley sometimes describes the sin that remains in more essentialist terms, as something that must be "rooted out,"[81] where Luther and the Confessions frequently use the language of the "old Adam" or "old creature" that remains.[82] Though weakened by repentance and the power of the Holy Spirit, the old creature must be wrestled with until death.

76. See Regin Prenter, *Spiritus Creator: Luther's Concept of the Holy Spirit*, trans. John M. Jensen (Philadelphia: Muhlenberg Press, 1953), 71, 73.

77. AP 4.115–16, 64–65, in *BC*, 139, 131.

78. AP 4.64A, in *BC*, 148.

79. Luther, Smalcald Articles 3.3.44, in *BC*, 319. The Formula likewise affirms that faith and the Holy Spirit can be lost through active sinning. SD FC, 4.33, in *BC*, 579.

80. Luther, Smalcald Articles 3.3.44, in *BC*, 318.

81. John Wesley, "The Scripture Way of Salvation (1765)," in *John Wesley's Sermons: An Anthology*, ed. Albert C. Outler and Richard P. Heitzenrater (Nashville: Abingdon, 1991), 373.

82. See, e.g., Martin Luther, "The Sacrament of Holy Baptism," 12, Small Catechism, in *BC*, 360; SD FC, 6.7, in *BC*, 588.

This struggle can even bring "victory" over the power of sin in Lutheran thought: "Although those born anew come *even in this life* to the point that they desire the good and delight in it and even do good deeds and grow in practicing them, this is not . . . a product of our own will or power, but the Holy Spirit, as Paul says himself, 'is at work in us to will and work' (Phil. 2[:13])."[83] Obviously, this is a far cry from Wesley's "entire sanctification," but it shows that Lutheran theology has room for a more transformative understanding of the Spirit's work in the sanctification of the believer than is commonly thought.

However, this transformation comes in ways that are not easily measurable or even always discernible. While "sanctification is a constant progress, a growing mastery of the Spirit over the flesh . . . *this* progress is not the same as the increase of empirical piety."[84] Empirical piety—the observable ways that faith expresses itself in prayer, praise, and service—is to be encouraged (see, e.g., Luther's *Treatise on Good Works*). However, Luther warns against identifying empirical piety with the progress of sanctification, for such piety "may in every moment be either an expression of the Spirit or of the flesh, whether the [believer] in that particular moment is either Spirit or flesh."[85] The Formula of Concord similarly observes, "For one can detect not only a great difference among Christians—one is weak, another strong in the Spirit—but within each Christian, who is at one moment resolute in the Spirit and at another fearful and afraid, at one moment ardent in love, strong in faith and hope, and at another cold and weak."[86]

Lutherans can define sanctification in terms of "progress," but they will do so in a significantly different way than Wesleyans. For both, progress involves a struggle with the "sin that remains"; however, for Luther the struggle is not between the "renewal" that has begun and the sin that remains—as if these were two parts of the same person—so that the believer, in their renewed self, battles the vestiges of sin in their "old self." Rather, as Prenter notes, the struggle is described as one between our whole selves—sinful and justified—and the power of the Holy Spirit, who unites us to the righteousness of Christ through faith, thereby empowering us in our groaning as the "old creature" is crucified.[87]

For Lutherans, this progress is more circular than linear. In fact, it is better described as a "progress of return," a constant going back to the alien righteousness

83. SD FC, 2.39, in *BC*, 551 (emphasis added).
84. Prenter, *Spiritus Creator*, 70.
85. Prenter, *Spiritus Creator*, 70.   ·
86. SD FC, 2.68, in *BC*, 557.
87. Prenter, *Spiritus Creator*, 98, 66.

of Christ. In this sense, it is not a progress marked by time, although it has its beginning in baptism (where the promise of justification traditionally is given) and its destination in the resurrection. The dynamic is one not of "getting better and better all the time" but of "losing all that is our own and starting anew again and again. This constant starting anew which embodies the essence of progress embraces the constant taking refuge in the righteousness of Christ."[88] Finally, for Wesley there can be a point at which the struggle against the old Adam (or Eve) comes to completion in this life, what he calls entire sanctification or Christian perfection. For Lutherans, this process ends only when the Christian dies, and perfection comes only at the resurrection on the last day.

What Lutherans Can Learn from Wesley about Sanctification

This brief comparison suggests a few things moving forward for Lutherans and other historic Protestants who have shied away from the doctrine of sanctification out of nervousness over works righteousness. First, sanctification is nothing to fear as long as we remember that it is the work of the Holy Spirit in and through the Christian's life. Wesley's theology offers a picture of sanctification that is thoroughly pneumatological. Even where there is a place for human "cooperation," we can do nothing apart from the work of the Holy Spirit. The Lutheran confessional writings have language to describe the Spirit's work in "making holy" that is strikingly similar to Wesleyan language, although this is not something of which many Lutherans are aware.

Second, there is "more" to the Christian life than being justified, or even, as Forde puts it, "getting used to justification." The new birth that the Spirit brings us does more than grant existential knowledge or eschatological hope; it inaugurates a renewal of life that can bring personal and social transformation. While Wesley is far more optimistic than Luther and the other Reformers about the possibility of "Christian perfection" in this life, the Wesleyan tradition reminds Lutherans that salvation from sin includes salvation from the power of sin over our lives in the present.

Finally, although the progress of sanctification may be defined in different ways, there is no standing still if one has received the Holy Spirit. The Christian life is dynamic. As God's personal presence, the Holy Spirit is constantly at work in Christians' lives, keeping them in faith and creating spiritual impulses

88. Prenter, *Spiritus Creator*, 74.

in their hearts. Lutherans do not need to fear believers "cooperating" with grace. Believers can have an active role as well as a passive role, as long as the focus remains on the work of the Holy Spirit as the source of love and good works.

A Pentecostal Perspective on Holiness and Sanctification

Wesley's ideas about holiness and sanctification are foundational for the branch of Pentecostalism with roots in the Holiness movement of the nineteenth century, including denominations such as the Church of God (Cleveland, TN) and the Church of God in Christ. Theologian Dale Coulter, of the Church of God (Cleveland, TN), is a major interpreter of holiness for contemporary Pentecostals. He acknowledges the uneasy history of this doctrine among Pentecostals, in terms of the theological divisions between Wesleyan and Keswickian views, but also the often-rigid enforcement of the doctrine through proper behavior. Coulter writes, "The word holiness conjures up ideas about following a set of laws or regulations as the means of maintaining moral purity before God without which a person could not enter heaven."[89] The misunderstanding that God's love for sinners is dependent on their holy living was, as we have seen, one of Luther's major critiques of the medieval system. This has led Coulter, among other Pentecostal scholars, to approach the doctrine in positive and life-giving ways.[90]

For Coulter, sanctification involves a "holistic transformation of the person that enables a deeper participation in the divine nature of holy love."[91] He sees sanctification as the work of the Holy Spirit in the Christian life between regeneration and ultimate glorification.[92] Coulter asserts that one cannot understand the Pentecostal approach to sanctification apart from a Wesleyan framework

---

89. Coulter, *Holiness*, 51. This book, originally published by Pathway Press (Church of God) in 2004, was written for a nonacademic audience and thus is not fully representative of the quality of his scholarship. Because Coulter does not engage in the theological debates over sanctification within holiness circles, one reviewer wrote that it is "difficult to consider this a serious contribution to or advancement in holiness theology." See Mark H. Mann's review in *Pneuma* 27, no. 2 (Fall 2005): 391–92. For my purposes, however, this book—read alongside Coulter, "Sanctification"— provides a contemporary, constructive Wesleyan-Pentecostal theology of holiness to discuss from a Lutheran perspective.

90. See, e.g., Green, "Not I, but Christ"; and Amos Yong, *Renewing Christian Theology: Systematics for a Global Christianity* (Waco: Baylor University Press, 2014), 59–74.

91. Coulter, "Sanctification," 237.

92. Coulter also notes that the Pentecostal outpouring of the Spirit is a counterpart to the sanctified life, focusing on the empowerment of believers to bear witness to the new work of God. Coulter, "Sanctification," 239.

"whereby the operations of the Spirit restore fully the image of God and turn the believer into the bride of Christ in anticipation of eschatological union and vision."[93]

As we have seen in our engagement with Wesley, sanctification is the heart of salvation; salvation includes but goes beyond justification.[94] Coulter makes the interesting suggestion that what historians of Pentecostalism have called "the full gospel" is another way of describing Wesley's view that modes of grace are different operations of the Holy Spirit. Drawing on Wesley's thoroughly pneumatological framing of sanctification, Coulter states that the "holy energy of divine love" that the believer receives in regeneration "makes possible the volitional activity of human love" in sanctification.[95] As an operation of the Spirit, sanctification thus includes healing, "a holistic transformation that begins in regeneration and prepares the soul for the proleptic realization of glorification in Spirit baptism. The Pentecostal understanding of sanctification entails an ontological change in the whole person."[96] Coulter's use of "ontological change" to describe this transformation goes beyond Wesley and raises red flags for most Lutheran theologians, but Lutherans can agree with his claim that sanctification is a manifestation of God's grace in the believer's heart.

This has two practical implications for the Christian. On the "negative side," the Spirit enables the believer to dispel wayward thoughts and resist sin. On the "positive side," the Spirit leads the believer to "perfection in love." There should not be a tension between these two aspects of the doctrine as applied to the Christian life, as both are grounded in the divine bestowal of love.[97] Sanctification is a process that includes being healed from sin and filled with new life, vitality, maturity. While this involves forgiveness of sins, Coulter begins his treatment by addressing "why forgiveness is not enough."[98]

For Coulter, forgiveness is not enough to heal the sinner because, while forgiveness addresses the guilt caused by sin, the Spirit's work extends to healing sinners themselves, specifically the damage that sin does to them.[99] Wesley

93. Coulter, "Sanctification," 243.
94. Coulter, Holiness, 51.
95. Coulter, "Sanctification," 240–41.
96. Coulter, "Sanctification," 244.
97. Coulter, "Sanctification," 245.
98. Coulter, Holiness, chap. 1.
99. Coulter, Holiness, 2. Coulter does not expand his discussion of healing to include victims, but one could understand the healing of victims to fall under the category of sanctification rather than justification (as Moltmann and Macchia have suggested). This coheres with Luther's notion of "the full forgiveness of sin," whereby forgiveness is not only something received by God

is well-known for using healing imagery to describe the transformation that happens in the process of sanctification that follows the sinner's justification: Jesus Christ is the Great Physician who heals our souls, diseased by sin, and who restores our human nature to God's original design.[100] Note that this healing does not lead to justification but follows justification. Following Wesley's understanding of sin as a disease that is not only self-inflicted but also inborn and socially conditioned, Coulter argues, "The damage our sinful choices inflict upon us cannot be repaired by simply asking for forgiveness."[101] Forgiveness brings absolution from guilt and restores our relationship with God, but sanctification brings healing from the damage of sin in our lives. This allows us to experience both a freedom from what Paul calls "the flesh," an orientation to worldly values, and a process of transformation by which we become more Christlike, which happens as we "live by the Spirit" (Gal. 5:16–26).[102]

Following Wesley, Coulter describes Christian perfection as the holy love that "adorns and beautifies, turning the believer into an icon of the Spirit." This includes a reordering of the affections so that we are able to love God (in our worship) and our neighbors (in our discipleship). Negatively, this involves a "separation from self-destructive patterns of thinking and behaving."[103] Positively, it involves "a union with God's own life such that we come to reflect that life in all that we do. God desires to bring us into a condition where we reflect all that he is, a being whose existence must be described as the beauty of perfection."[104] Coulter continues, "Holiness and sanctification are about the restoration of harmony and order where all we do reflects the perfect goodness of God."[105] The purpose of "being made holy" is to transform us to reflect God's design for the world, to become the human beings we were created to be (imago Dei), called to be in relationship and fellowship with God and one another. This happens in the holy community, the church, of which we become

---

but also something lived out in relationships, in the ways that we forgive, bear with, and aid one another. BC, 438.

100. See, e.g., John Wesley, "The One Thing Needful," in Sermons, 34–38; and John Wesley, "Original Sin," in Sermons, 326–34.

101. Coulter, Holiness, 7.

102. The Greek word that the NRSV here renders as "live" is περιπατεῖτε (peripateite). This word is more commonly, and more literally, rendered as "walk" (see NIV, KJV, and RSV). I will use "walk" alongside "live" because I believe "walk" better captures the dynamic movement of the Spirit's work in sanctification.

103. Coulter, Holiness, 65.

104. Coulter, Holiness, 67.

105. Coulter, Holiness, 70; see also 73–76.

members, fellow disciples of those who are learning to care for one another "in the power of the Spirit."[106]

The church is more than an instrument through which the Spirit calls believers to faith through the Word. The church is also the community in which believers begin to live out the promise of new life. Another way to put this is to say that the sanctified life—a way of living that Paul describes as living (or walking) "by the Spirit" (Gal 5:16)—requires a community of faith.[107] Coulter explores this walk vertically and horizontally: vertically, in how worship and prayer cultivate believers' passion for God and inflame their hearts with love; and horizontally, in how believers offer themselves in loving service to others.[108] The holy life is not defined by how one acts or dresses or by what activities one avoids; rather, it is a life conformed to Christ in which one loves one's neighbor spontaneously, as the Spirit leads.

Coulter addresses the development of the fruit of the Spirit as that which makes the holy life even possible. The fruit of the Spirit grows in the believer from the Spirit's working in the believer, but not without the believer's cooperation.[109] Fruit grows as the believer walks "by the Spirit." According to Coulter, "Paul's admonition that his readers must walk with the Spirit (Gal. 5:25) implies that this fruit grows gradually as the believer cooperates with the work of the Spirit."[110] For something to grow, attention is required: it must be nurtured (or in the case of Paul's list of character traits or virtues, practiced); and it must be pruned, freed of those things that would inhibit growth, such as sinful patterns in the believer's life. The Spirit works on both fronts to conform the believer into Christ's likeness, which the believer practices and experiences both in the community of faith and through neighbor love.[111]

A Lutheran Engagement with Dale Coulter

Although the title of Coulter's book, *Holiness: The Beauty of Perfection*, may give pause to most Lutherans, as these are not topics typically treated by Lutherans, Coulter's overall treatment resonates with much of what the Lutheran

---

106. Coulter, *Holiness*, 101.
107. Coulter, *Holiness*, 102. See also Green, "Not I, but Christ"; and Chris E. W. Green, *Sanctifying Interpretation: Vocation, Holiness, and Scripture*, 2nd ed. (Cleveland, TN: CPT, 2020).
108. Coulter, *Holiness*, 161, 183.
109. Coulter, *Holiness*, 184–85.
110. Coulter, *Holiness*, 186.
111. Coulter, *Holiness*, 189–93.

Confessions teach about sanctification. Additionally, Coulter shares many concerns Lutherans hold regarding misunderstandings about holiness. A key difference is one shared with Macchia regarding the broader definition of salvation, which can concern Lutherans who like to keep sanctification as a distinct movement of the Spirit to avoid works righteousness. Coulter's main challenge to Lutherans has to do with his claim that forgiveness is not enough, that healing of sin is an aspect of the Spirit's work in sanctification, removing what is in the way of the believer growing into Christ's likeness.

It is true that the forgiveness of sins features prominently in Luther's discussion of holiness in the Large Catechism. He speaks of the daily forgiveness of sins as the primary blessing believers receive through their participation in the holy community (through the means of grace through which the Spirit works— i.e., the Word and sacraments). Indeed, holiness for Luther depends on this daily experience. He writes, "All who would seek to merit holiness through their works rather than the gospel and the forgiveness of sins" separate themselves from the holy community.[112] Believers need forgiveness continually because they are never without sin in this life. It is important to note that, for Luther, forgiveness is both a blessing that the individual believer receives from God and a gift lived out in relationship with others. As Luther writes, the Christian experiences new life as "full forgiveness of sins, both in that God forgives us *and that we forgive, bear with, and aid one another.*"[113] This suggests a concept closer to reconciliation and restoration, which I explore more in the next chapter.

As we have seen, in Lutheran theology, justification is not only forensic but also effective. Forgiveness includes more than a declaration of God's mercy, a pardon of guilt; forgiveness of sins is an experience of God's love and mercy, bringing consolation and peace. Our relationship with God is restored on God's side. However, since the believer is "simultaneously justified and sinful," we will continue to struggle with sin from the human side of that relationship. Therefore, forgiveness of sins is needed daily. But this is not the only way that sin is dealt with, as we also have seen in the Lutheran Confessions. As we remain sinners throughout our lives, the Holy Spirit works in us to help us resist the power of sin, decreasing the effect of our sin on others. In his 1539 treatise, "On the Councils and the Church," Luther has strong words for "fine Easter preachers" who are "very poor Pentecost preachers" because they fail to teach sanctification by the Holy Spirit, dwelling exclusively on the redemption

112. Luther, "Creed," 56, Large Catechism, in *BC*, 438.
113. Luther, "Creed," 55, Large Catechism, in *BC*, 438 (emphasis added).

won by Christ on the cross. Christ redeemed us so that the Holy Spirit might transform us from the old Adam (or Eve) into new creatures, as we die to sin and live for righteousness. He writes, "Christ did not earn only *gratia*, 'grace,' for us, but also *donum*, 'the gift of the Holy Spirit,' so that we might have not only forgiveness of, but also cessation of, sin."[114] Rather than using the language of healing, Lutherans tend to describe this process in terms of a return to the waters of baptism, the daily cycle of death and rebirth and the ongoing struggle with sin.[115] The language of healing can lead one to view grace as a "medicine," which would be suggestive of "infused grace," which Luther rejects, as we have seen.

However, Luther draws on this image and the corresponding doctor/patient relationship in a striking passage from his commentary on Paul's Letter to the Romans in a way that avoids this danger and offers a way for Lutherans to recover this image.[116] He begins by likening justification to the case of a sick man who believes in his doctor's ability to heal him.[117] Not his own actions but, rather, his trust in the doctor's promise is the basis for his restoration to health. However, the man is not idle. He follows the doctor's orders so as not to hinder the fulfillment of his promise.[118] Luther asks, then, if this sick man is well. He answers, "The fact is that he is both sick and well. He is sick in fact, but he is well because of the sure promise of the doctor, whom he trusts who has reckoned him as already cured, because he is sure that he will cure him; for he has already begun to cure him and no longer reckons to him a sickness unto death."[119] The man's restoration is described not as an "increase" in health but as the existence of both illness and health simultaneously. Although a full cure will come only in "eternal life,"[120] the sinner lives in the present with God's promise to "continue to deliver him from sin until He has completely cured

---

114. *LW* 41:113–14.

115. The following paragraphs develop ideas I first explored in "Healing as an Image for the Atonement: A Lutheran Consideration," in *Justification in a Post-Christian Society*, ed. Carl-Henric Grenholm and Göran Gunner (Eugene, OR: Pickwick, 2014), 72–87. Used with permission of Wipf & Stock, www.wipfandstock.com.

116. *LW* 25:260–63. See also *LW* 25:336.

117. *LW* 25:260.

118. Luther adds that the sick man will not get healthy either if he decides that he likes his disease and does not want to be cured, or if he fails to recognize his illness and therefore rejects the promised cure. This, Luther says, "is the kind of operation that wants to be justified and made well its own works." *LW* 25:260.

119. *LW* 25:260. Prenter writes that Luther's emphasis here is on the certainty of the physician's promise of a complete recovery, not on the daily progress of healing. Prenter, *Spiritus Creator*, 77.

120. *LW* 25:260.

him.["]121 Such ones are sick in fact but "healthy in hope"122—a hope grounded
in the promise of the Physician, rather than in the empirical increase of health
within their bodies, but also "in the fact that they are beginning to be healthy,
that is, they are 'being healed.'"123

This healing relationship involves more than "getting used to being healed."
The "medicine" in this case is not the infused grace of medieval Catholicism; it
is, in fact, nothing other than the personal presence of the Holy Spirit. Believers
have the promise of full healing, but they live into this promise by hope and by
the power of the Holy Spirit in their lives—that is, by the power of the divine
companion who battles the sin within, allowing the fruit of the Spirit to grow,
so that believers may better love God and neighbor. In his last sermon in Wittenberg (January 17, 1546), on Romans 12:3, Luther uses the image of healing
in a striking way to describe the Christian life: "If Christ, the Samaritan, had
not come, we should all have had to die. He it is who binds our wounds, carries
us into the church and is now healing us. So we are now under the Physician's
care. The sin, it is true, is wholly forgiven, but it has not been wholly purged.
If the Holy Spirit is not ruling men [sic], they become corrupt again; but the
Holy Spirit must cleanse the wounds daily. Therefore this life is a hospital; the
sin has really been forgiven, but it has not yet been healed."124

The sinner's relationship with God is healed completely by the objective
act of the death and resurrection of Christ on the cross. The presence of the
indwelling Holy Spirit, who regenerates us and enables us to trust the Great
Physician (i.e., who justifies us), also heals our hearts so that we may weakly
cooperate with God's will and (imperfectly!) love God and the neighbor, so
that we may live in the promise of restored relationships in our daily lives (i.e.,
be sanctified). Lutherans can affirm healing as a motif for the Spirit's work in
justification and sanctification if healing is understood relationally through a
"meeting of persons." The believer's relationship with the Great Physician is
itself healing, bringing new life (and the person and presence of the Holy Spirit)
to the believer to transform not only their standing before God but also their
relationship with God, other people, and, indeed, all of creation. The basis for
healing is given in the relationship with and the promise of the Great Physician. However, that promise includes more than a declaration of a new reality;

121. LW 25:260, 336.
122. LW 25:260, 336.
123. LW 25:336.
124. LW 51:373.

it means being led into and walking in that new reality, accompanied by the Spirit, the giver of life, who removes that which hinders the relationship and enables good fruit and works.

A welcome emphasis in Coulter's treatment of holiness and sanctification is his attention to the role of the church. This finds echoes in Luther's Large Catechism, where he writes that "being made holy" involves being incorporated into the holy community in order to become "a part and member, a participant and co-partner in all the blessings it possesses."[125] Luther refers to the variety of gifts the Spirit gives the community and to the community's growth in the faith and "in its fruits," which the Spirit produces.[126] Luther addresses in some detail this aspect of the Spirit's work in his 1519 and 1535 lectures on Galatians.

His discussion of the fruit of the Spirit is preceded by a discussion of Paul's phrase "live [or walk] by the Spirit," which precedes Paul's list of the "fruit of the Spirit" (Gal. 5:16–26). In his 1519 lectures, Luther explains Paul's idea that we are to "make progress and become more spiritual."[127] This includes resisting temptation when we are enticed to "bite and devour." The Spirit can help us resist such promptings. We will continue to have the impulse to sin, even though we are justified. The point is not to gratify that impulse.[128] Indeed, as he also states in the Large Catechism, the Christian life is "a trial, warfare, and a struggle" on this side of the eschaton. "We are not yet spirit, but we are being led by the Spirit," meaning that the Spirit arouses impulses in believers to live according to God's ways and to desire what God desires.[129] Here he again speaks of healing as something God's grace both has accomplished and is still accomplishing. Sinners are righteous because "grace has worked healing in them; they are sinners in accordance with the fact that they still must be healed."[130]

Although faith alone justifies, Luther asserts that "because it is genuine, it obtains the spirit of love."[131] Sinners are transformed by love, and an aspect of this is the growth of the fruit of the Spirit. In his 1519 and 1535 lectures, Luther explicates Paul's list of fruit in Galatians 5:22–23.[132] In the earlier commentary, he understands "spirit" to refer to the "spiritual man [sic]," not to the Holy Spirit.

---

125. Luther, "Creed," 52, Large Catechism, in BC, 438.
126. Luther, "Creed," 53, Large Catechism, in BC, 438.
127. LW 27:360.
128. LW 27:361.
129. LW 27:366.
130. LW 27:372.
131. LW 27:371.
132. LW 27:372–78; and LW 27:93–96.

In Luther's mature work, he understands Paul to be speaking about the Holy Spirit. Love is listed first because love "expands into all the fruit of the Spirit."[133] Luther's description of joy as "joyful thoughts about Christ, wholesome exhortations, happy songs, praise, and thanksgiving, with which godly people exhort, arouse, and refresh one another"[134] would resonate with Pentecostal spirituality. His definition of peace includes bearing one another's burdens (Gal. 6:2), or what he elsewhere calls "the full forgiveness of sins."[135]

He lists the next two fruits by the Greek terms, defining *makrothymia* as "a persistent patience by which someone not only bears adversity, insults, injury, etc., but even waits patiently for some improvement in those who have harmed him."[136] *Chrēstotēs* means "a gentleness and sweetness in manner and in one's life": speaking charitably about others, including interpreting their actions as charitably as possible.[137] Goodness means to willingly help those in need, especially financially. Faithfulness he relates specifically to love, as the capacity to trust and befriend others. Gentleness "is the virtue by which one is not easily provoked to anger," even though life provides numerous occasions for such provocation!"[138] Finally, self-control refers not only to chastity in matters of sex but also to "sobriety, temperance, or moderation in every walk of life."[139] The fruit that the Spirit works in us benefits not only us; it gives glory to God and "by these virtues invite[s] others to the teaching and faith of Christ" (similar to the concept of "attraction, not promotion" found in Alcoholics Anonymous).

The Spirit works in us in a twofold way: to help us resist sin and to grow this fruit within us, enabling us to "walk by the Spirit" in the new life we received in justification. Luther clearly understands the work of the Spirit in us to be transformative: "For where the Spirit is present, [the Spirit] renews [people] and creates new attitudes in them. [The Spirit] changes [people] who are vainglorious, wrathful, and envious into [people] who are humble, gentle, and loving. Such [people] seek not their own glory but God's. They do not provoke and envy one another; they yield to one another and outdo one another in showing honor."[140]

---

133. *LW* 27:93.
134. *LW* 27:93.
135. Luther, "Creed," 55, Large Catechism, in *BC*, 438.
136. *LW* 27:94.
137. *LW* 27:94.
138. *LW* 27:95.
139. *LW* 27:95.
140. *LW* 27:98.

The Spirit is present in the preaching of the Word, among other means (the topic of chap. 6); and through the preaching of the Word, God "supplies the Spirit and performs powerful deeds in the hearers."[141] It is as if Paul were saying, "Through my preaching God has not only brought it about that you believed but also that you lived holy lives, produced much fruit of faith, and suffered evil. By the same power of the Spirit you, who used to be covetous, adulterous, angry, impatient, and hostile, have become generous, chaste, gentle, patient, and loving toward your neighbors."[142] Some Lutheran theologians, such as Robert Kolb, take this to mean that the Spirit does all the work, and we "dare not think that we are anything other than tools in his hands."[143] But Luther's meditation on Paul's phrase "let us walk by the Spirit"[144] suggests a more active role for the believer. Luther understands this phrase to mean forward movement, progress and perseverance, that we ought to "advance by the Spirit."[145] In his discussion of Galatians 6:1, he understands Paul's reference to "you who are spiritual" to be a reminder of their duty and instruction regarding what that duty consists of; he writes, "If they are spiritual, let them do what characterizes spiritual people. But what else does it mean to be spiritual than to be a child of the Holy Spirit and to have the Holy Spirit?"[146]

At this point, Luther refers to the Johannine term for the Spirit, the "Paraclete, the Advocate, the Comforter." Luther goes on to explain the work of the Paraclete as comforting our afflicted consciences, enabling our trust in God's mercy, forgiving our sins, and magnifying our faith and good works.[147] In his sermons on John, he describes the relationship of Jesus to his disciples in the image of the vine and the branches (John 15:1–11) and the love commandment (15:12–17). He suggests that bearing fruit is part of our witness in the world, a sign that we have been reborn by the Holy Spirit (15:5). He describes the fruit of the new birth as attending to the welfare and improvement of our neighbor; when one has received the new birth, one is "willing to risk life, goods, and honor for Christ's sake, is eager to bring all to the faith, serves [one's] neighbor faithfully, treats him justly and brotherly [sic]."[148] In short, when we have received the new birth, we will love one another as Christ has loved us (15:5).

141. LW 26:220.

142. LW 26:220.

143. Robert Kolb, "God's Word Produces Faith and Fruit: Reflections from Luther's Understanding of the Sermon on the Mount," Concordia Journal (Summer 2014): 222.

144. This is Luther's translation of Gal. 5:25. LW 27:382.

145. LW 27:386.

146. LW 27:388. "You who are spiritual" is Luther's translation of Gal. 6:1.

147. LW 27:388.

148. LW 24:263.

Conclusion: The Spirit as the Paraclete in the Movement of Sanctification

As Luther writes in the Large Catechism, the Holy Spirit is the one who has made us holy and still makes us holy. Sanctification is the movement of the Spirit who is "in us," inviting our cooperation, leading us to "walk by the Spirit," so that we might be transformed by the new life we received in justification. The Spirit does this by helping us resist sin and by growing in us the fruit of the Spirit, especially love, enabling us to love God and our neighbors in need.

I have proposed that we consider the Johannine image of Paraclete, or companion, for this movement of the Spirit's work. "Paraclete" in the Greek means, literally, "one alongside of one"—that is, one who accompanies. This is no ordinary companion because the Paraclete is God the Holy Spirit, who indwells us even as the Spirit leads us on our "walk" and accompanies us along the way. The evangelist John speaks of the Spirit both abiding with and indwelling the disciples. As the Paraclete, Advocate, and Counselor, the Spirit teaches and recalls to the disciples what Jesus said to them and guides them into all truth. As we will explore in the next chapter, the Spirit also witnesses to Christ and enables disciples to be witnesses.

As we saw in his lectures on Galatians, Luther makes the connection between the Pauline idea of the fruit of the Spirit and John's image of the Paraclete. As the evangelist John develops the image of the Spirit as another Paraclete (John 14–16), he inserts the idea of Jesus as the vine and the disciples as the branches who have been appointed by the Father to bear fruit—most of all, love. The Holy Spirit as the Paraclete, then, is the one by whom we "walk in newness of life" (Rom. 6:4), the one who brings growth and transformation within us.

The following chapter explores a third movement of the Spirit, one having to do with our mission to be disciples in the world. In one sense, this is simply an expansion of sanctification, for the work the Spirit does to enable us to resist sin and bear fruit of the Spirit is not only for us to experience the Spirit *in* us but also so that the Spirit can work *through* us, especially for the neighbor in need. Here the focus is on the Spirit as empowerer, drawing more from the narrative of the Acts of the Apostles. In Luke 24:49, Jesus refers to the Holy Spirit as "power from on high" for the sake of God's mission in the world, as the one who enables God's people to share the love of God through witnessing, serving others, and working for justice.

5

The Spirit through Us

Empowerment for Mission

In this chapter, I explore the work of the Holy Spirit in the individual Christian's call to participate in God's mission—that is, how the Spirit works *through* the believer, empowering and enabling them to bear witness to and participate in God's mission in the world. Lutherans speak of the Christian's calling, originating in baptism, and its goal: to serve God and the neighbor in works of charity and justice. But they usually do not use explicitly pneumatological terms, and they even less frequently make references to "power." On the other hand, Pentecostals historically have highlighted the role of the Spirit as empowering Christians for service, evangelism, and ministries of healing, prophecy, and so on. Pentecostals speak of the Holy Spirit as the needed "power from on high" (Luke 24:49), or as empowerment itself, to accomplish God's mission in the world, especially the task of evangelism and, more recently, the work of social justice.

Following the pattern of the previous chapters, where the Spirit's work in the believer is defined in personal and relational terms, I consider the Holy Spirit's role as the one who accompanies by empowering. In this movement, the Holy Spirit as empowerer works *through* the believer to enable and encourage the

Portions of this chapter first appeared in Cheryl M. Peterson, "A Lutheran Exploration of Spiritual Empowerment, Pentecostal-Style," *Lutheran Forum* 51, no. 2 (Summer 2017): 47–50; and Cheryl M. Peterson, "Rediscovering Pneumatology in the 'Age of the Spirit': A North American Lutheran Contribution," *Dialog* 58, no. 2 (Summer 2019): 102–8. Used with permission.

people of God to participate in God's mission in the world through word and deed. This movement of the Spirit can be considered an expansion of God the Spirit's sanctifying work. The Spirit's indwelling in the believer leads to an increase of love and the growth of spiritual fruit but also to empowerment in the form of spiritual gifts needed to witness to the love of God in Christ through word and deed. This empowerment may be thought of as a particular form of accompaniment or companionship.

While central to Pentecostal theology, the idea of spiritual empowerment is not characteristic of how Lutherans in North America and Europe speak of the Spirit's work in calling and empowering the believer for mission.[1] In what follows, I address the Lutheran neglect of this aspect of the Spirit's work in comparison with Pentecostal traditions. The idea of spiritual empowerment received some attention by Lutheran charismatics, as an aspect of the "baptism of the Holy Spirit," but this took second place to experiences of closeness and assurance of God's presence, especially through the gift of tongues.[2] Lutheran charismatics primarily interpreted spiritual gifts in relation to personal spiritual renewal, or sanctification. Carter Lindberg writes, "When all is said and done about charismata, what the charismatics see missing in the life of the church is the appropriation of the power to lead a new life in terms of a renewal of the whole person."[3] While the intense personal encounter of the Spirit experienced in the "baptism" led to a zeal for sharing that experience with others (which is a form of evangelism), the empowerment needed for such witness did not receive as much attention. As we will see, spiritual gifts and empowerment are mentioned in relation to mission in documents produced by the Lutheran World Federation but are not theologically explored in depth. Further, a theological treatment of the spiritual gifts from a pneumatological perspective has yet to appear from a contemporary Lutheran systematic theologian working in the US context, apart from Veli-Matti Kärkkäinen, who identifies as both

---

1. This is not the case in Lutheranism in the Southern Hemisphere, especially in the Ethiopian Evangelical Church Mekane Yesus, currently the fastest-growing Lutheran church. See, e.g., Hailu Yohannes Bulaka, "Theology of Holy Spirit: Experiences of the Ethiopian Evangelical Church Mekane Yesus," *Missio Apostolica* 23, no. 1 (May 2015): 126–39; and Wondimu L. Sonessa, "Simul Lutheran et Charismatic in Ethiopia," *Lutheran Forum* 51, no. 4 (Winter 2017): 23–27. Even in these contexts, the use of spiritual gifts is not without controversy.

2. Norwegian Lutheran missiologist Tormod Engelsviken's comprehensive study of the spiritual gifts illustrates this. Engelsviken, "The Gift of the Spirit: An Analysis and Evaluation of the Charismatic Movement from a Lutheran Theological Perspective" (PhD diss., Aquinas Institute of Theology, Dubuque, IA, 1981).

3. Carter Lindberg, *Charismatic Renewal and the Lutheran Tradition* (Geneva: LWF, 1985), 78.

Pentecostal and Lutheran. Indeed, of the representative Lutheran and Reformed theologians discussed in previous chapters, only Jürgen Moltmann addresses the charismata in his pneumatology.[4]

The Pentecostal tradition, on the other hand, has emphasized spiritual empowerment for mission, but as Frank Macchia points out, Pentecostals have not integrated this idea into their pneumatology or connected it to sanctification. In his work *Baptized in the Spirit: A Global Pentecostal Theology*, Macchia provides such a connection with the concept "outpouring of love," which he argues is central to the idea of Spirit baptism. A full examination of Macchia's argument is beyond the scope of this work, but his integration of sanctification and Spirit baptism (usually separated as two distinct "graces" in Pentecostal theology) echoes the argument I am making, which is that empowerment is another aspect of the Spirit's indwelling with which the believer cooperates. In sanctification, the believer cooperates with the indwelling Spirit, leading to the growth of love and fruit of the Spirit. In mission, the believer cooperates with the indwelling Spirit, the empowerer who enables them to share with others the love of God they themselves have received and experienced through spiritual gifts and moral courage.

My goal in this chapter is to bring the Pentecostal emphasis on spiritual empowerment, spiritual gifts, and the related theological idea of "baptism in the Holy Spirit" into conversation with Lutheran theology, suggesting ways that Lutherans can affirm the work of the Holy Spirit as empowerment through various charismata, or spiritual gifts. Specifically, I consider how the Spirit as empowerer gifts the believer for witnessing to the in-breaking kingdom of God, in terms of both evangelism and testimony as well as through prophetic speech, courageous truth-telling, and the work of justice.[5]

Mission, Empowerment, and Spirit Baptism in Pentecostal Theology

In a departure from the previous two chapters, I begin with the Pentecostal perspective on empowerment because of its centrality to Pentecostal theology

---

4. Jürgen Moltmann, *The Spirit of Life: A Universal Affirmation*, trans. Margaret Kohl (Minneapolis: Fortress, 1992), chap. 6, "The Charismatic Powers of Life."

5. The gift of healing could also be included here, especially in view of the prominence of healing in the Global South (even over tongues) as a sign of God's power over sickness and death, which has made it a significant aspect of the church's ministry and mission in many places. Because healing can also be viewed by Pentecostals as an aspect of salvation (Jesus as Healer is one of the four- or fivefold gospel), I will address the spiritual gift of healing in the following chapter, in my treatment of the means of the Spirit's work.

and practice. Mission in Pentecostal circles is understood foremost in terms of advancing the gospel through evangelistic means: sharing the gospel with others (unbelievers as well as those who do not yet know the "full" gospel) so that all might come to know the fullness of salvation available through Jesus Christ. Indeed, the spread and growth of Pentecostal Christianity around the globe are attributed to the Holy Spirit's empowerment. Juan Sepúlveda notes that "the key to this phenomenon from the perspective of Pentecostal churches themselves, is the presence of the Holy Spirit encouraging and giving thrust to the task of evangelization."[6] The Holy Spirit empowers believers both to evangelize others with the good news and to confront any opposition that faces them in this work—that is, "the world, the flesh, and the devil." On the one hand, this refers to empowering believers to resist the power of sin and evil in their own lives; on the other hand, it refers to the empowerment needed to oppose Satan by casting out demons from people who are possessed.[7] Pentecostal scholars often speak of the urgency felt by early Pentecostals regarding this call to mission, given by Jesus himself (Matt. 28:18–20; Acts 1:8). Other gifts of the Spirit are also given to enable believers to participate in the mission to share the gospel with the world: healing, prophecy, faith, and other gifts highlighted by Paul in 1 Corinthians 12–14 and Romans 12. More recently, Pentecostal scholars have begun to address mission in a more holistic way, to include working for justice along with sharing the gospel.

According to Pentecostal theologian Peter Althouse, "power" was a fundamental theme that undergirded the early Pentecostal movement, with the experience of the baptism of the Holy Spirit with speaking in tongues understood primarily as an experience and sign of this spiritual empowerment.[8] Pentecostals traditionally draw on the Acts of the Apostles, which connects the Spirit to power for evangelistic mission, to enable believers to witness to the gospel "to the ends of the earth" (Acts 1:8). Althouse argues that an ideology of power offered early Pentecostalism a hermeneutical key for interpreting God's action in the world and in the experience of individual believers. He points

6. Without denying this theological interpretation, Sepúlveda notes the sociological factors that play a role in facilitating this success, including its appeal to those living in poverty and other marginalized conditions, offering them a powerful experience of God that can transform their lives in positive ways. Juan Sepúlveda, "Reflections on the Pentecostal Contribution to the Church's Mission in Latin America," *Journal of Pentecostal Theology* 1 (1992): 98.

7. Peter Althouse, "The Ideology of Power in Early American Pentecostalism," *Journal of Pentecostal Theology* 13, no. 1 (2004): 104.

8. Althouse, "Ideology of Power," 96–97. See also David A. Dorman, "The Purpose of Empowerment in the Christian Life," *Pneuma* 7, no. 2 (Fall 1985): 147–65.

out, "Pentecostals not only believed in God's omnipotent power, they expected God to revive the believer with this power."[9] The experience of power was not an end to itself but a means of empowerment for service. Althouse notes that charismatic manifestations such as speaking in tongues were given primarily not for the purpose of spiritual enrichment but to inaugurate a life of ministry and mission in believers.[10] Believers experienced this "power from on high" (Luke 24:49) through conversion, sanctification, and especially the baptism of the Holy Spirit.

What distinguishes Pentecostals from earlier Holiness Christians is their construct of Spirit baptism as a distinct work of the Holy Spirit that empowers believers for mission and is evidenced by speaking in tongues.[11] This work of the Spirit follows conversion and sanctification. It is understood to be "an intense awareness of the Spirit's presence to empower Christian ministry and witness (Acts 1:8)."[12] The significance of Spirit baptism (the "crown jewel" of Pentecostal experience and theology) as a powerful experience of the Holy Spirit, David Perry writes, "is for most Pentecostals, simply assumed, and for those outside of Pentecostalism, often overlooked or undervalued."[13] Many contemporary Pentecostal theologians minimize the doctrinal necessity of subsequence and tongues as "initial evidence" in favor of a distinctive and powerful experience of the Spirit, whenever it happens and however it manifests in the believer.[14]

Spirit baptism has been closely connected to the missiological impulse in the Pentecostal movement, which was initially undergirded by an eschatological urgency that has given way to a greater emphasis on the in-breaking reign of God in more recent years. Pentecostals interpret the outpouring of the Holy Spirit in Spirit baptism as an eschatological event itself (Acts 2), thus providing an impetus for the evangelistic and missiological work of the early Pentecostal movement.[15] In the early years of the movement, this impetus produced what

9. Althouse, "Ideology of Power," 101.

10. Althouse, "Ideology of Power," 102.

11. For a succinct review of this doctrine in Pentecostal theology, see Frank Macchia, "Spirit Baptism: Initiation in the Fullness of God's Promises," in *The Routledge Handbook of Pentecostal Theology*, ed. Wolfgang Vondey (New York: Routledge, 2020), 247–56. See also Wolfgang Vondey, *Pentecostal Theology: Living the Full Gospel, Systematic Pentecostal and Charismatic Theology* (New York: Bloomsbury T&T Clark, 2017), 91–97.

12. Macchia, "Spirit Baptism," 247.

13. David Perry, *Spirit Baptism: The Pentecostal Experience in Theological Focus* (Leiden: Brill, 2017), 109.

14. Perry, *Spirit Baptism*, 6.

15. Perry, *Spirit Baptism*, 155.

historian Vinson Synan calls "missionaries of the one-way ticket."[16] Because of this connection, it is easy to see why empowerment for ministry and witness became the central motif identified with Spirit baptism. Indeed, Veli-Matti Kärkkäinen calls baptism of the Holy Spirit the "primary mission strategy of the Pentecostal movement."[17]

Several Pentecostal biblical scholars and theologians defended the missiological purpose of Spirit baptism in response to James Dunn's 1970 thesis that the New Testament view of "baptism in the Holy Spirit" is primarily soteriological. Dunn argues that the Holy Spirit is an agent of "conversion-initiation," one who primarily brings individual believers into the new eschatological age rather than empowering them for mission so that they might be effective witnesses.[18] Many charged Dunn with reading Luke-Acts with a "Pauline lens" and ignoring distinctive aspects of Luke's pneumatology, such as prophetic speech.[19] Pentecostal scholars such as Robert Menzies, Harold Hunter, and Roger Stronstad defend Luke's theology of Spirit baptism as having a distinctive charismatic and missiological focus, especially empowerment for witness, pointing to the link between witness and the promised "power from on high" (the Spirit) in Luke 24:49 and Acts 1:8, favorite passages among Pentecostals.

Dunn's challenge to the traditional understanding of Spirit baptism also led to new and expanded understandings of this doctrine from other Pentecostal scholars. For example, Macchia questions whether the classic view of Spirit baptism is too narrowly focused on empowerment and renewal, and he proposes a more expanded understanding that includes conversion, indwelling, and sanctification along with empowerment.[20] Perry agrees that this narrow

16. Quoted in L. Grant McClung, "Pentecostal/Charismatic Perspectives on Missiology for the Twenty-First Century," *Pneuma* 16, no. 1 (Spring 1994): 14.

17. Quoted in Perry, *Spirit Baptism*, 157. See also Wonsuk Ma, "The Holy Spirit in Pentecostal Mission: The Shaping of Mission Awareness and Practice," *International Bulletin of Mission Research* 41, no. 3 (2017): 227–38, esp. 231–32.

18. James D. G. Dunn, *Baptism in the Holy Spirit* (London: SCM, 1970), 32.

19. See esp. Harold D. Hunter, *Spirit Baptism: Pentecostal Alternative* (1983; repr., Eugene, OR: Wipf & Stock, 2009); and William W. Menzies and Robert P. Menzies, *Spirit and Power: Foundations of a Pentecostal Experience* (Grand Rapids: Zondervan, 2000). In this work, Menzies and Menzies claim that the distinctive contribution of Pentecostal theology is a recovery of an authentic Lukan pneumatology, not one obscured by reading Luke-Acts through a Pauline lens. Luke and Paul bring different understandings of the work of the Spirit, and theological integration cannot be done with integrity unless the distinctive teachings are acknowledged. For a current state of the debate, see Perry, *Spirit Baptism*, 9–20. Perry's contribution explores the phenomenological aspects of the experience itself.

20. See Frank D. Macchia, "Salvation and Spirit Baptism: Another Look at Dunn's Classic," *Pneuma* 24, no. 1 (Spring 2002): 1–6; and Macchia, *Baptized in the Spirit: A Global Pentecostal*

focus devalues the theological significance of this experience, but he challenges Macchia's broad interpretation as too nebulous and ultimately unhelpful for Pentecostal Christians trying to understand this "powerful experience."[21] For Perry, the central significance of the experience of Spirit baptism is "the relational and transformational encounter with the Holy Spirit," and yet it is indisputable that for Pentecostals this encounter results in, or at the very least includes, empowerment for ministry.[22] In other words, even an expanded view of Spirit baptism includes a focus on spiritual empowerment for mission. This category has also been revised by certain Pentecostal theologians such as Macchia who argue that Luke's understanding of empowerment for witness is more expansive than prophetic speech (Menzies) or charismatic gifting (Stronstad), in that it also includes "a certain quality of communal life that is reconciling and rich in praise and acts of self-giving (Acts 2 and 4)."[23]

I have suggested that this movement of the Spirit might be seen as an extension of the Spirit's work in sanctification, at the center of which is love. In a similar way, Pentecostals such as Perry, Amos Yong, and Macchia acknowledge that although empowerment is necessary for the enacting of this mission, at its center is the outpouring of divine love—which is experienced first by believers themselves, who then want to share it with others in lives of witness and service.[24] In other words, being baptized in the Spirit involves more than receiving renewed energy and particular gifts for doing the work of God in the world. Yong acknowledges that most people associate power, rather than love, with the Pentecostal movement, thanks to the centrality of Acts 1:8 for the missional mandate of the church.[25] However, the empowerment of the Spirit for mission must have at its core "the introduction of the gift of God's love in Christ to the world, so that the world may also come to experience and participate in the love of the Father and the Son. . . . Those who have been caught up in the baptism of love want others to experience that love for themselves."[26] Perry's proposal

Theology (Grand Rapids: Zondervan, 2006). According to Macchia, the challenge of relating empowerment for mission to sanctification in a broader pneumatological framework is ongoing for Pentecostal theologians. Macchia, *Baptized in the Spirit*, 28.

21. Perry, *Spirit Baptism*, 35.
22. Perry, *Spirit Baptism*, 147.
23. Macchia, *Baptized in the Spirit*, 16. See also Matthias Wenk, *Community-Forming Power: The Socio-Ethical Role of the Spirit in Luke-Acts* (Sheffield, UK: Sheffield Academic, 2000).
24. Perry, *Spirit Baptism*, 170–74; Macchia, *Baptized in the Spirit*; and Amos Yong, *Spirit of Love: A Trinitarian Theology of Grace* (Waco: Baylor University Press, 2012).
25. Yong, *Spirit of Love*, 40.
26. Yong, *Spirit of Love*, 156.

is that Spirit baptism is an "invitation to participate in the work of the Holy Spirit in the building up of the kingdom of God and enacting the love of God in the world."[27] This resonates with Lutheran and other mainline Protestant sensibilities, including in ways that connect to social justice, as we will see.

Spiritual Empowerment through the Spiritual Gifts in Pentecostal Theology

Although Macchia's theology of Spirit baptism expands beyond the traditional focus on "spiritual empowerment," he does helpfully note that "the connection between Spirit baptism and an expansive array of spiritual gifts helps us focus on the relatively neglected vocational dimension of the Christian life and the polyphonic and diverse charismatic structure of the church."[28] Here too Macchia wishes to expand beyond the singular focus on speaking in tongues, which from the beginning had a twofold purpose in Pentecostal experience of the Spirit. Speaking in tongues was seen both as a sign of one's experience of being baptized in the Spirit and as a spiritual gift to be exercised for the mission of the church, along with other spiritual gifts, such as healing and prophecy. Early Pentecostals focused more on the ability to speak in other known languages, or xenolalia, than on speaking in an unknown tongue, or glossolalia.

Despite the importance of spiritual gifts to the theology of Spirit baptism and empowerment for mission, it is ironic that "Pentecostals have not produced a comprehensive theology of spiritual gifts."[29] Matthias Wenk's contribution to *The Routledge Handbook of Pentecostal Theology* is a step in the right direction. Wenk identifies the experience of "the in-breaking kingdom of God" as the central thread in discussions about spiritual gifts as they relate to the church's ministry, specifically as "observable manifestations of God's presence attributed to the work of the Holy Spirit."[30] While there continues to be a fascination with the more unusual of the spiritual gifts, especially speaking in tongues, the spiritual gifts are not ends in themselves but rather something to be used for the mission of God's kingdom and the justice of God.[31] For Pentecostals, spiritual gifts play a key role in empowering Christians to participate in God's

---

27. Perry, *Spirit Baptism*, 149.
28. Macchia, *Baptized in the Spirit*, 32.
29. Matthias Wenk, "Spiritual Gifts: Manifestations of the Kingdom of God," in *The Routledge Handbook of Pentecostal Theology*, ed. Wolfgang Vondey (New York: Routledge, 2020), 301.
30. Wenk, "Spiritual Gifts," 302.
31. Wenk, "Spiritual Gifts," 304.

mission in the world. This power is not exercised as power over others, or a will-to-power. The goal is not to gain power over other people or situations but to receive power to minister to others and to face together life's struggles and challenges—be they spiritual, economic, health related, or otherwise. Wenk points to the need for spiritual discernment to expose claims of power that are not of the Holy Spirit and that oppose the "paradoxical power of God made manifest in kenosis."[32]

A ministerial orientation toward empowerment can be traced back to the origins of the Pentecostal movement. Pentecostalism first arose among the poor in 1906 at Azusa Street in Los Angeles, and it continues to appeal to many in impoverished contexts, among those who experience powerlessness over their lives and destinies on a regular basis. In this regard, it is important that Pentecostalism be characterized as a religion of the poor, not for the poor. Wonsuk Ma writes, "The very fact that the Holy Spirit chose to visit them through powerful experiences such as healing, baptism in the Spirit, prophecy and miracles, as well as drastic conversion experiences, was in itself a social upliftment."[33] Pentecostalism teaches that people can overcome such situations of powerlessness by exercising the New Testament spiritual gifts, especially healing and speaking in tongues. Healing is experienced as the power of the Holy Spirit to change a bad situation or to oppose evil. Not only do believers experience the power of God in the healing event itself, but "in Pentecostal churches, healings are part of the empowerment of the church to spread the good news; they are a visible sign that the kingdom of God is coming."[34] Historically, Pentecostals viewed tongues as related to their success in missionary efforts to spread the gospel, although the emphasis shifted early on from xenolalia (speaking other known languages) to glossolalia (speaking in a heavenly language). Ma points out the democratizing function of ministry in Pentecostalism through the gifting of all believers, proposing the term "prophethood of all believers" in contrast to the more common Reformation refrain of the "priesthood of all believers."[35]

Although Pentecostals view tongues as a sign of empowerment for worldwide evangelism, Wenk notes that this connection is assumed rather than

---

32. Wenk, "Spiritual Gifts," 309.

33. Wonsuk Ma, "'When the Poor Are Fired Up': The Role of Pneumatology in Pentecostal-Charismatic Mission," *Transformation* 24, no. 1 (January 2007): 29. See also Robert Mapes Anderson's important study, *Vision of the Disinherited: The Making of American Pentecostalism* (Peabody, MA: Hendrickson, 1979).

34. Wenk, "Spiritual Gifts," 303.

35. Ma, "When the Poor Are Fired Up," 30.

argued. Further, most Pentecostals speak in tongues in private prayer, emphasizing other spiritual gifts for mission work, such as teaching, leadership, and healing.[36] Wenk, a New Testament scholar, offers an intriguing reading of Luke-Acts to support "the missionary power of glossolalia." He points to the contrast between the Roman Empire and God's kingdom, in which there is no dominating culture or language and "no attempt to overpower particularity, plurality, diversity, or any other form of cultural expression."[37] In other words, the gift of tongues is more than a personal experience of God's power, enjoyed by the believer; it also manifests the plurality and diversity of the inbreaking kingdom of God.[38] The narrative arc of the Spirit's work in Acts is one of increasing inclusion into God's people, signaled by the "falling" of the Holy Spirit on various groups—Samaritans, gentiles, and so on—overcoming religious and ethnic barriers.

In a similar way, Wolfgang Vondey argues that "the restriction of the charismatic life to the church alone is particularly problematic in the speaking of tongues and prophetic gifts."[39] From the earliest days of the movement at Azusa Street, tongues have been viewed as a social disturbance by others. Indeed, the sights and sounds of tongues not only confront the established culture but also can contribute "to the building of an alternative public and symbolic narrative," even when the content is no more than groaning in the Spirit.[40]

A more standard argument for the relation of tongues to mission is made by Jerry Michael Ireland. He calls for Pentecostals to reclaim the missionary nature of interpretation of tongues, arguing that glossolalia is central to missiology in Acts in its "proclamational role" to the nations. He writes, "Specifically, Luke utilizes tongues speech in order to convey the ultimate trajectory of the church—namely a concern for the nations. Understanding this trajectory helps temper

36. Wenk, "Spiritual Gifts," 304. See also Janet Evert Powers, "Missionary Tongues?," *Journal of Pentecostal Theology* 17 (2000): 39–55.

37. Wenk, "Spiritual Gifts," 304.

38. This has not always been the case, especially in the charismatic movement among Lutherans and other mainline Protestants in the 1960s, '70s, and '80s, when tongues were often experienced as divisive, a concern Paul himself addressed to the Corinthians (1 Cor. 12). While there are still vestiges of the charismatic movement in American Lutheranism and other mainline Protestant denominations, it has significantly declined in numbers and influence since the 1980s. See John Dart, "Charismatic and Mainline," *Christian Century* (March 7, 2006): 22–27; and Christopher J. Richmann's excellent analysis, "Lutheran Charismatics and the 'Chief Article': A Historical-Theological Assessment," *Journal of the Lutheran Historical Conference* 3 (2013): 46–73.

39. Vondey, *Pentecostal Theology*, 213.

40. Vondey, *Pentecostal Theology*, 214.

narrowly individualistic interpretations of tongues as initial evidence, as well as holistic mission paradigms that often fail to articulate this key characteristic of God's people."[41] In contrast to the more holistic understandings of mission that have become prominent in Pentecostal theology of late, Ireland views mission in more narrow terms, as the Spirit-empowered proclamation of the gospel to all nations, based on his reading of Acts. Rather than de-emphasizing the role that tongues plays in Pentecostalism (especially as "initial evidence"), Ireland believes a fresh focus on speaking in tongues is needed to "reorient the church to its cross-cultural mandate."[42]

Along with tongues, prophetic speech is another spiritual gift that is traditionally linked to evangelism and mission. The Holy Spirit speaks through believers, enabling them to share the Word of God with others. Wenk points out that prophetic speech has another function in Pentecostal theology: to expose and confront sin. This is one way that Pentecostals connect "the transformational orientation of spiritual gifts" to the work of justice.[43] Cheryl Sanders writes, "For the liberationists, the manifestation of the Spirit empowers social change by mandating a witness against injustice and a holy boldness that compels speaking truth to power in the public square."[44] Recently, a number of Pentecostal scholars have begun to explore how the spiritual gifts build up not only the church but also the wider community and how they serve the work of justice as an aspect of God's mission in the world.

The Holy Spirit and Mission in Lutheran Theology

Because power and mission are not topics typically addressed—much less connected—in Lutheran theology, I initially treat these topics separately. The Lutheran movement was not born out of the same missiological urgency as Pentecostalism. As a result, as Gustav Warneck observes, Luther's Reformation lacked not only mission action but the very idea of missions itself.[45] Warneck's

---

41. Jerry Michael Ireland, "The Missionary Nature of Tongues in the Book of Acts," *PentecoStudies* 18, no. 2 (2019): 201–2. See also Ireland, *The Missionary Spirit: Evangelism and Social Action in Pentecostal Missiology* (Maryknoll, NY: Orbis Books, 2021).

42. Ireland, "Missionary Nature of Tongues," 213.

43. Wenk, "Spiritual Gifts," 304.

44. Cheryl J. Sanders, "Social Justice: Theology as Social Transformation," in *The Routledge Handbook of Pentecostal Theology*, ed. Wolfgang Vondey (New York: Routledge, 2020), 433.

45. Gustav Warneck, *Outline of the History of Protestant Missions from the Reformation to the Present Time* (New York: Revell, 1901), 9. See also Ray Van Neste, "The Mangled Narrative of Missions and Evangelism in the Reformation," *Southeastern Theological Review* (2017): 1–7.

understanding of "mission" was typical of nineteenth-century missionaries: to preach the gospel to the "heathen world."[46] Others, such as James A. Scherer, have defended against this charge by pointing out that Luther's "mission field" was limited to Christendom. Scherer's definition of mission is also centered in the proclamation of the gospel, but he points out that Luther's reform was aimed at his fellow Germans who had been led astray by false teachings.[47] Reformation historian Scott Hendrix notes that "the Reformers saw themselves in a missionary situation in which the faith had to be taught to a populace they judged to be inadequately informed."[48] Scherer further explains, "And since the distortion of the Gospel message had led to the degeneration of mission into ecclesiastical propaganda, forced conversions, crusades, and non-evangelical methods, Luther's obedience to the mission command meant re-establishing the church on its one true foundation of Jesus Christ and the Gospel."[49]

Later Lutherans did discover a world outside of Christendom, however, and formed missionary societies in the eighteenth and nineteenth centuries. Spurred in large part by the emergence of Pietism in Germany and northern Europe, they began to send missionaries around the world to share the good news of Jesus Christ.[50] The commitment of Pietists to missionary outreach led them to work outside of official church structures for this work.[51] By the eighteenth century, Lutheran missionaries were spreading the gospel in places like India, Indonesia, Tanzania, and beyond. The mixed legacy of the modern missionary movement is a sensitive topic among contemporary Lutherans due to its historical entanglement with colonialism. As a result, the term "mission" has subsequently been defined more holistically by Lutherans, incorporating diaconal and development work along with evangelism, which is increasingly understood in terms of "accompaniment." Rafael Malpica Padilla explains, "Accompaniment is walking together in solidarity which is characterized by mutuality and interdependence. The basis for this accompaniment, what the New Testament calls *koinonia*, is found in the God-human relationship in

46. Warneck, *Outline of the History of Protestant Missions*, 9.

47. James A. Scherer, "Luther and Mission: A Rich but Untested Potential," *Missio Apostolica* 2, no. 1 (May 1994): 18.

48. Scott H. Hendrix, *Recultivating the Vineyard: The Reformation Agendas of Christianization* (Louisville: Westminster John Knox, 2004), 172.

49. Scherer, "Luther and Mission," 18.

50. Robert Kolb, "'So Much Began in Halle': The Mission Program That Sent Mühlenberg to America," *Concordia Historical Institute Quarterly* 84, no. 3 (Fall 2011): 26–35.

51. F. Ernest Stoeffler, *The Rise of Evangelical Pietism* (Leiden: Brill, 1965), 19.

which God accompanies us in Jesus Christ through the power of the Holy Spirit."[52]

An important shift in missiological thinking occurred in the mid-twentieth century whereby the *missio Dei* (mission of God) was distinguished from the *missio ecclesia* (mission of the church). The term "mission" originated in patristic debates over the Trinity, and until the end of the sixteenth century, it referred exclusively to the "missions" ("sendings") of the Son and the Spirit within the Godhead.[53] This trinitarian foundation of the term is significant, especially because it was largely neglected in the modern missionary movement, which viewed mission as an activity of the church to spread the gospel and care for those in need.

In the emerging missiology, however, mission is not primarily an activity of the church but instead God's work into which the church is invited to participate. South African missiologist David Bosch explains, "The classical doctrine of the *missio Dei* as God the Father sending the Son, and God the Father and the Son sending the Spirit [is] expanded to include yet another 'movement': Father, Son, and Holy Spirit sending the church into the world."[54] This makes mission "the result of God's initiative, rooted in God's purposes to restore and heal creation. 'Mission' means 'sending' and it is the central biblical theme describing the purpose of God's action in human history."[55]

The Lutheran World Federation (LWF)[56] has embraced this shift to understanding God's mission in terms of reconciling all creation to God's self and, since 1977, has increasingly emphasized the holistic nature of mission. At the Fourth LWF Assembly (Helsinki, 1963), mission was still understood exclusively in terms of evangelism and conversion, with the goal of bringing people from unbelief to faith. Since the Sixth LWF Assembly (Dar es Salaam, 1977), mission has been understood and practiced in a holistic way that encompasses proclamation, advocacy, and service to the whole person. The Tenth LWF Assembly (Winnipeg, 2003) emphasized that participation in the mission of

52. Rafael Malpica Padilla, "Accompaniment as an Alternative Model for the Practice of Mission," *Trinity Seminary Review* 29, no. 2 (Summer–Fall 2008): 88.

53. David J. Bosch, *Transforming Mission: Paradigm Shifts in Theology of Mission* (Maryknoll, NY: Orbis Books, 1991), 1.

54. Bosch, *Transforming Mission*, 390.

55. Darrell L. Guder et al., eds., *Missional Church: A Vision for Sending the Church in North America* (Grand Rapids: Eerdmans, 1998), 4.

56. The majority of the seventy-seven million Lutherans worldwide belong to the LWF, including the largest Lutheran denomination in the United States, the Evangelical Lutheran Church in America (ELCA). For more information on the LWF, see https://www.lutheranworld.org.

God involves three interconnected dimensions: *diakonia* (service), proclamation, and dialogue.

The Lutheran World Federation—Mission in Context

In 2004, the LWF produced its most comprehensive document to date on mission: *Mission in Context: Transformation, Reconciliation, Empowerment; An LWF Contribution to the Understanding and Practice of Mission* (MIC).[57] The consultation that led to this document "envisioned transformation as an important mission imperative. This understanding of mission as transformation—of both the individual and society—deepens the empowering dimension of service as *diakonia*. Mission as transformation challenges the church to undergo transformation itself in order to be an instrument of transformation in the world."[58] The document also proposes a model of "accompaniment" for the work of mission, illustrated well by the biblical model for mission highlighted by the document, the Emmaus story (Luke 24). Accompaniment is defined as sharing with others in their struggles as part of one's witness to God's redeeming love in Jesus Christ.

In the first section, the document explores mission in a trinitarian framework, centered in the incarnation of the Son. The work of the Holy Spirit is to bring repentance and make Christ present in faith to the believer, create *koinonia*, and empower believers through Word and sacraments with spiritual gifts needed for the transforming mission of God in the world. "Equipped with these spiritual gifts (charismata), they are able to proclaim the gospel and share the life described by the gospel with all peoples in every place. All of the Spirit's gifts—preaching, teaching, healing, prophecy, administration, and others given to women and men—are intended to strengthen the communities of God's gathered people, congregations, for inner growth and holistic mission."[59]

Notably absent is the gift of tongues, which, as we have seen, is central to a Pentecostal understanding of spiritual empowerment. However, the document states that the Spirit "awakens, inspires and guides" the church and continually

---

57. *Mission in Context: Transformation, Reconciliation, Empowerment; An LWF Contribution to the Understanding and Practice of Mission* (Geneva: LWF, 2004), hereafter cited as MIC. (This is a revision of a 1988 document.) I have also proposed framing the church's mission in terms of transformation. See Cheryl M. Peterson, "The Church Transformed," *Seminary Ridge Review* 17, no. 1 (Autumn 2014): 16–37.

58. *MIC*, 7.

59. *MIC*, 27. Healing is mentioned again in a later section on salvation (p. 39).

revives and renews the church for mission. "Church renewal may take the form of creative worship and liturgical, structural, missiological, and charismatic renewal, all of which are the working of the Holy Spirit using different gifts for different purposes."[60] The document distinguishes the term "charismatic" from "Pentecostal"; these are not interchangeable. However, a "charismatic church" will use all the gifts of the Spirit for the mission of God, including "proclamation of the gospel, deliverance from evil powers, prayer for healing, community building, service, and advocacy." At the same time, the document echoes the urging of the Tenth LWF Assembly to find ways "to engage with Pentecostal churches and charismatic movements within our own churches," explaining that such engagement could help the church participate more faithfully in God's mission.[61]

The second major section of the document outlines mission in terms of "transformation, reconciliation, and empowerment." The Holy Spirit is referred to as the agent of transformation "in and through the church to the whole world," both in individuals (Rom. 6:4–14) and in structures of social and political oppression and economic exclusion. The Spirit is also identified as the agent of empowerment for the church's mission (Acts 1:8). As the document states, "Empowerment refers here primarily to God sharing power (*dynamis*) with people for participation in God's mission. God empowers individual Christians and the whole church through the leading of the Holy Spirit and the bestowing of spiritual gifts necessary to carry out the holistic mission of the church."[62] The Spirit empowers believers to share the gospel of justification and the message of hope in God's grace for a suffering and broken world. Further, the Spirit calls the church to resist power for its own sake, "power over" others, and empowers all the baptized to instead exercise their gifts "in the way of Christ" for the building up of the church and the holistic mission of God. In this way, the church is called to point "to the in-breaking of God's reign in Christ in the world, using all the spiritual gifts (charismata) that the Holy Spirit has generously bestowed upon it."[63] Citing 1 Corinthians, the document stresses the church's spiritual empowerment for its mission of accompaniment to be a worshiping, nurturing, messenger, serving, healing, and ecumenical community.

---

60. *MIC*, 31.
61. *MIC*, 32. As noted, the LWF began a "proto-dialogue" with classical Pentecostals from the Pentecostal World Fellowship.
62. *MIC*, 35.
63. *MIC*, 46.

The MIC document is an important first step in incorporating spiritual empowerment with a theology of mission, but more exploration is needed from a Lutheran theological perspective. While some Lutheran theologians have begun to explore the Spirit's role as "sending" the church in mission,[64] for the most part they have not investigated the Spirit's role as the one who empowers members of the church for mission, nor have they made explicit the connection between the Holy Spirit and power when addressing mission and evangelism, as have Pentecostals.

The Holy Spirit and Power in Lutheran Theology

As we have seen, power is not the primary category that Lutherans use to frame the work of the Holy Spirit. In fact, Lutherans tend to be wary of power talk in general, due to Luther's negative experiences with ecclesiastical power in the sixteenth century and the church hierarchy's exercise of power to oppose the free proclamation of the gospel. In two of the Lutheran confessional documents, Melanchthon distinguishes between spiritual and worldly power—that is, between the power and authority to proclaim the gospel, announce the forgiveness of sins, and administer the sacraments and the power to wield the sword and establish or depose political heads.[65] The Reformers were concerned with the church's entanglement with secular powers and neglect of its own God-given calling and "spiritual power" to preach the gospel. Such concerns continue into the present day, as seen in the MIC document, which names the abuse, misuse, and lack of power as important contextual factors for mission. "Understanding contexts requires naming the realities and powers that are operative in the world; this includes naming both the powers of evil and the power of God."[66] This includes the abuse of power in Christian congregations. Power need not be defined only in negative terms, however. Annemie Dillen writes, "Having power is possessing the capacity

---

64. See, e.g., Cheryl M. Peterson, *Who Is the Church? An Ecclesiology for the Twenty-First Century* (Minneapolis: Fortress, 2013); and Richard H. Bliese and Craig Van Gelder, eds., *The Evangelizing Church: A Lutheran Contribution* (Minneapolis: Augsburg Fortress, 2005).

65. See Augsburg Confession, art. 28, in *The Book of Concord: The Confessions of the Evangelical Lutheran Church*, ed. Robert Kolb and Timothy J. Wengert (Minneapolis: Fortress, 2000), 90–103. The Augsburg Confession will hereafter be cited as CA, and page references to *The Book of Concord* will be supplied with the abbreviation BC. See also Philip Melanchthon, "Treatise on the Power and Primacy of the Pope," in BC, 329–44.

66. *MIC*, 11.

to influence and/or to control oneself and/or others and is closely connected with the influence exercised by others. Power refers to a circular process."[67] It is present in all relationships, including our relationship with God. The question is how one exercises power in those relationships, in one's ministry and mission. The LWF document promotes mutual empowerment in ministries of koinonia, kerygma, and diakonia instead of the exercising of "power over" others.

For the Reformers, "spiritual power" related primarily to kerygma, the proclamation of the gospel, of God's Word. One receives power—or perhaps better, authority—to preach the gospel.[68] When addressing this idea, however, the Reformers focused more on who should exercise power—that is, on who has the authority to exercise power—than on the necessary abilities and gifts. Lutherans also tend to focus more on "set apart" ministries in the church: the public office of ministry (or pastoral office) and the authority of pastors to publicly preach the gospel, preside at the Eucharist, and pronounce the forgiveness of sins (the office of the keys).

The phrase "power of God" appears in several places in the Lutheran Confessions. The most significant reference is to the power of the gospel to save. Romans 1:16 is frequently cited in the Lutheran Confessions and by Luther in several of his sermons: "For I am not ashamed of the gospel; it is the power of God for salvation to everyone who has faith, to the Jew first and also to the Greek."[69] In the Large Catechism, after acknowledging that the Word is the "power of God," Luther writes, "Indeed, the power of God . . . burns the devil's house down, and gives us immeasurable strength, comfort, and help."[70]

As we have seen, Lutherans affirm that the Holy Spirit enables believers not only to trust in God's Word but also to obey it. The Lutheran Confessions

67. Annemie Dillen, "The Complexity of Power in Pastoral Relations: Challenges for Theology and Church," ET Studies 4, no. 2 (2013): 222.

68. Richmann points out the irony in how Larry Christenson failed to make this connection in Luther, when he seemingly denigrated proclamation as a means of grace. In discussing Paul's ministry in Malta, Christenson insisted that they "were cured because the gospel Paul preached was not a gospel of mere words: it was a gospel of power." Quoted in Richmann, "Lutheran Charismatics and the 'Chief Article,'" 62–63.

69. This verse is cited in CA 28.9, in BC, 92–93; Apology of the Augsburg Confession (hereafter cited as AP), 4.67, 13.11, in BC, 131, 220; the preface to the Large Catechism, in BC, 381; Epitome, Formula of Concord (hereafter cited as Ep. FC), 2.5, in BC, 492; and Solid Declaration, Formula of Concord (hereafter cited as SD FC), 5.22, 11.29, in BC, 585, 635. See also Luther's "Easter 4 Sermon on James 1:16–21," in Sermons of Martin Luther, ed. John Nicholas Lenker, 8 vols. (Grand Rapids: Baker, 1988), 2:248.

70. Martin Luther, Large Catechism, in BC, 381.

teach that while the law commands us to obey God's Word and live a holy life, the ability to do so comes only from the Holy Spirit, who accompanies us in the new life. The Holy Spirit works through the law to teach us how to live, exhorting and reproving us, raising us up when we stumble and fall, comforting us with the promise of the gospel.[71] Thus the Lutheran Confessions teach that those who have been set aside for the ministry of the Word are given authority to preach and administer the sacraments, and receive "spiritual power" for these specific tasks, but that all the baptized receive the Spirit's power, which gives them faith in the gospel and enables them to obey God in holiness of life.

The question remains, however: What about power for the ministry and mission of all baptized believers, not only those set apart for the public office of ministry? What about power that is received not only to believe and obey but also to be exercised by the believer for the sake of the kingdom? Is there a place for this kind of "spiritual power" for mission in Lutheran theology? What might Lutherans learn from Pentecostals in this regard?

A Lutheran Theology of Empowerment for Mission

Baptism and Vocation

The most obvious avenue for a Lutheran engagement of this topic would appear to be Luther's concept of the "priesthood of all believers," as it has come to be known, in spite of the fact that the phrase is nowhere to be found in Luther's own writings.[72] In Luther's 1520 treatise, "To the Christian Nobility of the German Nation," he cites 1 Peter 2:9 to make the point that "we are all consecrated priests through baptism" and that ministry belongs to the baptized.[73] The "priesthood of all believers" has come to mean, in the minds of many, that anyone can do the pastor's job. But that is not what Luther claimed. While Lutherans do not hold a sacerdotal view of ordination, the Lutheran Confessions teach that one should not regularly preach or preside without a "call," which Lutherans have always defined ecclesiastically through ordination.[74] It

---

71. SD FC, 6.13–14, in BC, 589.

72. See Timothy J. Wengert, Priesthood, Pastors, Bishops: Public Ministry for the Reformation and Today (Minneapolis: Fortress, 2008), 1.

73. Martin Luther, "To the Christian Nobility of the German Nation," in Three Treatises, 2nd rev. ed. (Philadelphia: Fortress, 1970), 12.

74. See CA 14, in BC, 46–47.

is important to remember that Luther used the concept of the royal priesthood to oppose the notion that priestly ordination or monastic vows "consecrate" someone to a different and higher spiritual estate. When Luther affirms that all the baptized are "priests," he is affirming that there is one "spiritual estate" and that one becomes "spiritual" through baptism and faith.[75] In other words, there are not two classes of Christians, only one.[76]

Lutherans teach that baptism is a gift that involves not only a new "standing" before God but also a "call," or a vocation, to ministry. Lutherans speak of vocation in two ways: first, in terms of a general calling to discipleship and service that all Christians receive in baptism and, second, as the "place" to which God calls one to exercise that general calling (e.g., being a mother, a shoemaker, a governor, etc.). In other words, no "calling" is higher than baptism for Lutherans; all baptized believers are consecrated and set apart for lives of loving service to God and the neighbor. Lutheran studies on vocation, however, have often tended to focus more on the "station" of life and gifts for "creation" and the affirmation that callings such as parenthood and secular work (such as teaching, nursing, governing, etc.) are faithful ways to live out one's Christian vocation and contribute to the common good.

Less often is vocation considered in relation to the call of the baptized explicitly to serve the gospel in their daily lives. Lutheran theology is clear on what this *does not* mean (i.e., that "anyone can/should do the pastor's job"), but it is not as clear on what this *does* mean. Christopher Richmann's recent treatment of vocation helpfully navigates this topic in a way that affirms both the call of the ordained pastor to preach publicly and the call of all the baptized to proclaim and teach God's Word to one another, especially within the circles of friends and family, along with the role of the church to equip them for this call.[77]

75. In addition to Luther's treatise, "To the Christian Nobility," see Martin Luther, "Answer to the Hyperchristian, Hyperspiritual, and Hyperlearned Book by Goat Emser in Leipzig—Including Some Thoughts Regarding His Companion, the Fool Murner" (1521), in *Luther's Works*, American ed., 55 vols. (Philadelphia: Fortress; St. Louis: Concordia, 1955–86), 39:139–224. *Luther's Works* is hereafter cited as *LW*.

76. See Luther, "To the Christian Nobility," 14–15.

77. Christopher J. Richmann, *Called: Recovering Lutheran Principles for Ministry and Vocation* (Minneapolis: Fortress, 2022). Interestingly, Richmann grew up in the Lutheran Church–Missouri Synod, then was active in Pentecostal and charismatic groups for ten years before returning to Lutheranism as a member, and later ordained pastor, of the ELCA. See also Craig L. Nessan, "Universal Priesthood of All Believers: Unfulfilled Promise of the Reformation," *Currents in Theology and Mission* 46, no. 1 (2019): 8–15.

Exercising the Spiritual Gifts

Lutherans could learn something from Pentecostals regarding the Spirit's empowerment of the baptized. When Pentecostals speak of "empowerment for mission," they mean the ministry and mission that is done by all believers, not just by those who are set aside as pastors, deacons, missionaries, or other professional church workers. The Spirit empowers and enables all for ministry so that the full gospel may be experienced by all, and the Spirit does this through the impartation of spiritual gifts. Apart from the Lutheran charismatic movement in the 1970s and 1980s (which focused primarily on the spiritual gift of tongues) and, more recently, "spiritual gift inventories" used in some congregations, the topic of "spiritual gifts" has not been explored regarding the ministry of the "common priesthood." Indeed, if all baptized Christian believers are called to participate in the *missio Dei* and bear the good news of Jesus Christ in word and deed to a hurting world, then an exploration of how the Spirit empowers the baptized for this work seems overdue.

At the 2019 LWF consultation in Addis Ababa, Kärkkäinen, who identifies as Lutheran and Pentecostal, raised this very question in his plenary address: "What are some of the ways the Spirit of God is empowering, gifting, and inspiring the people of God in order for them to live out the central Reformation vision of the priesthood of all believers? What is the Spirit's role in our Christian missional vocation?"[78] Kärkkäinen defends Lutheranism against ignoring the Third Person of the Trinity but also recognizes that "we Lutherans have neglected, minimized, or outright resisted the ministry of the Holy Spirit in charismatic endowment, spiritual gifts, and dynamic spirituality—all profoundly important themes for the global Lutheran community of the third millennium."[79] This can be traced back to Luther's polemical writings against Andreas Karlstadt and others, such as Thomas Müntzer, who claimed that the Spirit spoke through them apart from the Word of God. Against what he perceived as their direct, unmediated experience of the Spirit, Luther insisted that the Spirit does not work apart from God's Word (the gospel) and external means of proclamation and the sacraments. However, Luther's primary concern with these "enthusiasts" is not that they claim to hear the Spirit outside of Word and Sacrament but that

---

78. Veli-Matti Kärkkäinen, "Transformed, Freed, Empowered: The Spirit's Work in the Gifting and Vocation of All Believers," in *"We Believe in the Holy Spirit": Global Perspectives on Lutheran Identities*, ed. Chad M. Rimmer and Cheryl M. Peterson (Leipzig: Evangelische Verlangsanstalt, 2021), 193.

79. Kärkkäinen, "Transformed, Freed, Empowered," 197.

they have not tested that inspiration against God's Word and so have confused God's Spirit with their own.[80] I agree with Kärkkäinen that it is counterproductive and even harmful to use Luther's polemic as the basis to reject the reception of the charismata, or spiritual gifts.[81]

Martin Luther on Miracles and the Spiritual Gifts

Kärkkäinen also notes Luther's suspicion of miracles in general, due to the role they played in medieval Catholicism, leading many to characterize Luther as a "cessationist." Cessationists are those who believe that while miracles and signs were needed for the early apostolic ministry, they ceased once the church was established and were replaced with God's Word alone. Kärkkäinen argues that while this is true, Luther is more of a "soft" cessationist as compared to later Protestants, such as B. B. Warfield, who were "hard" cessationists.[82] Luther did not deny that miracles could happen in his day, but he found them to have little value. The real miracle for Luther is faith, which is accomplished through the Holy Spirit working through the Word to bring believers to Christ. He writes, "Is this not an immeasurably greater and more glorious work and miracle than if (God) were in a bodily or temporal way to raise the dead again to life, or help the blind, deaf, dumb, and leprous here in the world, in this transitory life?"[83] In a similar vein, he responds to those who charge that Lutherans "lack completely the gift of miracles": "For even nowadays the blind receive their sight when minds obsessed by Satan are brought to know Christ. The deaf hear the Gospel, and the lame, who sat in their superstitions, and the idolaters arise with an upright faith and walk about happily. . . . The dumb, too, now sing and proclaim the praise of God. Those who are not moved by these miracles would not believe even Christ if He were to perform these miracles bodily, for they are no less significant than raising the dead and restoring sight to the blind."[84]

---

80. See LW 40:146–49. Whether this is a fair assessment of Karlstadt and others is debatable, and evaluation of this question is beyond the scope of this book. For a fuller examination of this historical trajectory, see Carter Lindberg, *The Third Reformation? Charismatic Movements and the Lutheran Tradition* (Macon, GA: Mercer University Press, 1983).

81. Kärkkäinen, "Transformed, Freed, Empowered," 201.

82. Kärkkäinen, "Transformed, Freed, Empowered," 199.

83. Martin Luther, "A Sermon on Keeping Children in School" (1530), quoted in Richard G. Ballard, "Lutheran Ambivalence toward Healing Ministry," *Lutheran Forum* (Advent 1987): 18.

84. Martin Luther, "Sermon on Isaiah 35:5–6" (1532), quoted in Ballard, "Lutheran Ambivalence toward Healing Ministry," 18.

The term "spiritual gifts" itself provides another challenge for Lutherans because that term is often used in Lutheranism to refer to God's salvific grace, and not to special power or abilities. Luther himself speaks of the gifts of baptism and the Lord's Supper in terms of the spiritual benefits received: forgiveness of sins, life, and salvation. However, in a sermon on 1 Corinthians 12, Luther refers to the diverse offices and gifts that emanate from the Spirit as the work of God and "the expression of [God's] power."[85]

Regarding the exercise of such spiritual gifts, while Luther presumes Paul is directing his words regarding the spiritual gifts in Romans 12 and 1 Corinthians 12 primarily to clergy and other church authorities, he does not *restrict* spiritual gifts to the office of ministry.[86] In a sermon on 1 Peter 4:7–11, he specifies that spiritual gifts "are bestowed for the good of the entire Church and *particularly* for its spiritual offices or government. [Peter] would have the Spirit's gifts used in the service of others, and admonishes Christians to consider all they have as given of God." He continues, "Let Christians know they are under obligation to serve God with their gifts; and God is served when they employ them for the advantage and service of the people—reforming them, bringing them to a knowledge of God, and thus building up, strengthening and perpetuating the Church."[87]

In a sermon on 1 Corinthians 12, Luther distinguishes between "administrations" (which he ties to specific ecclesial offices), "workings" (remarkable works of God wrought through certain individuals), and the spiritual gifts themselves, including wisdom, knowledge, prophecy, the power to discern spirits, the capacity to speak in tongues and to interpret them, extraordinary faith, and the power to work miracles. While Luther stresses the ordinary gifts more than the extraordinary gifts in his sermons on 1 Corinthians 12, in his 1522 Ascension Day sermon he does acknowledge the exercise of miraculous gifts among Christians, making this a favored text among Lutheran charismatics. The context is Jesus's commission to the disciples in Mark 16:15: "Go into all the world and proclaim the good news to the whole creation." Luther uses the image of a stone thrown into water, creating waves that move outward, to illustrate the preaching of the Word begun by the disciples, which will continue

85. Martin Luther, "The Tenth Sunday after Trinity," in *Sermons of Martin Luther*, 8:211.
86. That Luther relegates the spiritual gifts to the clergy alone is the key argument made in one of the few in-depth treatments available on Luther's theology of spiritual gifts. See Robert Kingston Wetmore, "The Theology of Spiritual Gifts in Luther and Calvin: A Comparison" (PhD diss., Concordia Seminary, 1992), 65–73.
87. Martin Luther, "Sunday after Ascension Day," in *Sermons of Martin Luther*, 7:323.

to ripple out until the gospel has come to all of creation.[88] This framing is important for understanding the rest of the passage because it presumes that subsequent generations of disciples will continue this work. As Luther states, "Thus generally and publicly shall it be proclaimed, and preached in all the world, being withheld from no one, till it reaches the ends of the world."[89] By adding "generally" to "publicly," Luther suggests that this commission will be fulfilled by all Christians, not just those ordained to preach publicly (i.e., pastors). To emphasize the point, he refers to Paul's list of spiritual gifts/offices in Ephesians 4:11–13, which includes offices beyond that of pastor, such as teachers and evangelists.

Luther then addresses the signs of Mark 16:17–18. As charismatic Lutheran pastor Larry Christenson rightly notes, Luther clearly understands that these signs should be interpreted as applying to all Christians, not just to the original twelve or to the church as a whole.[90] As Luther writes, "If there is a Christian who has faith, he shall have the power to do these accompanying miracles, and they shall follow him," citing John 14:12. Christians have this power, but they should exercise it only "if it is necessary"—that is, when needed to prove or confirm the Word of God.[91] Luther's next statement reflects his "soft" cessationism. He claims that there should be no need to work miracles, as in the time of the apostles, since the gospel already has been made known to the world. Here Luther seems to contradict his earlier point regarding Jesus's commission, where Luther states that the work of spreading the gospel is not yet finished, adding this quip: "For I know not whether Germany has ever heard of the Word of God."[92] Even so, he does not prohibit the working of miracles, especially in cases where the gospel is "derided and suppressed."[93] Without a pressing need, it is best not to work miracles, in Luther's view. He specifically mentions the gift of tongues (which he interprets as xenolalia, not glossolalia) as being unnecessary in most cases, "since you all can well hear and understand me; but if God should send me where the people could not understand me, he could easily grant me their speech of language, that I

---

88. Martin Luther, "Ascension Day Sermon," in *Sermons of Martin Luther*, 3:202.

89. Luther, "Ascension Day Sermon," 3:205.

90. Mentioned in Richmann, *Called*, 69n45. See also Karlfried Froehlich, "Charismatic Manifestations and the Lutheran Incarnational Stance," in *The Holy Spirit in the Life of the Church: From Biblical Times to the Present*, ed. Paul D. Opsahl (Minneapolis: Augsburg, 1978), 151.

91. Luther, "Ascension Day Sermon," 207.

92. Luther, "Ascension Day Sermon," 205.

93. Luther, "Ascension Day Sermon," 207.

might be understood."[94] He ends the sermon with a specific cautionary tale regarding exorcism.

In a sermon on 1 Corinthians 12, Luther focuses on the specific spiritual gifts of prophecy, knowledge, and faith because these relate closest to the proclamation of God's Word. As he concludes the sermon, he connects the exercise of these gifts (along with administrations and workings) to the Great Commission of Matthew 28:19 and suggests that the devil himself will flee from the confident faith that God's command and power inspire in a Christian. Further, God's "gifts and works in his Church must effect inexpressible results, taking souls from the jaws of the devil and translating them into eternal life and glory."[95] The implication is that the Spirit works gifts in all believers for the sake of the gospel's witness and mission.[96]

The Holy Spirit as the Empowerer

For Evangelism and Testimony

While Lutherans have begun to develop the notion of the "evangelizing church,"[97] Lutherans in the United States could learn from Pentecostals and charismatic Lutherans in the Global South about sharing personal testimony and gain inspiration for more fully developing a theology of lay evangelism that draws on the biblical idea of spiritual gifts. Charismatic Lutherans globally have focused more on the connection between spiritual gifts and empowerment for mission than have US charismatic Lutherans. For example, the mission statement of the largest member church in the Lutheran World Federation, the Ethiopian Evangelical Church Mekane Yesus, speaks about how the Spirit works through the proclamation of the gospel to enable the church to become "an embodiment of God's love in holistic service to the world, planting congregations, empowering ministers, nurturing believers, and making disciples in Ethiopia."[98] There is a clear and strong reliance on the Holy Spirit not only as the one who empowers for "supernatural living" through the fruit of the Spirit but also as the one who gives gifts for "supernatural ministry." Indeed, the Spirit alone empowers believers for the task of ministry. "If a person doesn't

94. Luther, "Ascension Day Sermon," 208.
95. Luther, "Tenth Sunday after Trinity," 8:220.
96. David J. Courey discusses the relationship between the charismata and the Lutheran concept of the common priesthood from the other direction; see Courey, *What Has Wittenberg to Do with Azusa? Luther's Theology of the Cross and Pentecostal Triumphalism* (New York: T&T Clark, 2015).
97. See, e.g., Bliese and Van Gelder, *Evangelizing Church*.
98. Bulaka, "Theology of Holy Spirit," 129.

have the supernatural gift of evangelism, how can he even begin to carry out the apostolic task, planting the Church of Christ in places where it is not? The Holy Spirit is central for missionary life and service. It is He who energizes the evangelists."[99] In the same way, the Holy Spirit empowers disciples through other spiritual gifts, such as healing and exorcism. Many people whose lives have been transformed by such works of the Spirit respond in faith and service, giving testimony to the power of the Holy Spirit.[100]

In contrast, Lutheran charismatics in the United States, such as Larry Christenson and Theodore Jungkuntz, tend to connect the experience of Spirit baptism, and especially the gift of tongues, to an assurance of one's salvation rather than to empowerment for ministry. While one does not need to speak in tongues to be saved, they argue that such an experience strengthens one's faith and brings an assurance of salvation and God's promises.[101] Noncharismatic Lutheran treatments that address spiritual gifts for ministry are rare, apart from "spiritual gift inventories," which do not always distinguish between natural abilities, or skills, and spiritual gifts, leading some to critique such tools.[102] The ELCA currently offers a "Spiritual Gifts Assessment" on its website in a tab for "Spiritual Renewal" as a tool for congregational renewal. This assessment does focus more on how the Holy Spirit is gifting people for ministry, but it is unclear if or how Lutheran congregations are using this tool for mission.[103]

Those contemporary US Lutherans writing on the topics of evangelism and testimony tend to focus on providing a theological rationale for evangelism, as well as strategies for sharing the gospel, since many Lutherans are uncomfortable with these practices.[104] Lutherans in the United States associate

99. Bulaka, "Theology of Holy Spirit," 132.
100. Bulaka, "Theology of Holy Spirit," 132.
101. Richmann argues that by insisting that faith must be completed by charismatic experiences, these charismatic leaders decenter the central doctrine of Lutheran theology, that of justification, and contribute to the waning of this movement in US Lutheranism. Richmann, "Lutheran Charismatics and the Chief Article,'" 46–73. Sarah Hinlicky Wilson points to the failure of the charismatics and church bureaucrats to listen to each other, which led most of the charismatic Lutherans to leave the Lutheran church. Wilson, "How Is Your Revival Going?," *Lutheran Forum* 50, no. 2 (Summer 2016): 4.
102. When I was in seminary, I did my internship project (1989–90) using a spiritual gifts inventory that focused more on natural abilities and interests than actual gifts of the Spirit. This is one of Robert W. Schaibley's criticisms of older forms of spiritual gift inventories. See Schaibley, "Measuring Spiritual Gifts," *Lutheran Quarterly* 3, no. 4 (Winter 1989): 423–41.
103. "Spiritual Gifts Assessment Tool," Evangelical Lutheran Church in America, accessed February 10, 2023, https://www.elca.org/Our-Work/Congregations-and-Synods/Faith-Practices/Spiritual-Renewal.
104. See, e.g., Mark C. Mattes, "A Lutheran Case for Evangelism," *Word & World* 39, no. 4 (Fall 2019): 295–308; Frederick J. Gaiser, "'I Will Tell You What God Has Done for Me' (Psalm

these practices with revivalism, emotionalism, and coercion, and most have no
practice sharing their faith—whether in worship, in small groups, or in public.
And yet Scripture admonishes believers—not just pastors and other set-apart
ministers—to "do the work of an evangelist" (2 Tim. 4:5). Evangelism is simply
sharing the good news of God's love in Jesus Christ with others, and a testimony
is sharing one's personal encounter with God's love in Christ.

Overall, US Lutherans are more comfortable sharing their faith in "deed"
than in "word," by doing or contributing to social-service work, often by sub-
scribing to the saying, wrongly attributed to St. Francis, "Preach the gospel at
all times, and if necessary, use words." According to Kathryn Schifferdecker,
the leadership of the Ethiopian Evangelical Church Mekane Yesus chastised
the Western churches in a 1972 letter for separating development work from
evangelism to alleviate a guilty conscience about colonialism. Humanitarian aid
is part of the church's holistic mission, but if the church does not proclaim the
gospel, who else will attend to people's spiritual hunger?[105] Luther saw testimony
as flowing naturally from one's rebirth in the gospel: "'Sing to the Lord a new
song. Sing to the Lord all the earth.' For God has cheered our hearts and minds
through his dear Son, whom he gave for us to redeem us from sin, death, and
the devil. [Those who believe] this earnestly cannot be quiet about it. But [they]
must gladly and willingly sing and speak about it so that others also may come
and hear it."[106] Unlike public proclamation of the gospel, which for Lutherans is
reserved for ordained ministers, giving testimony is something all Christians
can and should do. In the Smalcald Articles, Luther notes that such "mutual
conversation and consolation" among siblings in Christ is one of the means
of grace, along with proclamation, the sacraments, and the office of the keys.[107]

In his sermons on the Gospel of John, Luther points to the Holy Spirit as
the power for such testimony, as the one who also will "impel you to testify of
me."[108] Luther believed that the church's gospel witness would be opposed, even
by the devil himself. His references to the devil in his writings are numerous
and well-known, and Luther often spoke of the opposition of the devil to the

---

66:16): A Place for Testimony in Lutheran Worship?," *Word & World* 26, no. 2 (Spring 2006):
138–48; and Craig L. Nessan, *Beyond Maintenance to Mission: A Theology of the Congregation*, 2nd
ed. (Minneapolis: Fortress, 2010), 113–25.

105. Kathryn Schifferdecker, "Learning from the Global South," *Word & World* Supplement
Series 7 (2017): 180–82.

106. *LW* 53:333.

107. See Martin Luther, "Concerning the Gospel," Part 3, Smalcald Articles, Article 4, in *BC*, 319.

108. *LW* 24:294.

Word of God.[109] While the Reformers were certain that the devil would do everything in his power to oppose the advancement of the gospel, they were equally confident in the power of the Holy Spirit to defend and strengthen the church's witness in the face of such opposition.

In such situations, the Holy Spirit "will fill us with a courage that is called a divine, holy, and bold defiance."[110] As the Spirit of truth, the Holy Spirit not only teaches us about the one who is Truth (i.e., Christ) but also gives us the courage needed to stand in and testify to the truth and to oppose all lies and false gospels.[111] Luther first refers to the "Spirit of truth" in his Johannine writings in a section about the persecution Christians will face as followers of Jesus (John 15:18–25). He also describes the Holy Spirit as the "comforter of all the weak, not only for us, but for everyone in the world."[112] This "comfort" makes believers "defiant and courageous in the face of all kinds of terror."[113] Luther assures his readers that the Holy Spirit "will not stop fortifying our hearts" against such attacks and will inspire us with "a courage that will overcome it all."[114]

The Holy Spirit keeps the Christian in the truth and emboldens the Christian to stand against those who teach a false gospel. While Luther had in mind the papacy, the progenitors of false gospels today in the United States are primarily those Christian preachers who forget the theology of the cross and identify the gospel with messages of prosperity and national strength. Luther's idea of the Spirit as the courage by which we testify to the truth we have received in Jesus Christ offers a resource to all those seeking "spiritual revolution," both inside and outside the church.

For the Work of Social Justice

A number of years ago, Lutheran ethicist Cynthia Moe-Lobeda wrote a paper on the Holy Spirit as the "power for confessing faith in the midst of empire."[115] Moe-Lobeda quotes Luther's sermon on the sixteenth Sunday after the Trinity

---

109. For an interesting discussion of Luther's view of spiritual warfare in dialogue with Pentecostal ideas, see Courey, *What Has Wittenberg to Do with Azusa?*, 116–21.

110. *LW* 24:118.

111. *LW* 24:292, 357.

112. *LW* 24:116.

113. *LW* 24:117.

114. *LW* 24:116.

115. Cynthia Moe-Lobeda, "The Holy Spirit: Power for Confessing Faith in the Midst of Empire," in *Being the Church in the Midst of Empire: Trinitarian Reflections*, ed. Karen L. Bloomquist (Minneapolis: Lutheran University Press, 2010), 125–46.

in which he, very much in the vein of his sermons on John, calls the Spirit "bold, undaunted courage."[116] She examines the gulf between this powerful description of the Spirit (which she shows is rooted in the scriptural witness) and the failure of churches in North America to act on it, instead falling into complicity with the forces of empire. She points out how the Spirit has been "interiorized," and so domesticated, by Western Christianity, starting with Augustine and perhaps culminating in some forms of "seeker" spiritualties today not associated with justice (although, as we have seen, that does not characterize all those who claim to be SBNR).

In a more recent essay, Moe-Lobeda outlines a pneumatology for spiritual empowerment to reverse the horrific trajectory of climate change, pointing to resources in Scripture and theology that teach that "the Holy Spirit empowers human beings to participate in God's healing and liberating engagement with the world."[117] This is an "unclaimed power," she argues, giving moral agency to follow God's will (as in sanctification) and "strength, courage to proclaim Jesus as Lord in the face of other gods, prophecy, speaking in tongues, discernment, intercessory prayer, generosity, faith, love, and healing."[118] She adds, "Many of these gifts are useful for neighbor-love."[119] She discusses several factors that hinder or impede Christians' ability "to receive, trust, and heed the Holy Spirit as moral-spiritual power for countering the ways of life that breed climate injustice and for building more just and regenerative alternatives."[120] One such factor is ecclesial fear of the Spirit's power, especially as manifested in charismatic and prophetic movements. She writes, "Perhaps in our day another threat that the Spirit presents to structures of power and privilege is the insistence by Paul that the gifts of the Spirit are meant to be used for the common good, not for the private good."[121] This flies in the face of the mandates and norms of profit-driven global capitalism, which too often do not count the social and ecological costs of wealth accumulation. The Holy Spirit gives courage for another way of life, one that draws people to an allegiance to God

---

116. Moe-Lobeda, "Holy Spirit," 127.
117. Cynthia Moe-Lobeda, "The Spirit as Moral-Spiritual Power for Earth-Honoring, Justice-Seeking Ways of Shaping Our Life in Common," in *Planetary Solidarity: Global Women's Voices on Christian Doctrine and Climate Justice*, ed. Grace Ji-Sun Kim and Hilda P. Koster (Minneapolis: Fortress, 2017), 250.
118. Moe-Lobeda, "Spirit as Moral-Spiritual Power," 252, 256.
119. Moe-Lobeda, "Spirit as Moral-Spiritual Power," 256.
120. Moe-Lobeda, "Spirit as Moral-Spiritual Power," 258.
121. Moe-Lobeda, "Spirit as Moral-Spiritual Power," 264.

over earthly authorities and enables believers to follow the way of Jesus and to confront powers that oppose it.

Moe-Lobeda concludes her essay by exploring ways that the Spirit might work through us, transforming people to respond to social and ecological injustices in the world today. As the Spirit of Truth, the Holy Spirit cultivates moral vision as a spiritual practice. Such vision can expose the truth about climate change and other injustices and reveal more ecologically sustainable ways of living. The Spirit can also open our eyes to see that humans are not alone in the quest for a more just world. The Spirit "is with and within Earth's elements and creatures, luring creation toward God's intent that all may have life and have it abundantly (John 10:10),"[122] opening our eyes to see goodness and beauty in all things.

Although Moe-Lobeda shifts between speaking of the Spirit in terms personal (as the one who empowers) and impersonal (as moral-spiritual power itself), her turn to pneumatology to address this aspect of the church's holistic mission—the work of social justice—is fresh and compelling. It also provides an interesting point of connection with the work of Wenk and other Pentecostal theologians who have also turned to pneumatology as a resource for doing the work of justice.[123]

Conclusion: The Spirit as the Empowerer for the Movement of God's Mission in the World

The movement of the Holy Spirit to empower believers to participate in the mission of God in ministries of evangelism and justice historically has not received the same attention in Lutheran theology as it has in Pentecostal theology, with its emphases on spiritual empowerment, spiritual gifts, and the related theological idea of "baptism in the Holy Spirit." I have suggested some ways that we Lutherans can learn from our Pentecostal siblings in this regard and thereby affirm the work of the Holy Spirit as empowerment through various charismata, or spiritual gifts, within a Lutheran framework. I have proposed viewing the Holy Spirit as the one who accompanies through empowerment—as

122. Moe-Lobeda, "Spirit as Moral-Spiritual Power," 269.

123. See, e.g., Michael Wilkinson and Steven M. Studebaker, eds., *A Liberating Spirit: Pentecostals and Social Action in North America* (Eugene, OR: Pickwick, 2010); Antipas Harris, ed., *The Mighty Transformer: The Holy Spirit Advocates for Social Justice* (Irving, TX: GIELD Academic, 2019); and Antipas Harris and Michael Palmer, eds., *The Holy Spirit and Social Justice: Scripture and Theology* (Lanham, MD: Seymour Press, 2019).

the empowerer gifting believers to be witnesses in word and deed to God's in-breaking kingdom.

Whenever Lutherans speak about the Holy Spirit and power regarding the church's mission, it is important not to lose sight of the cross. The apostle Paul, who wrote about the spiritual gifts in Romans 12 and 1 Corinthians 12, also claimed to preach nothing more or less than Christ crucified (1 Cor. 2:2). For Luther, God's power is most mightily manifested at the cross, not in displays of signs and wonders. A theologian of the cross will view power from the foot of the cross, not from the heights of heaven. Pentecostal David Courey suggests that this is at the root of Luther's ambiguity of human experience and caution about exercising the spiritual gifts, quoting Luther: "Among Christians there have been many who had fine charismatic gifts (Gnadengaben). Some were able to do miracles, and yet this served the devil."[124] Even so, as Luther states, citing St. Peter, we are called to "use the gifts called spiritual—gifts of the Holy Spirit—in the Christian Church 'as good stewards of the manifold grace of God'" and in obedience "to the particular calling and work assigned of God."[125]

In the next chapter, we consider the means through which the Spirit works to justify, sanctify, and empower. We consider the proclamation of the Word and the sacraments as well as the other "means" mentioned by Luther in the Smalcald Articles, including the "mutual conversation and consolation" of siblings in Christ. In this context, we revisit how Pentecostal and charismatic Christians experience the Holy Spirit through the Spirit's visitation in worship and praise and through the spiritual gifts themselves.

124. Courey, *What Has Wittenberg to Do with Azusa?*, 120.
125. Luther, "Sunday after Ascension Day," 7:323.

6

The Means of the Spirit's Work

Word, Sacraments, and Charisms

In this chapter, I consider the means through which the Spirit works in the life of the Christian in all three movements: in justification (as the giver of life), in sanctification (as the companion who dwells in us), and in mission (as the companion who empowers us, or the empowerer). We have already seen references to such means in previous chapters. For example, Pentecostals expect to encounter the Holy Spirit in worship, as they share the Word, praise God, and pray for one another, including laying on hands for healing and other spiritual gifts. Through such means, but less often through the sacraments of water baptism and the Eucharist (which most Pentecostals understand as ordinances), the Spirit converts, sanctifies, heals, and Spirit-baptizes God's people. Lutherans also see the Spirit at work in worship, but more narrowly: through the proclamation of the gospel and the celebration of the sacraments.[1] The focus

---

Portions of this chapter first appeared in Cheryl M. Peterson, "Theology of the Cross and the Experience of God's Presence: A Lutheran Response to Pentecostal Wonderings," *Dialog* 55, no. 4 (Winter 2016): 316–23; and Sarah Heaner Lancaster and Cheryl M. Peterson, "Table Grace: Communion Distinctions in the Lutheran and Methodist Traditions," *Sacramental Life* 22, no. 1 (Winter 2010): 22–30. Used with permission.

1. For the purposes of this chapter, we will consider the sacraments of baptism and the Eucharist, although penance was one of the Roman Catholic sacraments that Luther and the Reformers

of the Spirit's work through these means also tends to be narrower—that is, the justification of the sinner. However, as we have seen, baptism can provide Lutherans a focal point for sanctification (in terms of a daily return to baptism in repentance) and mission (in terms of a call to service and mission).

I have two goals in this chapter. The first is to bring the Lutheran understanding of the Word and sacraments as embodied "means of the Spirit's work" into conversation with recent Pentecostal scholarship on the sacraments, which is moving in this direction—that is, toward a more sacramental view of water baptism and the Eucharist. The second is to examine, from a Lutheran perspective, the Pentecostal understanding of worship, praise, and spiritual gifts as means through which the Spirit works. I explore how Lutherans might affirm other means of the Spirit's transforming work—especially in sanctification and empowerment—through spiritual gifts like tongues and healing. Through this, we will begin to discover what each tradition might learn from the other regarding the means of the Spirit's work.

The Word and Sacraments as Means of the Spirit's Work: A Lutheran Perspective

Lutherans do teach that Christians experience the presence and person of God the Holy Spirit through the Word in proclamation (and hearing) and more visibly in the sacraments—to bring Christ to the believer, giving them new birth and the faith that receives new life, and to empower them in the new life, in sanctification and mission. Although most Lutherans speak of the Word and sacraments as "means of grace," Article 5 of the Augsburg Confession is clear that the Word and sacraments are means *of the Spirit*. Both the original Latin and German texts specify that it is the Holy Spirit who is given through the Word and sacraments "as through means" or "as through instruments" to produce faith in those who hear.[2] The gospel and sacraments are described as means

---

sometimes included along with baptism and the Eucharist as a means of the Holy Spirit's work, specifically the absolution of sin after confession (following John 20:22–23). Few Lutherans today seek out individual confession and forgiveness, even though it was retained by the Reformers, and a liturgy for this rite appears in recent Lutheran hymnals. See, e.g., *Evangelical Lutheran Worship* (Minneapolis: Augsburg Fortress, 2006), 243–44. It is more common for ELCA members to hear the absolution in corporate worship as part of a "brief order for confession and forgiveness" at the beginning of the Service of Holy Communion. See, e.g., *Evangelical Lutheran Worship*, 94–95.

    2. Augsburg Confession, art. 5 (German text), in *The Book of Concord: The Confessions of the Evangelical Lutheran Church*, ed. Robert Kolb and Timothy J. Wengert (Minneapolis: Fortress, 2000), 40–41. The Augsburg Confession will hereafter be cited as CA, and page references to

and media of the Spirit's personal, salvific, and sanctifying activity, as opposed to the medieval notion of created grace.[3] In this context, by "the Word" Luther means the living, proclaimed Word that actualizes the promises of Christ in the embodied event of speaking and hearing. Faith is produced through hearing the Word, as Melanchthon states.[4] Because the ear is regularly accosted by sounds that it does not choose to hear, the passivity of the believer, the one who receives faith by hearing, is emphasized in the Spirit's justifying action—the action of God "for us." The Word of God is given voice by the preacher on behalf of a congregation as a means of encounter with Christ and his benefits.[5] Through the proclamation of the gospel, the Spirit works to bring believers to faith, as Luther famously states in the Small Catechism: "The Holy Spirit has called me through the gospel."[6] The Holy Spirit enables both the speaking and the hearing of the Word.

Lutherans also speak of baptism and the Eucharist as "visible Words" through which the same promise is given and experienced.[7] As Luther writes, baptism "brings about forgiveness of sins, rescues from death and the devil, and gives eternal salvation to all who believe this, as the words and promises of God declare."[8] Regarding the Eucharist, or Sacrament of the Altar, he writes, "These words, 'Given and shed for you for the forgiveness of sins,' show us that in the Sacrament forgiveness of sins, life, and salvation are given us through these words. For where there is forgiveness of sins, there is also life and salvation."[9] The gospel is proclaimed and received in a visible way: "This is my body, given

---

The Book of Concord will be supplied with the abbreviation BC. Although the Kolb and Wengert translation uses nearly identical language in translating the Latin and German texts, Bernd Oberdorfer points out slight differences in the original languages, whereby the Latin speaks of the Holy Spirit working through these means (as the actor), compared to the German, which speaks of God (the Father) giving the Spirit to the believer through these means. Oberdorfer, "Embodied Spirit: Outlines of Lutheran Pneumatology," in "We Believe in the Holy Spirit": Global Perspectives on Lutheran Identities, ed. Chad M. Rimmer and Cheryl M. Peterson (Leipzig: Evangelische Verlangsanstalt, 2021), 49–51.

3. See the discussion of Regin Prenter's treatment of Luther's pneumatology in chap. 3.

4. Apology of the Augsburg Confession (hereafter cited as AP), 4.74, in BC, 132.

5. See, e.g., Robert W. Jenson, Visible Words: The Interpretation and Practice of Christian Sacraments (Philadelphia: Fortress, 1978). As an aside, this Lutheran understanding of the office of ministry (that privileges the preaching of the Word) provided the rationale that led several Lutheran churches in the United States to begin ordaining women in 1970. Simply put, women also have voices to speak God's Word. See Paul Hinlicky, "Whose Ministry? Whose Church?," Lutheran Forum (2008): 48–53.

6. Martin Luther, "The Creed," 6, Small Catechism, in BC, 355.

7. See Jenson, Visible Words.

8. Martin Luther, "The Sacrament of Holy Baptism," 5–6, Small Catechism, in BC, 359.

9. Martin Luther, "The Sacrament of the Altar," 5–6, Small Catechism, in BC, 362.

for you." Indeed, Luther calls the Sacrament "a short summary" of the whole gospel: "For the Gospel is nothing but a proclamation of God's grace and of the forgiveness of all sins, granted us through the sufferings of Christ. . . . And this same thing, as we have seen, is contained in the words of this testament."[10]

In both sacraments, Lutherans teach and confess that God—not the believer—is the primary actor and is present to give life, salvation, and the forgiveness of sins. As Luther writes in the Small Catechism, in baptism it is not the water that does these things "but the Word of God, which is with and alongside the water, and faith, which trusts this Word of God in the water. . . . With the Word of God it is a baptism, that is, a grace-filled water of life and a 'bath of the new birth in the Holy Spirit.'"[11] In the Eucharist, the bread becomes Christ's own body because of the promise of the gospel attached to it ("This is my body"); it is no longer bread alone but a life-giving means of grace for those who eat and drink. Christ comes to us *in* the bread and the wine, and we receive the whole Christ (human and divine, crucified and risen) and the benefits that come with him (forgiveness of sins, life, and salvation) when we partake of the meal.

Robert Jenson writes, "The main thing to remember is that what Lutheranism says about sacraments is always a specification of what it says about the gospel communication event in general."[12] What the gospel communicates and promises is God's self-giving love in and through the risen Christ, as a present reality. In the visible Word of the Lord's Supper, the gospel is communicated in a real and embodied way—by Christ's true presence in and under the bread and wine.[13]

However, for a sacrament to be efficacious or beneficial to someone (i.e., to work in someone's life to bring them life, salvation, and the forgiveness of sins), faith is needed. As we have seen, for Lutherans faith itself is understood as a gift of the Holy Spirit, who is given through these means to the Christian. On the one hand, "faith alone" is the means through which we receive the salvation won by Christ. On the other hand, the Word and the sacraments—in this case, especially baptism—are God's external means through which God the Holy Spirit engenders that saving faith in us. Although faith alone saves, this

---

10. Martin Luther, "A Treatise on the New Testament, that is, The Holy Mass," *Luther's Works*, American ed., 55 vols. (Philadelphia: Fortress; St. Louis: Concordia, 1955–86), 35:106. *Luther's Works* is hereafter cited as LW.

11. Luther, "Sacrament of Holy Baptism," 9–10, Small Catechism, in *BC*, 359.

12. Eric W. Gritsch and Robert W. Jenson, *Lutheranism: The Theological Movement and Its Confessional Writing* (Philadelphia: Fortress, 1976), 85.

13. Gritsch and Jenson, *Lutheranism*, 86.

faith comes to us by the Holy Spirit working through these external means or instruments. The Eucharist was instituted "to awaken our faith and comfort our consciences."[14] When God's people receive the Sacrament, they receive the assurance of the forgiveness of sins, which Luther calls "food for the soul, for it nourishes and strengthens the new creature."[15]

The focus in Lutheran sacramental theology tends to be on the Spirit's first movement in the Christian life, whereby sinners are justified and forgiven. German Lutheran theologian Wolfhart Pannenberg has criticized what he calls "the Lutheran distortion of the meaning of the Eucharist," in celebrating it as "primarily a visible and touchable assurance to the individual of the forgiveness of sins."[16] It is important to remember that Luther's distinctive emphasis on the evangelical promise "for you, for the forgiveness of sins" was developed in view of certain late medieval practices (such as masses for the dead), which obfuscated the supper as "pure gospel" and the priority of God's action in the meal.

The focus on forgiveness is still central to Lutheran piety, but since the late twentieth century it has been broadened to include other aspects such as reconciliation, communion-fellowship, and participation in Christ's life. What has received less attention is the Spirit's sanctifying and empowering work through the means of grace; however, as we have seen, Luther is quick to remind us, "For where there is forgiveness of sins, there is also life and salvation." If the Eucharist is "food for the soul" that "nourishes and strengthens the new creature,"[17] surely the Holy Spirit is not only strengthening the believer in their faith through this means but also strengthening and empowering them in their new life with Christ, a new life received in justification, on account of Christ. Luther speaks of the strength needed to face hindrances and temptations so that our faith grows stronger and the new life in us "continually develops and progresses." Through regular reception of the Eucharist, one receives not only comfort but also "new strength and refreshment."[18]

Luther reasons that since children are received into the church through baptism, they too "should enjoy this communion of the sacrament, in order that they may serve us and be useful to us; for they must all indeed help us to believe, love, pray and fight against the devil."[19] We also recall Luther's understanding

14. CA 24.30, in BC, 70.
15. Luther, "Sacrament of the Altar," 23, Large Catechism, in BC, 469.
16. Wolfhart Pannenberg, Christian Spirituality (Philadelphia: Westminster, 1983), 40–41.
17. Luther, "Sacrament of the Altar," 23, Large Catechism, in BC, 469.
18. Luther, "Sacrament of the Altar," 24–27, Large Catechism, in BC, 469.
19. Luther, "Sacrament of the Altar," 87, Large Catechism, in BC, 476.

of the "full forgiveness of sins," which includes not only our being forgiven by God in Christ but also our forgiving, bearing with, and aiding one another. In an earlier treatise, the 1519 "Sermon on the Sacrament of the Holy and True Body of Christ," Luther explains how the Spirit works through us, by means of the Sacrament, to serve the neighbor. Luther speaks of an "interchange of [Christ's] blessings and our misfortunes," by which Christ takes upon himself our form (i.e., our sin and infirmity), and we take on his form (i.e., his righteousness). He goes on to say, "Through this same love, we are to be changed and to make the infirmities of all other Christians our own; we are to take upon ourselves their form and their necessity, and all the good that is within our power we are to make theirs, that they may profit from it. . . . In this way we are changed into one another and are made into a community by love."[20]

The Sacraments in Recent Pentecostal Theology

For most Pentecostals, the Spirit's presence and power are experienced primarily through worship/singing, laying on of hands, prayer (including tongues), and altar calls. Although Lutherans will speak of experiencing God intimately in worship (especially at the Eucharist and in singing), for Pentecostals the time of worship and praise is explicitly identified as a time "where God is invited to be present" and "to have His way." The "means of grace" for Pentecostals include all the ways God is present to heal and make whole, not just through the forgiveness of sins, as tends to be the Lutheran focus. For example, Pentecostals believe that prayer and the laying on of hands bring God's healing grace and presence to someone in physical or emotional pain.

Pentecostals also center their worship on God speaking through the Word to those gathered. God's love and power are encountered through preaching and sharing of testimonies, although the sermon can also have a didactic role. For most Pentecostals, baptism and the Lord's Supper are viewed as ordinances, done in response to Jesus's scriptural command as signs of what grace God has already worked in the believer's heart, rather than as means through which God offers grace. However, an increasing number of Pentecostal theologians have begun to embrace the sacramentality of baptism, the Lord's Supper, and other embodied practices. Charismatic theologian Chris Green offers a helpful overview of what he calls the "sacramental turn" in Pentecostal

20. LW 35:58.

theology.[21] He acknowledges the widespread perception that Pentecostals are not sacramental, or are even anti-sacramental. However, sacraments held a more prominent place in early Pentecostalism than they do today. Pentecostal spirituality, by definition, is "inherently sacramental"—that is, it already holds the view that the visible can reveal that which is invisible or spiritual.[22] This is something that struck me when I began to worship with Pentecostals and study the Pentecostal movement. If God could work through someone's hands or a blessed handkerchief to heal, for example, then why couldn't the Holy Spirit work also through water, bread, and wine? It is simply not the case that Pentecostals advocate an "unmediated encounter with God," as Frank Macchia points out.[23] Pentecostals believe and teach that the Holy Spirit works through embodied means to save, sanctify, heal, and empower God's people. Amos Yong argues that Pentecostals need not fear the more traditional sacraments because there is already a "unique sacramentality" in Pentecostal spirituality that is experiential and incarnational.[24] Indeed, as Daniel Tomberlin puts it, it should be an "easy leap of faith" for Pentecostals to affirm the sacraments as a means of grace through which the Holy Spirit is encountered.[25] Green shows how this "turn" is actually a return to the sacramental practices of many early Pentecostal leaders.[26] He laments the movement away from the celebration of the Eucharist as an "efficacious participation in the divine life" to one of re-membrance and imitation of Jesus's actions on the night of his betrayal, a shift he attributes to "the influence of a low-church, conversionist evangelicalism."[27] Although informed by church tradition and ecumenical dialogue partners, a return to sacramental practices need not be feared as "too Catholic," ritualistic,

---

21. Chris E. W. Green, "Sacraments: Rites in the Spirit for the Presence of Christ," in *The Routledge Handbook of Pentecostal Theology*, ed. Wolfgang Vondey (New York: Routledge, 2020), 311–20. In his popular treatment of the subject, Daniel Tomberlin agrees that Pentecostalism is "essentially sacramental." See Tomberlin, *Pentecostal Sacraments: Encountering God at the Altar* (Cleveland, TN: Center for Pentecostal Leadership and Care, 2010), 73–74. Green's roots are Pentecostal, but he is currently an ordained priest in the Continuing Evangelical Episcopal Communion, a charismatic Anglican church. For more information, see https://ceec.church /ceec/.

22. Green, "Sacraments," 311.

23. Frank D. Macchia, "Tongues as a Sign: Toward a Sacramental Understanding of Pentecostal Experience," *Pneuma* 15, no. 1 (1993): 76.

24. Amos Yong, *The Spirit Poured Out on all Flesh: Pentecostal and the Possibility of Global Theology* (Grand Rapids: Baker Academic, 2005), 136.

25. Tomberlin, *Pentecostal Sacraments*, 82.

26. Green, "Sacraments"; also, Green, *Toward a Pentecostal Theology of the Lord's Supper: Fore-tasting the Kingdom* (Cleveland, TN: CPT, 2012).

27. Green, "Sacraments," 314–15.

or mechanistic, Green insists, if the focus is on "practicing the sacraments *as* Pentecostals."[28]

This shift in thinking began when certain Pentecostal scholars, especially John Christopher Thomas and Frank Macchia, began to explore foot washing and speaking in tongues in sacramental terms.[29] Drawing on Macchia and his own previous work, Thomas developed a schema that connects a sacramental sign to each pillar of the fivefold gospel for Wesleyan Pentecostals: water baptism as a sign of salvation (Jesus as Savior), foot washing as a sign of sanctification (Jesus as Sanctifier), speaking in tongues as a sign of Spirit baptism (Jesus as Baptizer), the laying on of hands as a sign of healing (Jesus as Healer), and the Lord's Supper as a sign of eschatological hope (Jesus as the Coming King).[30] Subsequently, several Pentecostal scholars—including Macchia, Yong, Kenneth Archer, Wolfgang Vondey, Jean-Daniel Plüss, and Lisa Stephenson—have encouraged Pentecostals to take more seriously the historic church's traditional teachings on sacraments and practices and have made proposals in that direction.[31]

However, even with all this renewed attention to sacraments, Green admits, "no single sacramental definition or ritual has been agreed upon."[32] Further, although these scholars agree that the believer encounters Christ through the power of the Spirit in these sacramental acts, the purpose of that encounter can vary. For example, Green and Vondey connect the Eucharist, rather than foot washing, to the Spirit's work in sanctification, both as a means of encountering

28. Green, "Sacraments," 317.

29. In addition to Macchia, "Tongues as a Sign," see John Christopher Thomas, *Footwashing in John 13 and the Johannine Community* (Sheffield, UK: Sheffield Academic, 1991); and Macchia's response to Thomas, "Is Footwashing the Neglected Sacrament? A Response to John Christopher Thomas," *Pneuma* 19, no. 2 (1997): 239–49. Steven Studebaker also attributes the increase in appreciation for the sacraments by Pentecostals to their more than fifty-year official dialogue with Roman Catholics, which is also seen in Macchia's piece on tongues. See Studebaker, "Baptism among the Pentecostals," in *Baptism: Historical, Theological, and Pastoral Perspectives*, ed. Gordon L. Heath and James D. Dvorak (Eugene, OR: Wipf & Stock, 2011), 209.

30. See John Christopher Thomas's 1998 presidential address to the Society for Pentecostal Studies, "Pentecostal Theology in the Twenty-First Century," *Pneuma* 20, no. 1 (1998): 18–19.

31. Kenneth Archer further developed Thomas's proposal of five sacraments to correspond to the fivefold gospel. See Archer, "Nourishment for the Journey: The Pentecostal *Via Salutis* and Sacramental Ordinances," *Journal for Pentecostal Theology* 13, no. 1 (2004): 76–96, esp. 88–95. See also Tomberlin, *Pentecostal Sacraments*, who develops this proposal further still in his popular treatment but does not include a chapter on tongues as sacrament. See also Jean-Daniel Plüss, "Sacrament or Ordinance: A Pentecostal Approach to a Contentious Issue," in *Pentecostals in the Twenty-First Century: Identity, Beliefs, Praxis*, eds. Corneliu Constantineanu and Christopher J. Scobie (Eugene, OR: Cascade Books, 2018), 59–75.

32. Green, "Sacraments," 314.

the divine presence and as a means of transforming the believer to walk in the new life of the Spirit.[33] In a similar vein, Macchia writes, "Jesus is present through the Holy Spirit during the eucharistic meal to commune with believers, to transform them toward greater love and holiness, and to heal them in body and mind."[34] Tomberlin also connects the Eucharist to sanctification and healing, recalling that early Pentecostals "affirmed the ancient understanding of the eucharist as therapeutic," arguing that through the connection to divine healing, Pentecostals can affirm the Lord's Supper as a sacrament, a "means of grace in which Christ is present."[35] Interestingly, Tomberlin highlights the altar as the place of encounter for Pentecostals, not only through the traditional "altar call" but also as the place where we present ourselves to God in worship, to be baptized and to receive the Lord's Supper. Tomberlin even suggests that the celebration of the sacraments may be considered an "on-going altar call."[36]

In summary, the shift to a more sacramental understanding of the ordinances is rooted in the expectation of those who gather for worship "that they will encounter the presence of Christ through the Spirit in these celebrative activities."[37] If Pentecostals expect to encounter God in the church's worship, then why not also in the bread and wine of Holy Communion and in the water of Holy Baptism?

A Lutheran Engagement with Recent Pentecostal Sacramental Theology

As a Lutheran, I affirm this sacramental shift in Pentecostal theology and recognize that there are more points of connection between our traditions than is commonly thought. This was acknowledged in the document produced by the "proto-dialogue" of the Lutheran-Pentecostal dialogue in 2010, which focused

33. Green, "Sacraments," 317; and Wolfgang Vondey, *Pentecostal Theology: Living the Full Gospel, Systematic Pentecostal and Charismatic Theology* (New York: Bloomsbury T&T Clark, 2017), 60–67.

34. Frank D. Macchia, *Baptized in the Spirit: A Global Pentecostal Theology* (Grand Rapids: Zondervan, 2006), 189.

35. Tomberlin, *Pentecostal Sacraments*, 244, 177.

36. Tomberlin, *Pentecostal Sacraments*, 27, 103. To this point, see also Vondey, *Pentecostal Theology*, esp. 5–10, 40–43. Space does not permit a full discussion of the sacrament of "water baptism," including its relationship to Spirit baptism. For more on this, see Sarah Hinlicky Wilson, *A Guide to Pentecostal Movements for Lutherans* (Eugene, OR: Wipf & Stock, 2016), 34–61; Studebaker, "Baptism among the Pentecostals," 201–24; and Anthony Ray Williams, *Washed in the Spirit: Toward a Pentecostal Theology of Water Baptism* (Cleveland, TN: CPT, 2021).

37. Archer, "Nourishment for the Journey," 18.

on how both traditions encounter Christ. While acknowledging the variety of Pentecostal understandings on Christ's presence in the Lord's Supper, the document suggests that "practical experience and piety indicate that Pentecostals actually believe in some kind of real presence beyond a strictly symbolic or memorial understanding of the Supper."[38] Although there is no agreed-on definition of a sacrament, by and large these Pentecostal theologians emphasize that the Spirit works to encounter the believer through embodied and material means and that grace is received through these encounters.

Because Lutherans have a more precise definition of a sacrament, any additional proposed sacraments must meet this criterion. As noted above, the Reformers often included absolution as a third sacrament. In "The Babylonian Captivity of the Church" (1520), Luther initially proposes three sacraments— "baptism, penance, and the bread"—but by the end of the treatise he limits the number to only two, baptism and the Lord's Supper, since only they have "divinely instituted visible sign[s]" (water in baptism and bread and wine in the Eucharist).[39] However, in the Apology of the Augsburg Confession, Melanchthon writes that "the sacraments are actually baptism, the Lord's Supper, and absolution (the sacrament of repentance)."[40] He says, "No intelligent person will argue much about the number or terminology, as long as those things are retained that have the mandate and promises of God."[41] For Lutherans, a sacrament is not just an embodied means of an invisible or supernatural grace; that grace must be grounded in the Word of God. Luther connects the Word of God to the elements in two ways: as divinely commanded or instituted in Scripture, and as having a divine promise of salvation attached to it. The grace that it effects, in other words, must be salvific. What makes a sacrament is not only that the Spirit works through material means but also that the Spirit attaches the Word of promise, the gospel, to these means and through them brings "life, salvation, and the forgiveness of sins." Gordon Jensen writes, "Luther came to emphasize the connection of the outward sign—the earthly elements—to the proclaimed word of gospel, a grace that was dynamic rather than a static

38. *Lutherans and Pentecostals in Dialogue* (Strasbourg, France: Institute for Ecumenical Research, 2010), 17–18. https://ecumenical-institute.org/wp-content/uploads/2022/06/Lutherans-and-Pentecostals-in-Dialogue-Text-FINAL.pdf.

39. *LW* 36:18, 124. See also Gordon A. Jensen, "Sacramental Theology," in *The Oxford Encyclopedia of Martin Luther*, vol. 3, ed. Derek R. Nelson and Paul R. Hinlicky (New York: Oxford University Press, 2017), 309–11.

40. AP 13.4, in *BC*, 219.

41. AP 13.17, in *BC*, 221.

commodity to be possessed inwardly."[42] This would be affirmed by Melanch-thon, in Article 5 of the Augsburg Confession, who wrote that through these means the Spirit works to bring the gospel and create faith in the believer.

Foot washing is commanded by Jesus and has an earthly element (water); however, it does not contain a promise of salvific grace. Jesus explains that he washed his disciples' feet to provide an example for them (John 13:15). Lu-therans traditionally observe this practice liturgically on Maundy Thursday, the same night that Jesus instituted the love commandment (John 13:34–35). This action could be connected to sanctification in providing an example of holy servanthood, but not as a means by which one receives the indwelling of the Spirit. On this basis, most Lutherans would not accept foot washing as a sacrament in the technical sense. In a Maundy Thursday sermon on John 13, Luther addresses foot washing as an example of humility Christ gives to his disciples. He fears that foot washing has, in his day, become an empty ritual, an outward show of care for the poor that is performed without substantially addressing or changing the material poverty of those whose feet are washed. At the end of the sermon, he seems to contrast the practice of foot washing with the "washing of sin" by Jesus's blood shed on the cross, received through Holy Baptism.[43] The other two practices proposed as sacraments by Thomas and others, laying on of hands / anointing for healing and speaking in tongues, come closer to but do not fully fit the Lutheran understanding. However, they can and should be affirmed as signs and means of the Spirit's work, especially in sanctification and mission.

Laying on of Hands / Anointing for Healing

Of the distinctive Pentecostal practices, laying on of hands / anointing for healing comes the closest to meeting Luther's criteria for a sacrament. There are physical means and, when oil is used, a material element through which the Spirit works. There is a scriptural basis. Although Jesus does not command his followers to heal, he expects them to, and James does exhort the disciples to anoint the sick with oil and pray for them, that they may be healed (James 5:13–16). Also, a salvific promise is attached to the act, if one considers healing as an aspect of salvation, as many Wesleyans and Pentecostals do. In the healing

42. Jensen, "Sacramental Theology," 308.
43. See Martin Luther, "Thursday before Easter," in *Dr. Martin Luther's House-Postil, or Sermons on the Gospels*, vol. 2 (Columbus, OH: J. A. Schultz, 1884), 24–41, esp. 36, 41.

stories in the Gospels, a clear-cut distinction does not always exist between spiritual healing (including forgiveness of sins) and physical healing. When Jesus heals someone, he makes them whole in mind, spirit, and body. For example, in Mark, Jesus tells a paralytic man "Your sins are forgiven" before healing him with the command "Stand up, take your mat and go to your home" (Mark 2:5, 11). Lutheran theologian Christoffer Gundemann writes, "The simple fact that Jesus healed clearly indicates that to him salvation had an unquestionable bodily dimension."[44] Although healing is not synonymous with salvation (not everyone who was healed came to faith in Jesus or became his disciples, as we see in Mark 2), salvation can include healing as one legitimate corporeal aspect of salvation.

The International Lutheran-Pentecostal Dialogue statement addresses healing, noting that "we should pray faithfully and ardently for healing," following Luther's commendation of prayer in the Large Catechism "as strictly and solemnly commanded as all the other commandments." However, the report cautions against identifying the communion with the triune God that is promised through the gospel now and in eternity with the promise of complete physical healing in this life to those who are "truly faithful." Such a "promise" falsely suggests that if someone is not healed, it is because they do not have enough faith.[45]

This conditionality creates difficulties for Lutherans for considering anointing and prayers for healing as a sacrament. Salvation can include physical healing, but it does not always. Not everyone we pray for and anoint will be physically healed by God's healing grace. Bodily healing is not something we can promise to all whom we pray for and anoint, the way we can promise that forgiveness of sins, life, and salvation are offered through the sacraments of baptism and the Lord's Supper. Many people are not healed bodily by these means, but those who are healed experience God's grace and power and can witness to that experience. As in the Gospel accounts, when one is healed physically, it is a sign to them—and others—of the presence of God and God's in-breaking kingdom. Jan-Olav Henriksen writes, "Experiences of healing should not be seen as an opportunity to escape the conditions of this world but as signs of a reality that is not yet realized. As concrete and broken symbols, such healings testify to

44. Christoffer Grundmann, "He Sent Them Out to Heal: Reflections on the Healing Ministry of the Church," *Currents in Theology and Mission* 33, no. 5 (October 2006): 374.

45. Dirk G. Lange, Paula Mumia, Jean-Daniel Plüss, and Sarah Hinlicky Wilson, eds., *International Lutheran-Pentecostal 2016–2022 Dialogue Statement: "The Spirit of the Lord Is Upon Me"* (Geneva: LWF, 2023), 36, §78. https://www.lutheranworld.org/resources/publication-spirit-lord-upon-me. See also Jensen, "Sacramental Theology," 310.

and *reveal* the care, compassion, and love of God that is not yet realized fully in the world. Furthermore, their finite and broken character warns us, in good Lutheran fashion, against any *theologia gloriae*."[46]

Healing also can be a means by which God's transforming grace is experienced in a human body, "enabling nature to become fulfilled or to be realized in new ways that are beyond the measures and capacities that the body can provide by itself."[47] Finally, while for Lutherans faith is not a condition for God's healing, faith can be strengthened and transformed by it. "As the Spirit is the one who creates life, and life is always embodied life, healing of the body is for the sake of the fullness of the human being's life," enabling us to become more fully the people God created us to be. But this is true also for the one who remains ill. They too are "recognized in the kingdom as a whole person, created in the image of God." Even in their condition of being ill, they are also "a witness to the gifts of God, and a receiver of God's caring love and compassion."[48]

Lutherans can affirm healing as the Spirit's work to accompany the believer in sanctification (growing in love of God and neighbor) and as the fruit of the Spirit. Healing can be experienced as an extension of God's grace working in our lives, to rid us not only of physical ailments but also of obstacles to experiencing God's love. However, as Henriksen reminds us, it is important to affirm that God's presence is also experienced when healing does not come quickly, or at all. In such cases, God may be present as the one who suffers with us, or as a "middle Spirit" (as Shelly Rambo has suggested, especially for survivors of trauma). The role of the Spirit here is to enable survivors of trauma to remember not only the events of the past but also the memory of Jesus, and then to accompany them into a new life that does not hide their scars but brings them forward in witness.[49]

Speaking in Tongues

Several scholars, both Pentecostal and non-Pentecostal, have noted a sacramental element in the Pentecostal practice of speaking in tongues, "making

---

46. Jan-Olav Henriksen, "Towards a Lutheran Theology of Bodily Healing," *Ritröð Guð-fræðistofnunar* (*Studia Theologica Islandica*) 50 (2020): 11–12.
47. Henriksen, "Towards a Lutheran Theology of Bodily Healing," 12.
48. Henriksen, "Towards a Lutheran Theology of Bodily Healing," 14.
49. For an engagement of Rambo's idea with Pentecostal theology, see Cheryl M. Peterson, "Pneumatology in the Age of #MeToo: An Exploration of the Spirit's Role in Suffering," in *Sisters, Mothers, Daughters: Pentecostal Perspectives on Violence against Women*, ed. Kimberly Irvin Alexander et al. (Boston: Brill, 2022), 13–32.

God present for Pentecostals in a special, audibly identifiable way."[50] Macchia makes a compelling case for considering tongues as a sacramental experience, if not as a sacrament in the classic sense. His caution regarding the latter reflects the Pentecostal fear that such a designation would imply "an understanding of sacramental efficacy as necessitated by a causative dynamic intrinsic to the element, thereby institutionalizing or formalizing the free Spirit or grace of God."[51] Macchia further discusses the issue of "causation," and while not referring to the Latin term *ex opere operato* (effected by the work performed), this seems to be what he has in mind. Luther also challenged such mechanical views of the sacrament. For him, it is the Word of God with the elements that make something a sacrament, and for the believer to receive the sacrament's benefits (i.e., for the sacrament to be efficacious), faith must be present. Tongues are clearly an embodied encounter with the Holy Spirit and, in this regard, have a sacramental quality.

Although tongues feature in Acts and 1 Corinthians as a sign of the Spirit's outpouring on the disciples (and other groups and individuals), nowhere in Scripture are tongues commanded; indeed, they are not even promoted by Paul in his discussion of the spiritual gifts in 1 Corinthians 12:1–11. Paul clearly believes that other spiritual gifts are more useful for the ministry of the church, and yet it is hard to argue with the impact that speaking in tongues has on people. This is the case not only for Pentecostals but also for Lutheran (and other mainline) charismatics, as we saw in the previous chapter. Speaking in tongues is a powerful embodied experience of God's love and power in one's life that often leads to personal transformation in other ways. However, this experience does not have a promise of salvation attached to it; it is not "necessary" for salvation the way that conversion is for Pentecostals, which comes through hearing the Word of God. In Macchia's more expansive understanding of Spirit baptism, one could connect tongues to salvation in a broader sense, as a means not of receiving salvation but of enjoying, participating in, and experiencing it. In classical trinitarian Pentecostalism, of course, tongues are also the initial evidence of Spirit baptism, which historically has been connected to empowerment for mission, as discussed in the previous chapter. Macchia writes, "Pentecostals regard tongues as a kind of primary sacrament or Kairos event that signifies, while participating in, the empowerment of the Spirit in the Christian life."[52]

50. Macchia, "Tongues as a Sign," 61.
51. Macchia, "Tongues as a Sign," 61–62.
52. Macchia, "Tongues as a Sign," 69.

Macchia notes a significant difference between the "sacramentality" of tongues and that of the ecclesial sacraments, such as baptism and the Eucharist. "Tongues represent a spontaneous charismatic sign that accents the free and unforeseen aspects of the divine/human encounter," whereas ecclesial sacraments occur in an ordered liturgy of the church, overseen by set-apart ministers (priests or pastors).[53] Macchia fears that by emphasizing the institutional and ecclesial aspects of sacramental worship, the free movement of the Holy Spirit can be restricted and prevented from encountering believers in "surprising and disturbing" ways.[54] He proposes that these theological emphases—ecclesial sacraments celebrated in liturgical worship and a more "inchoate" sacramentality of the charisms, especially tongues—are more complementary than not.

As we have seen, Macchia's proposal is being explored from the Pentecostal side, as Pentecostals reconceive their sacramental theology in ways that embrace the "ecclesial sacraments" of baptism and the Eucharist, along with more distinctively Pentecostal practices with a sacramental character (such as healing, tongues, and foot washing) as means through which the Spirit encounters believers. Now I wish to explore his proposal from the Lutheran side by asking how Lutherans might affirm the Spirit's work through means other than the Word and sacraments, such as the experience of worship itself and the charisms, especially when we move beyond the work of the Spirit in justification as God "for us," to the work of the Spirit in sanctification as God "in us," and to the work of the Spirit in mission as God "through us."

The Spirit's Work through the Charisms: A Lutheran Consideration

While Lutherans rightly emphasize the proclaimed Word and sacraments as the indispensable, primary means through which the Holy Spirit works, it is hard to deny that the presence of God is experienced by Christians through other means, such as prayer and worship.[55] As we saw in chapter 1, not only do Pentecostals experience God in tangible, transformative ways, but they also come to worship with the expectation that God will meet them there. This has

53. Macchia, "Tongues as a Sign," 72.
54. Macchia, "Tongues as a Sign," 73.
55. When discussing the number of sacraments, Melanchthon asks, perhaps rhetorically, if everything that has the command of God and a promise of grace attached to it could be called a sacrament, then why not include prayer? "Were it included among the sacraments, as though in a more exalted position, it would encourage people to pray." See AP 13.16–17, in BC, 221.

led to several distinctive worship practices, including the giving of testimonies, as witness to the work of God in believers' lives, and the altar call, an invitation to prayer at the altar, which can be for any number of things (e.g., to commit one's life to Christ or to ask for healing or another spiritual gift). Pentecostal congregations receive the proclamation of the minister, but "the response of the congregation to the word is itself part of the proclamation."[56] In addition, Pentecostals believe that the laying on of hands and prayer can serve as "means of empowerment" through which the Holy Spirit empowers someone for ministry with spiritual gifts.

While Lutherans enjoy and can be moved by worship, especially through hymnody, it is not a common practice for Lutherans to invite God "into this space" or to expect to have an "experience" of God's power during worship. Lutheran Christians gather for worship to hear God's Word and to receive assurance and comfort in the gospel message, and then to respond to God's promises with songs of praise, prayers for those in need, and service to their neighbors. It is even less common for Lutherans (apart from charismatic Lutherans) to experience worship as the place where they can be spiritually empowered for that service. However, the idea is found in Lutheran worship, especially in post-communion prayers that connect spiritual empowerment to service. For example, one prayer reads, "O God, we give you thanks that you have set before us this feast, the body and blood of your Son. By your Spirit strengthen us to serve all in need." Another reads, "God of abundance, with this bread of life and cup of salvation you have united us with Christ, making us one with all your people. Now send us forth in the power of your Spirit, that we may proclaim your redeeming love to the world and continue forever in the risen life of Jesus Christ, our Lord."[57] While Lutherans who worship regularly will hear this theme each week, it is, at best, an underdeveloped idea and practice and, at worst, a rote prayer that does not impact worshipers' daily lives. The idea that the Holy Spirit would actualize this empowerment with physical manifestations, as experienced by Pentecostals through impartation and anointing, likely would make most Lutherans (at least those in North America and Europe) uncomfortable and nervous.

If in worship Lutherans tend to focus more on receiving God's promise (and experiencing forgiveness because of it—God "for us"), Pentecostals tend to focus

56. *Lutherans and Pentecostals in Dialogue*, 12.
57. E.g., the second and third of the suggested post-communion prayers in *Evangelical Lutheran Worship*, 114.

more on receiving God's presence and power (God "in us" and "through us"). The Lutheran focus tends to emphasize the passivity of the believer in receiving God's promise of forgiveness of sins rather than the transforming power to make changes in one's own life and, for that matter, to become an agent of change and healing in the world. This focus on being "receivers" rather than "doers" of the Word leads to the oft-made charge that Lutherans are antinomian. However, it is *not* only through the pastor's proclamation in the sermon and the sacraments that the promise of new life in Christ is to be experienced, according to Luther. In the Smalcald Articles, Luther offers a longer list of the ways that the gospel comes to us. Not surprisingly, he begins with the traditional external means of grace—the Word and sacraments—to which he adds the office of the keys (the absolution of sin given by the pastor), which, as noted, was sometimes considered a third sacrament by the Reformers. He goes on to name one more means of grace: the mutual conversation and consolation of the brothers and sisters.[58] Although some scholars believe this phrase refers strictly to the practice of mutual confession,[59] others propose that Luther means something that includes *but goes beyond* the act of confession.[60] I imagine that this mutual conversation and consolation happens whenever Christians speak and enact God's promise of new life to one another, empowered by the Holy Spirit—possibly, as is traditional in Pentecostal worship, by the laying on of hands and praying for and with one another, asking for spiritual gifts to enable one another to serve God and love the neighbor.

According to Heiko Oberman, the chief rediscovery of the Reformation had to do not with Scripture's authority or with the sole efficacy of grace but rather with "the Holy Spirit as the dynamic presence of God."[61] The dynamic personal presence of the Holy Spirit is experienced most powerfully in worship, not only bringing the Christian the Word of promise and the faith to cling to it but also

58. Martin Luther, "Concerning the Gospel," Part 3, Smalcald Articles, Article 4, in *BC*, 319. To this we would add "siblings" to include gender-queer and nonbinary persons.

59. Paul Althaus recognizes that Luther distinguishes the office of the keys (priestly absolution) from "mutual conversation and consolation," but he goes on to argue that the latter cannot be separated from absolution because, according to the Wittenberg Concordia, the goal of conversation is absolution, "and the consolation of the sinner consists in the forgiveness of sins." Althaus, *The Theology of Martin Luther*, trans. Robert C. Schultz (Philadelphia: Fortress, 1979), 318n110.

60. E.g., Julius Köstlin understands this phrase to mean the totality of ministry to someone in distress who is in need of comfort and advice, including but not limited to private absolution. Köstlin, *Theology of Luther in Its Historical Development and Inner Harmony*, 2 vols. trans. Charles E. Hay (Philadelphia: Lutheran Publication Society, 1897), 2:527–32.

61. Heiko A. Oberman, "Preaching and the Word in the Reformation," *Theology Today* 18, no. 1 (April 1961): 21.

moving the Christian to action. This offers a contrast to the medieval tradition of Luther's day that saw the worship service as a place of refuge from the evils of this world, a place of respite for pilgrims on their journey. However, for the Reformers, the congregation "does not flee the world for the sanctuary, nor for that matter does it bring the world into the church, but the service takes place in the world. The world as God's creation, with its needs and promises, is not lost from sight for one moment."[62]

Historically, Lutherans have focused on *diakonia* (service) as the way God's people address the needs of the world, whereas Pentecostals—hearing the same cries of pain in the world—add to *diakonia* prayers of healing, words of wisdom, prophecy, and other charismatic gifts to bring comfort and healing to those in pain and empowerment to others to become healers and speakers of the truth. However, might Lutherans affirm these charismatic gifts together with *diakonia* as ways to experience God's presence in and for the world, as the Spirit "through us"?

A prominent Lutheran liturgist once told a Lutheran pastor friend of mine that it would be inappropriate to have a Pentecostal-style "time of ministry" for prayers for the spiritual gifts following the Eucharist because "we receive everything we need in the Eucharist." However, what if we were to think of the fruit and gifts of the Spirit as ways to experience the presence and grace of God in and through us? What if we thought of these means as enabling us to walk in the Spirit and bear the Spirit's fruit, and empowering us with spiritual gifts to strengthen us as the body of Christ that we receive as a community through Christ's presence with his church in the Eucharist (and Word)? We have already discussed how healing can be an extension of the grace given through Word and Sacrament to be shared by believers for the sake of the body and the world. We have also pointed out that Lutherans have the language, if not the practice, of spiritual empowerment through the Eucharist in their liturgy. These could be ways to live out what Luther means by the "mutual consolation" of siblings in Christ. If mutual confession is a component of that, there is no reason to think that mutual prayers for healing and the empowerment of the Spirit could not also be.

Conclusion

As we have seen, the primary concern Lutherans have about "experience" is that experience itself might become normative for Christian life and theology and

62. Oberman, "Preaching and the Word," 22.

take the place of Scripture as the unnormed and norming norm. The concern is that Scripture, not experience, should always have the last word. The Reformers' primary concern regarding charismatic manifestations of the Holy Spirit was less about the manifestations themselves than about the spiritual elitism of those who claimed them, their disdain for Holy Scripture as norm and judge of all spiritual experiences, and "an insistence on the possession of this Spirit as an inward reality apart from all outward 'means.'"[63]

Regarding all of the spiritual gifts, Karlfried Froehlich offers this helpful perspective. By seeing God only in their own spiritual world, "enthusiasts" such as Andreas von Karlstadt missed seeing God in the "cradle of earthly reality"— that is, incarnationally. If the Spirit is not "found in the lofty world of unreal dreams, then the gifts do not transport us into such a realm either."[64] Froehlich argues that those who yearn to experience the Holy Spirit in sacramental and bodily ways, including through the charismatic phenomena, may reflect "the incarnational emphasis so deeply embedded in the Lutheran tradition, as a longing for the consolation of the Spirit down here on earth, in the concrete experience of our limited human existence."[65] I expect the same might be said of many SBNRs who are seeking a "grounded" spirituality. This brings us back to the concern raised by Luther regarding a theology of glory: that one might boast in one's own reason and experience, making reason and experience normative for knowing who God is. Neither human reason nor human experience can be the basis for our knowledge of God, but only the cross and resurrection of Christ made present to us by the Holy Spirit.

63. Karlfried Froehlich, "Charismatic Manifestations and the Lutheran Incarnational Stance," in *The Holy Spirit in the Life of the Church: From Biblical Times to the Present*, ed. Paul D. Opsahl (Minneapolis: Augsburg, 1978), 141.
64. Froehlich, "Charismatic Manifestations," 149.
65. Froehlich, "Charismatic Manifestations," 149.

Epilogue

As I completed the manuscript for this book, the Holy Spirit seemed to be stirring on several university campuses, starting with Asbury University in Wilmore, Kentucky. On February 8, 2023, the Asbury chapel service did not end but continued for hours, and then days, and then weeks. Other colleges and universities reported similar outpourings of the Spirit.

Revivals are nothing new to Pentecostals. After all, the Pentecostal movement was born out of revival, especially the one at Azusa Street. Pentecostal and charismatic Christians regularly pray for the Spirit to renew the church and its members. Some Pentecostal preachers regularly preach about revival. A Pentecostal scholar once told me that he was frustrated with the pastor at his home church because that is all he ever preached about. He did not disagree on the need for revival but felt that his pastor's sermons should focus on other messages from Scripture as well.

Conversely, it would be difficult to find an American Lutheran pastor who preached on revival even once in a sermon—much less a Lutheran pastor interested in planning and leading one! Indeed, Lutheran Sarah Hinlicky Wilson was caught off guard when asked by Lutherans in Madagascar, "How is your revival going?" When she admitted, "We don't have a revival," they were astonished. After being with the Malagasy Lutheran Church for a few days and experiencing their ministries of healing and deliverance, she began to see that the question might not be so odd after all. Revival is integral to the life of the church in Madagascar, which counts four major revivals since the late nineteenth century. The Malagasy term they use is "fifohazana," which means to be awake, to be alive, and to be active.[1]

When I wrote the epilogue to my first book, *Who Is the Church?*, I proposed that what the church needed was not a "plan for survival" but rather a "vision for revival."[2] I knew the use of this word would be provocative for most Lutherans and many mainline Protestant Christians in the US. Many Lutherans associate revivals with worship practices that are usually nonsacramental, overly concerned with individual salvation, associated with "decision theology" and emotionalism, and that often lack decorum and good order. Or as Wilson puts it, since revivals are inherently anti-institutional, anti-intellectual, and anti-liturgical, they "perfectly embody everything Lutherans oppose."[3]

However, by using the term "revival," I simply wanted to retrieve its most basic meaning—that is, to "bring back to life," like the fifohazana in the Malagasy Lutheran Church. I contemplated what it might look like to be revived by the Spirit. What would it mean for congregations to reclaim an identity as a Spirit-breathed people, to consider that the same Spirit who raised Jesus from the dead is also raising them to new life—a life to be shared with the world? In this book, I have explored the work of the Holy Spirit in the Christian life in terms of who the Holy Spirit is *for* us, *in* us, and *through* us as *giver of life*, *companion*, and *empowerer*. The Bible teaches us that the Holy Spirit is the one who awakens, makes alive, and renews us—and through us, the world.

The last chapel sermon I preached as a faculty member at Trinity Lutheran Seminary at Capital University was for the Fifth Sunday in Lent. I did not preach a "revival" sermon, exactly, but I did preach about the Spirit as the giver of new life. The Epistle appointed for the day (Lent 5, Year A), Romans 8:6–11, has been a touchpoint for this book, especially verses 9–11: "But you are not in the flesh; you are in the Spirit, since the Spirit of God dwells in you. Anyone who does not have the Spirit of Christ does not belong to him. But if Christ is in you, though the body is dead because of sin, the Spirit is life because of righteousness. If the Spirit of him who raised Jesus from the dead dwells in you, he who raised Christ from the dead will give life to your mortal bodies also through his Spirit that dwells in you."

1. Sarah Hinlicky Wilson, "How Is Your Revival Going?," *Lutheran Forum* 50, no. 2 (Summer 2016): 4.

2. Cheryl M. Peterson, *Who Is the Church? An Ecclesiology for the Twenty-First Century* (Minneapolis: Fortress, 2013), 143–44.

3. Wilson, "How Is Your Revival Going?," 3.

As I read about what was happening on the Asbury campus, I wondered (as many others did): Was this really a revival, a movement of the Holy Spirit to bring new life? In a piece penned for the *New York Times*, Aaron Griffith, a professor of history at Whitworth University and a Public Fellow at the Public Religion Research Institute, wrestled with the question behind my question, one that many generations have wrestled with before: How can we be sure that it is God we are experiencing? Could it be simply the result of some form of manipulation or collective experience, or a natural response to the longing for "a deeper sense of connection to God and to each other," perhaps one partly fueled by the "political and social fragmentation" that we have all experienced "coming out of a global pandemic, a time of really deep isolation" (as Frank Yamada has suggested)?[4]

Most scholars contend that the answer lies in the fruit born by a revival, specifically lives that have been "demonstrably changed" and "oriented toward holiness and justice."[5] Griffith points to Frederick Douglass's experience as a cautionary tale of revivals. In his 1845 *Narrative of the Life of Frederick Douglass, an American Slave*, Douglass wrote about how his enslaver attended a revival meeting and experienced a conversion. Douglass hoped that this experience might lead his enslaver to be a kinder man, or even lead him to grant Douglass manumission. But instead, he became crueler and more hateful to those whom he enslaved.

How can we invite the Spirit to revive us—in a new life, a holy life, and one in which we are empowered for ministry in a world that is broken by human sinfulness, including greed, ecological degradation, racism, sexism, homophobia, and transphobia?

The question of spiritual discernment—"How will we know when the Holy Spirit comes?"—is not only for those experiencing revival but for all who seek to understand the rhythm of the movement of the Spirit in their lives, whether they be Lutheran Christians, Pentecostal Christians, or SBNRs. Kirsteen Kim points out that such discernment "is a matter for ecumenical debate as well as individual conscience."[6]

---

4. Quoted in Sara Weissman, "The Aftershocks of the Asbury Revival," Inside Higher Ed, March 2, 2023, https://www.insidehighered.com/news/2023/03/02/asbury-revival-comes-close#.ZB84ChSOxTo.link.

5. Aaron Griffith, "What Asbury's Christian Revival Says about America's Need for Connection," *New York Times*, February 28, 2023, https://time.com/6258703/asbury-christian-revival-america-connection.

6. Kirsteen Kim, "Case Study: How Will We Know When the Holy Spirit Comes? The Question of Discernment," *Evangelical Review of Theology* 33, no. 1 (January 2009): 94.

This book did not include a chapter on discernment, but there have been hints throughout: the Holy Spirit is present where the gospel is being proclaimed (with the criterion of justification), where the fruit of the Spirit (especially love) is present and growing, and where believers are empowered to participate in the *missio Dei*, for holistic mission, sharing the good news of the divine liberation in word and deed.

Kim proposes four biblical criteria for discerning the Spirit's presence, none of which alone is determinative confirmation of the Holy Spirit's presence. The three movements of the Spirit I have explored align with her criteria:

1. Ecclesial/christological: The confession that Jesus is Lord, made possible by the Spirit (1 Cor. 12:3; 1 John 4:2). This aligns with the Spirit's role in justification, giving us faith that receives Christ and leads to our confession that he is Lord.

2. Ethical: The evidence of the fruit of the Spirit (Gal. 5:22), which aligns with the Spirit's role in sanctification, dwelling in us to increase in us love and the fruit of the Spirit.

3. Charismatic: The practice of the gifts of the Spirit (1 Cor. 12:4–11).

4. Liberational: Being on the side of the poor (Luke 4:18). Both this and the previous criterion (charismatic) align with the Spirit's empowering us for God's mission in the world, including witnessing and working for social justice.[7]

It is too soon to know if the Asbury University and other campus revivals will bear the kind of fruit that will not only change individual lives but also lead to societal transformation. Griffith ponders whether we will ever know and, further, if it is even possible for those of us who are outsiders to understand if and how God is at work in this or any revival. He then suggests that "we might then carefully embrace the possibility of spiritual awakening even if we aren't exactly sure from whence it came or where it is going."[8] Maybe the purpose of a revival is simply to remind us that God is present and active in people's lives today. This is a message Pentecostals try to get across to anyone who will listen, not to mention many of those who call themselves "spiritual but not religious," even though they would use different language to describe God's presence.

7. Kim, "Case Study," 95.
8. Griffith, "What Asbury's Christian Revival Says."

This is something Lutherans can learn from these two groups. As Wilson notes, we Lutherans have excelled in our theology, but too often we address our theological understanding to people who are not ready for it. We would rather talk about the theology of the cross than give a testimony or share the love of Jesus with someone, either because we assume they already know him or, more likely, because we are too embarrassed to. This is not to dismiss the importance of the theology of the cross. For Lutherans, the cross is an important additional criterion of a true revival, of a revival that "neither proclaims false promises of victory in this lifetime nor makes a fetish of its own failures."[9]

But maybe Griffith is right when he says that the response need not be "interrogation or critique"; instead, one can respond with admiration, or even aspiration, when one "sees a person overcome with the Spirit, who knows that God loves them and is working to transform their life for the good."[10]

Come, Holy Spirit!

9. Wilson, "How Is Your Revival Going?," 6.
10. Griffith, "What Asbury's Christian Revival Says."

Abbreviations

AP   Apology of the Augsburg Confession. In *The Book of Concord: The Confessions of the Evangelical Lutheran Church*, edited by Robert Kolb and Timothy J. Wengert. Minneapolis: Fortress, 2000.

BC   *The Book of Concord: The Confessions of the Evangelical Lutheran Church.* Edited by Robert Kolb and Timothy J. Wengert. Translated by Charles Arand, Eric Gritsch, Robert Kolb, William Russell, James Schaaf, Jane Strohl, and Timothy J. Wengert. Minneapolis: Fortress, 2000.

CA   The Augsburg Confession. In *The Book of Concord: The Confessions of the Evangelical Lutheran Church*, edited by Robert Kolb and Timothy J. Wengert. Minneapolis: Fortress, 2000.

CD 2   *Christian Dogmatics*, vol. 2. Edited by Carl E. Braaten and Robert W. Jenson. Philadelphia: Fortress, 1984.

Ep. FC   Epitome, Formula of Concord. In *The Book of Concord: The Confessions of the Evangelical Lutheran Church*, edited by Robert Kolb and Timothy J. Wengert. Minneapolis: Fortress, 2000.

LW   *Luther's Works.* American ed. 55 vols. Edited by Jaroslav Pelikan and Helmut T. Lehmann. Philadelphia: Fortress; St. Louis: Concordia, 1955–86.

LWF   Lutheran World Federation

MIC   *Mission in Context: Transformation, Reconciliation, Empowerment; An LWF Contribution to the Understanding and Practice of Mission.* Geneva: LWF, 2004.

SD FC   Solid Declaration, Formula of Concord. In *The Book of Concord: The Confessions of the Evangelical Lutheran Church*, edited by Robert Kolb and Timothy J. Wengert. Minneapolis: Fortress, 2000.

Sermons   *John Wesley's Sermons: An Anthology.* Edited by Albert C. Outler and Richard P. Heitzenrater. Nashville: Abingdon, 1991.

Bibliography

Abdullah, Melina. "The Role of Spirituality and Prayer in the Black Lives Matter Movement." Interview by Jonathan Bastian. June 25, 2020. https://www.kcrw.com/culture /shows/life-examined/religion-slavery-black-lives-matter/black-lives-matter-blm -melina-abdullah-hebab-ferrag-interview.

Albrecht, Daniel E. *Rites in the Spirit: A Ritual Approach to Pentecostal/Charismatic Spirituality.* New York: Bloomsbury T&T Clark, 1999.

Althaus, Paul. *The Theology of Martin Luther.* Translated by Robert C. Schultz. Philadelphia: Fortress, 1979.

Althouse, Peter. "The Ideology of Power in Early American Pentecostalism." *Journal of Pentecostal Theology* 13, no. 1 (2004): 97–115.

Ammerman, Nancy. "Spiritual but Not Religious? Beyond Binary Choices." *Journal for the Scientific Study of Religion* 52, no. 2 (June 2013): 258–78.

Anderson, Allan Heaton. "Pentecostal Theology as a Global Challenge: Contextual Theological Constructions." In Vondey, *Routledge Handbook of Pentecostal Theology,* 18–28.

Anderson, Robert Mapes. *Vision of the Disinherited: The Making of American Pentecostalism.* Peabody, MA: Hendrickson, 1979.

Archer, Kenneth J. "Nourishment for the Journey: The Pentecostal *Via Salutis* and Sacramental Ordinances." *Journal for Pentecostal Theology* 13, no. 1 (2004): 76–96.

———. *A Pentecostal Hermeneutic: Spirit, Scripture and Community.* Cleveland, TN: CPT, 2009.

Archer, Kenneth J., and L. William Oliverio Jr., eds. *Constructive Pneumatological Hermeneutics in Pentecostal Christianity.* New York: Palgrave Macmillan, 2016.

Ballard, Richard G. "Lutheran Ambivalence toward Healing Ministry." *Lutheran Forum* (Advent 1987): 17–21.

Barrett, David B., George T. Kurian, and Todd M. Johnson, eds. *World Christian Encyclopedia.* 2nd ed. New York: Oxford University Press, 2001.

Basil of Caesarea. *On the Holy Spirit*. Translated by David Anderson. Crestwood, NY: St. Vladimir's Seminary Press, 1997.

Bass, Diana Butler. *Christianity after Religion: The End of Church and the Birth of a New Spiritual Awakening*. San Francisco: HarperOne, 2013.

———. *Grounded: Finding God in the World—A Spiritual Revolution*. San Francisco: HarperOne, 2015.

Beck, Richard. "The Spiritual Dimensions of Justice Work." *Experimental Theology*, September 27, 2016. http://experimentaltheology.blogspot.com/2016/09/the-spiritual -dimensions-of-justice-work.html.

Bellah, Robert Neelly, Richard Madsen, William M. Sullivan, Ann Swidler, and Steven M. Tipton. *Habits of the Heart: Individualism and Commitment in American Life*. Berkeley: University of California Press, 1985.

Bliese, Richard H., and Craig Van Gelder, eds. *The Evangelizing Church: A Lutheran Contribution*. Minneapolis: Augsburg Fortress, 2005.

Boff, Leonardo. *Come, Holy Spirit: Inner Fire, Giver of Life, Comforter of the Poor*. Translated by Margaret Wilde. Maryknoll, NY: Orbis Books, 2015.

Bosch, David J. *Transforming Mission: Paradigm Shifts in Theology of Mission*. Maryknoll, NY: Orbis Books, 1991.

Braaten, Carl E. *The Principles of Lutheran Theology*. Philadelphia: Fortress, 1983.

Bulaka, Hailu Yohannes. "Theology of Holy Spirit: Experiences of the Ethiopian Evangelical Church Mekane Yesus." *Missio Apostolica* 23, no. 1 (May 2015): 126–39.

Callen, Barry L., ed. *The Holy River of God: Currents and Contributions of the Wesleyan Holiness Stream of Christianity*. Glendora, CA: Aldersgate, 2016.

Carey, Jeremiah. "Spiritual, but Not Religious? On the Nature of Spirituality and Its Relation to Religion." *International Journal for Philosophy of Religion* 83 (2018): 261–69.

Carlfeldt, C. G. "The Work of the Holy Spirit." In *What Lutherans Are Thinking: A Symposium on Lutheran Faith and Life*, edited by E. C. Fendt, 219–46. Columbus, OH: Wartburg Press, 1947.

Cartledge, Mark J., and Mark A. Jumper, eds. *The Holy Spirit and the Reformation Legacy*. Eugene, OR: Pickwick, 2020.

Castelo, Daniel. *Pentecostalism as a Christian Mystical Tradition*. Grand Rapids: Eerdmans, 2017.

Christenson, Larry. *Speaking in Tongues and Its Significance for the Church*. Minneapolis: Bethany Fellowship, 1968.

Clark, Matthew S., and Henry I. Lederle. *What Is Distinctive about Pentecostal Theology?* Pretoria: University of South Africa, 1983.

Collins, Kenneth J. *The Scripture Way of Salvation: The Heart of John Wesley's Theology*. Nashville: Abingdon, 1997.

"Confessing Our Faith Together: A Proposal for Full Communion between the Evangelical Lutheran Church in America and the United Methodist Church." Chicago: Evangelical Lutheran Church in America, 2008.

Coulter, Dale M. *Holiness: The Beauty of Perfection.* Lanham, MD: Seymour Press, 2021.

———. "Sanctification: Becoming an Icon of the Spirit through Holy Love." In Vondey, *Routledge Handbook of Pentecostal Theology,* 237–46.

———. "What Meaneth This? Pentecostals and Theological Inquiry." *Journal of Pentecostal Theology* 10, no. 1 (2001): 38–64.

Courey, David J. *What Has Wittenberg to Do with Azusa? Luther's Theology of the Cross and Pentecostal Triumphalism.* New York: T&T Clark, 2015.

Cox, Harvey G., Jr. *Fire from Heaven: The Rise of Pentecostal Spirituality and the Reshaping of Religion in the Twenty-First Century.* Reading, MA: Addison-Wesley, 1995.

———. *The Future of Faith.* San Francisco: HarperOne, 2010.

———. "Make Way for the Spirit." In *God's Life in Trinity,* edited by Miroslav Volf and Michael Welker, 93–100. Minneapolis: Fortress, 2006.

———. *The Secular City: Secularization and Urbanization in Theological Perspective.* New York: Macmillan, 1965.

———. "Some Personal Reflections on Pentecostalism." *Pneuma* 15, no. 1 (1993): 29–34.

———. "Spirits of Globalization: Pentecostalism and Experimental Spiritualities in a Global Era." In *Spirits of Globalization: The Growth of Pentecostalism and Experiential Spiritualities in a Global Age,* edited by Sturla J. Stålsett, 11–22. London: SCM, 2006.

Cross, Richard. "Deification in Aquinas: Created or Uncreated?" *Journal of Theological Studies* 69, no. 1 (April 2018): 106–32.

Cross, Terry L. "The Divine-Human Encounter: Toward a Pentecostal Theology of Experience." *Pneuma* 31 (2009): 3–34.

Dabney, D. Lyle. "Naming the Spirit: Toward a Pneumatology of the Cross." In *Starting with the Spirit,* edited by Stephen Pickard and Gordon Preece, 28–58. Adelaide: Australian Theological Forum, 2001.

Dahill, Lisa E. "Spirituality in Lutheran Perspective: Much to Offer, Much to Learn." *Word & World* 18, no. 1 (Winter 1998): 68–75.

———. "Spirituality: Overview." In *The Encyclopedia of Christianity,* 5 vols. edited by Erwin Fahlbusch, Jan Milič Lochman, John Mbiti, Jaroslav Pelikan, and Lukas Vischer, vol. 5 (*Sh–Z*), 159–61. Grand Rapids: Eerdmans, 1999–2007.

Dart, John. "Charismatic and Mainline." *Christian Century* (March 7, 2006): 22–27.

Davis, Caroline Franks. *The Evidential Force of Religious Experience.* Oxford: Clarendon, 1989.

Dayton, Donald W. *Theological Roots of Pentecostalism.* Peabody, MA: Hendrickson, 1987.

Dillen, Annemie. "The Complexity of Power in Pastoral Relations: Challenges for Theology and Church." *ET Studies* 4, no. 2 (2013): 221–35.

Dorman, David A. "The Purpose of Empowerment in the Christian Life." *Pneuma* 7, no. 2 (Fall 1985): 147–65.

Drescher, Elizabeth. *Choosing Our Religion: The Spiritual Lives of America's Nones.* New York: Oxford University Press, 2016.

Dunn, James D. G. *Baptism in the Holy Spirit.* London: SCM, 1970.

Engelsviken, Tormod. "The Gift of the Spirit: An Analysis and Evaluation of the Charismatic Movement from a Lutheran Theological Perspective." PhD diss., Aquinas
Institute of Theology, Dubuque, IA, 1981.

Evangelical Lutheran Worship. Minneapolis: Augsburg Fortress, 2006.

Fahmy, Dalia. "Key Findings about Americans' Belief in God." Pew Research Center,
April 25, 2018. https://www.pewresearch.org/fact-tank/2018/04/25/key-findings
-about-americans-belief-in-god.

Forde, Gerhard O. "The Christian Life." In *Christian Dogmatics,* vol. 2, edited by Carl E.
Braaten and Robert W. Jenson, 391–469. Philadelphia: Fortress, 1984.

———. "Forensic Justification and the Christian Life: Triumph or Tragedy?" In *A More
Radical Gospel: Essays on Eschatology, Authority, Atonement, and Ecumenism,* edited
by Mark C. Mattes and Steven D. Paulson, 114–36. Grand Rapids: Eerdmans, 2004.

———. *Justification by Faith: A Matter of Death and Life.* 1982. Reprint, Ramsey, NJ:
Sigler, 1991.

———. "Law and Gospel as the Methodological Principle of Theology." In *Theological
Perspectives: A Discussion of Contemporary Issues in Lutheran Theology,* edited by E. D.
Farwell et al., 50–69. Decorah, IA: Luther College Press, 1967.

———. "Law and Gospel in Luther's Hermeneutic." *Interpretation* 37 (1983): 240–52.

———. "*Lex Semper Accusat?* Nineteenth-Century Roots of Our Current Dilemma."
Dialog 9, no. 4 (Fall 1970): 265–74.

———. "The Lutheran View." In *Christian Spirituality: Five Views of Sanctification,* edited
by Donald L. Alexander, 14–32. Downers Grove, IL: InterVarsity, 1988.

———. *Theology Is for Proclamation.* Minneapolis: Fortress, 1990.

———. "The Work of Christ." In *Christian Dogmatics,* vol. 2, edited by Carl E. Braaten
and Robert W. Jenson, 35–99. Philadelphia: Fortress, 1984.

Frey, Jörg. "How Did the Spirit Become a Person?" In *The Holy Spirit, Inspiration, and the
Cultures of Antiquity, Ekstasis: Religious Experience from Antiquity to the Middle Ages,*
vol. 5, edited by Jörg Frey and John R. Levison, 343–71. Berlin: De Gruyter, 2014.

Froehlich, Karlfried. "Charismatic Manifestations and the Lutheran Incarnational
Stance." In *The Holy Spirit in the Life of the Church: From Biblical Times to the Present,*
edited by Paul D. Opsahl, 136–57. Minneapolis: Augsburg, 1978.

Fuller, Robert. *Spiritual but Not Religious: Understanding Unchurched America.* Oxford:
Oxford University Press, 2001.

Gabriel, Andrew K. *The Lord Is the Spirit: The Holy Spirit and the Divine Attributes.*
Eugene, OR: Pickwick, 2011.

———. "Pneumatology: Eschatological Intensification of the Personal Presence of God."
In Vondey, *Routledge Handbook of Pentecostal Theology,* 206–15.

Gaiser, Frederick J. "'I Will Tell You What God Has Done for Me' (Psalm 66:16): A Place
for Testimony in Lutheran Worship?" *Word & World* 26, no. 2 (Spring 2006): 138–48.

Genia, Vicky. "The Spiritual Experience Index: A Measure of Spiritual Maturity." *Journal of Religion and Health* 30 (1991): 337–47.

———. "The Spiritual Experience Index: Revision and Reformulation." *Review of Religious Research* 38, no. 4 (June 1997): 344–61.

"The Global Catholic Population." Pew Research Center, February 13, 2013. https://www.pew research.org/religion/2013/02/13/the-global-catholic-population/#:~:text=Of%20 the%20estimated%2075.4%20million,the%20United%20States%20(30%25).

Green, Chris E. W. "'Not I, but Christ': Holiness, Conscience, and the (Im)possibility of Community." In *A Future for Holiness: Pentecostal Explorations*, edited by Lee Roy Martin, 127–44. Cleveland, TN: CPT, 2013.

———. "Sacraments: Rites in the Spirit for the Presence of Christ." In Vondey, *Routledge Handbook of Pentecostal Theology*, 311–20.

———. *Sanctifying Interpretation: Vocation, Holiness, and Scripture*. 2nd ed. Cleveland, TN: CPT, 2020.

———. *Toward a Pentecostal Theology of the Lord's Supper: Foretasting the Kingdom*. Cleveland, TN: CPT, 2012.

Grey, Mary C. *Sacred Longings: The Ecological Spirit and Global Culture*. Minneapolis: Fortress, 2004.

Griffith, Aaron. "What Asbury's Christian Revival Says about America's Need for Connection." *New York Times*, February 28, 2023. https://time.com/6258703/asbury -christian-revival-america-connection.

Gritsch, Eric W., and Robert W. Jenson. *Lutheranism: The Theological Movement and Its Confessional Writing*. Philadelphia: Fortress, 1976.

Groh, John E. "Revivalism among Lutherans in America in the 1840s." *Concordia Historical Institute Quarterly* 43, no. 1 (February 1970): 29–43.

Grundmann, Christopher. "He Sent Them Out to Heal: Reflections on the Healing Ministry of the Church." *Currents in Theology and Mission* 33, no. 5 (October 2006): 372–78.

Guder, Darrell L., Lois Barret, Inagrace T. Dietterich, George R. Hunsberger, Alan J. Roxburgh, and Craig Van Gelder, eds. *Missional Church: A Vision for Sending the Church in North America*. Grand Rapids: Eerdmans, 1998.

Hahn, Jennifer Lois. "'God as We Understood Him': Being Spiritual but Not Religious in Alcoholics Anonymous, Past and Present." *Implicit Religion* 22, no. 2 (2019): 101–21.

Harran, Marilyn J. *Luther on Conversion: The Early Years*. Ithaca, NY: Cornell University Press, 1983.

Harris, Antipas L., ed. *The Mighty Transformer: The Holy Spirit Advocates for Social Justice*. Irving, TX: GIELD Academic, 2019.

Harris, Antipas L., and Michael D. Palmer, eds. *The Holy Spirit and Social Justice: Scripture and Theology*. Lanham, MD: Seymour, 2019.

Hegstad, Harald. "United with Christ in the Spirit: The Pneumatological Dimension of the Doctrine of Justification." *Dialog* 60, no. 1 (March 2021): 79–85.

Helmer, Christine. "Luther's Theology of Glory." *Neue Zeitschrift für Systematische Theologie und Religionsphilosophie* 42, no. 3 (2000): 237–45.

———. *The Trinity and Martin Luther*. Rev. ed. Bellingham, WA: Lexham, 2017.

———. *The Trinity and Martin Luther: A Study on the Relationship between Genre, Language and the Trinity in Luther's Works, 1523–1546*. Mainz: Philipp von Zabern, 1999.

Hendrix, Scott H. *Recultivating the Vineyard: The Reformation Agendas of Christianization*. Louisville: Westminster John Knox, 2004.

Henriksen, Jan-Olav. *Life, Love, and Hope: God and Human Experience*. Grand Rapids: Eerdmans, 2014.

———. "Towards a Lutheran Theology of Bodily Healing." *Ritröð Guðfræðistofnunar* (*Studia Theologica Islandica*) 50 (2020): 4–14.

Henry, James Daryn. *The Freedom of God: A Study in the Pneumatology of Robert Jenson*. Lanham, MD: Lexington Books / Fortress Academic, 2018.

Herms, Eilert. *Luthers Auslegung des Dritten Artikels*. Tübingen: Mohr Siebeck, 1987.

Hill, William J. *The Three-Personed God: The Trinity as a Mystery of Salvation*. Washington, DC: Catholic University Press, 1988.

Hinlicky, Paul. "Whose Ministry? Whose Church?" *Lutheran Forum* (2008): 48–53.

Hollenweger, Walter J. "From Azusa Street to the Toronto Phenomenon." In *Pentecostal Movements as an Ecumenical Challenge*, vol. 3, edited by Jürgen Moltmann and Karl Josef Kuschel, 3–14. Maryknoll, NY: Orbis Books, 1996.

———. *Pentecostalism: Origins and Developments Worldwide*. Peabody, MA: Hendrickson, 1997.

———. *The Pentecostals: The Charismatic Movement in the Churches*. Minneapolis: Augsburg, 1972.

Hughes, Robert Davis, III. *Beloved Dust: Tides of the Spirit in the Christian Life*. New York: Continuum, 2008.

Hunter, Harold D. *Spirit Baptism: Pentecostal Alternative*. 1983. Reprint, Eugene, OR: Wipf & Stock, 2009.

Ireland, Jerry Michael. "The Missionary Nature of Tongues in the Book of Acts." *PentecoStudies* 18, no. 2 (2019): 200–223.

———. *The Missionary Spirit: Evangelism and Social Action in Pentecostal Missiology*. Maryknoll, NY: Orbis Books, 2021.

Jacobsen, Dennis G. *Thinking in the Spirit: Theologies of the Early Pentecostal Movement*. Bloomington: Indiana University Press, 2003.

Jensen, Gordon A. "Sacramental Theology." In *The Oxford Encyclopedia of Martin Luther*, vol. 3, edited by Derek R. Nelson and Paul R. Hinlicky, 307–19. New York: Oxford University Press, 2017.

Jenson, Robert W. *God after God: The God of the Past and the Future as Seen in the Work of Karl Barth*. New York: Bobbs-Merrill, 1969.

————. *Story and Promise: A Brief Theology of the Gospel about Jesus.* Philadelphia: Fortress, 1973.

————. *Systematic Theology.* Vol. 1, *The Triune God.* New York: Oxford University Press, 1997.

————. *The Triune Identity: God according to the Gospel.* Philadelphia: Fortress, 1982.

————. *Visible Words: The Interpretation and Practice of Christian Sacraments.* Philadelphia: Fortress, 1978.

Johnson, Todd M. "Counting Pentecostals Worldwide." *Pneuma* 36 (2014): 265–88.

————. "The Global Demographics of the Pentecostal and Charismatic Renewal." *Society* 46 (2009): 479–83.

Johnson, Todd M., and Gina A. Zerlo. *World Christian Encyclopedia.* 3rd ed. Edinburgh: Edinburgh University Press, 2019.

Jungkuntz, Theodore R. "Secularization Theology, Charismatic Renewal, and Luther's Theology of the Cross." *Concordia Theological Monthly* 42, no. 1 (1972): 5–24.

Kärkkäinen, Veli-Matti. *A Constructive Christian Theology for the Pluralistic World.* Vol. 4, *Spirit and Salvation.* Grand Rapids: Eerdmans, 2016.

————. *One with God: Salvation as Deification and Justification.* Collegeville, MN: Liturgical Press, 2004.

————. "Transformed, Freed, Empowered: The Spirit's Work in the Gifting and Vocation of All Believers." In Rimmer and Peterson, *"We Believe in the Holy Spirit,"* 197–210.

————. "The Working of the Spirit of God in Creation and the People of God: The Pneumatology of Wolfhart Pannenberg." *Pneuma* 26, no. 1 (Spring 2004): 17–35.

Keaty, Anthony. "The Holy Spirit Proceeding as Mutual Love: An Interpretation of Aquinas' Summa Theologiae, I.37." *Angelicum* 77, nos. 3/4 (2000): 533–57.

Kim, Grace Ji-Sun. *Embracing the Other: The Transformative Spirit of Love.* Grand Rapids: Eerdmans, 2015.

————. *The Holy Spirit, Chi, and the Other: A Model of Global and Intercultural Pneumatology.* New York: Palgrave Macmillan, 2011.

————. *The Homebrewed Christianity Guide to the Holy Spirit: Hand-Raisers, Han, and the Holy Ghost.* Minneapolis, Fortress: 2018.

————. *Reimagining Spirit: Wind, Breath, and Vibration.* Eugene, OR: Cascade Books, 2019.

Kim, Kirsteen. "Case Study: How Will We Know When the Holy Spirit Comes? The Question of Discernment." *Evangelical Review of Theology* 33, no. 1 (January 2009): 93–96.

————. *The Holy Spirit in the World: Global Conversations.* Maryknoll, NY: Orbis Books, 2007.

————. Review of *The Holy Spirit, Chi, and the Other: A Model of Global and Intercultural Pneumatology,* by Grace Ji-Sun Kim. *Pneuma* 35 (2013): 112–13.

Kohli, Candace L. "Grasping at the Human as Human: The Human Person after Justification, according to Martin Luther's Pneumatological Lens," in *T&T Clark Handbook of Theological Anthropology*, edited by Mary Ann Hinsdale and Stephen Okey, 183–91. London: T&T Clark, 2021.

———. "Help for Moral Good: The Spirit, the Law, and Human Agency in Martin Luther's Antinomian Disputations (1537–40)." PhD diss., Northwestern University, 2019. https://arch.library.northwestern.edu/concern/generic_works/4q77fr419 ?locale=en.

Kolb, Robert. "God's Word Produces Faith and Fruit: Reflections from Luther's Understanding of the Sermon on the Mount." *Concordia Journal* (Summer 2014): 217–24.

———. "'So Much Began in Halle': The Mission Program That Sent Mühlenberg to America." *Concordia Historical Institute Quarterly* 84, no. 3 (Fall 2011): 26–35.

Kolb, Robert, and Timothy J. Wengert, eds. *The Book of Concord: The Confessions of the Evangelical Lutheran Church*. Translated by Charles Arand, Eric Gritsch, Robert Kolb, William Russell, James Schaaf, Jane Strohl, and Timothy J. Wengert. Minneapolis: Fortress, 2000.

Köstlin, Julius. *Theology of Luther in Its Historical Development and Inner Harmony*. 2 vols. Translated by Charles E. Hay. Philadelphia: Lutheran Publication Society, 1897.

Kurtz, Ernest. "Whatever Happened to Twelve-Step Programs?" In *The Collected Ernie Kurtz*. 1999. Reprint, Bloomington, IN: iUniverse, 2008.

Lancaster, Sarah Heaner, and Cheryl M. Peterson. "Table Grace: Communion Distinctions in the Lutheran and Methodist Traditions." *Sacramental Life* 22, no. 1 (Winter 2010): 22–30.

Land, Steven J. *Pentecostal Spirituality: A Passion for the Kingdom*. Sheffield, UK: Sheffield Academic, 1993.

Lange, Dirk G., Paula Mumia, Jean-Daniel Plüss, and Sarah Hinlicky Wilson, eds. *International Lutheran-Pentecostal 2016–2022 Dialogue Statement: "The Spirit of the Lord Is Upon Me."* Geneva: LWF, 2023. https://www.lutheranworld.org/resources/publica tion-spirit-lord-upon-me.

Lenker, John Nicholas, ed. *Sermons of Martin Luther*. 8 vols. Grand Rapids: Baker, 1988.

Leonard, Bill. *A Sense of the Heart: Christian Religious Experience in the United States*. Nashville: Abingdon, 2014.

Lindberg, Carter. *Charismatic Renewal and the Lutheran Tradition*. Geneva: LWF, 1985.

———. *The Third Reformation? Charismatic Movements and the Lutheran Tradition*. Macon, GA: Mercer University Press, 1983.

Lundblad, Barbara K. "Do You See This Woman?" In *Lutheran Women in Ordained Ministry 1970–1995: Reflections and Perspectives*, edited by Gloria E. Bengston, 86–92. Minneapolis: Augsburg, 1995.

Luther, Martin. *Luther's Works*. American ed. 55 vols. Edited by Jaroslav Pelikan and Helmut T. Lehmann. Philadelphia: Fortress; St. Louis: Concordia, 1955–86.

———. "Thursday before Easter." In *Dr. Martin Luther's House-Postil, or Sermons on the Gospels*, vol. 2, 24–41. Columbus, OH: J. A. Schultz, 1884.

———. *Three Treatises*. 2nd rev. ed. Philadelphia: Fortress, 1970.

Lutherans and Pentecostals in Dialogue. Strasbourg, France: Institute for Ecumenical Research, 2010. https://ecumenical-institute.org/wp-content/uploads/2022/06/Lutherans-and-Pentecostals-in-Dialogue-Text-FINAL.pdf.

Ma, Wonsuk, "The Holy Spirit in Pentecostal Mission: The Shaping of Mission Awareness and Practice." *International Bulletin of Mission Research* 41, no. 3 (2017): 227–38.

———. "'When the Poor Are Fired Up': The Role of Pneumatology in Pentecostal Charismatic Mission." *Transformation* 24, no. 1 (January 2007): 28–34.

MacArthur, John F., Jr. *Charismatic Chaos*. Grand Rapids: Zondervan, 1993.

———. *Strange Fire: The Danger of Offending the Holy Spirit with Counterfeit Worship*. Nashville: Thomas Nelson, 2013.

Macchia, Frank D. *Baptized in the Spirit: A Global Pentecostal Theology*. Grand Rapids: Zondervan, 2006.

———. "Discerning the Spirit in Life: A Review of *God the Spirit* by Michael Welker." *Journal of Pentecostal Theology* 10 (1997): 3–28.

———. "Is Footwashing the Neglected Sacrament? A Theological Response to John Christopher Thomas." *Pneuma* 19, no. 2 (1997): 239–49.

———. *Jesus the Spirit Baptizer: Christology in Light of Pentecost*. Grand Rapids: Eerdmans, 2018.

———. "Justification and the Spirit: A Pentecostal Reflection on the Doctrine by Which the Church Stands or Falls." *Pneuma* 22, no. 1 (2000): 3–21.

———. "Justification through New Creation: The Holy Spirit and the Doctrine by Which the Church Stands or Falls." *Theology Today* 58, no. 2 (July 2001): 207–12.

———. *Justified in the Spirit: Creation, Redemption, and the Triune God*. Grand Rapids: Eerdmans, 2010.

———. "Salvation and Spirit Baptism: Another Look at Dunn's Classic." *Pneuma* 24, no. 1 (Spring 2002): 1–6.

———. "Spirit Baptism: Initiation in the Fullness of God's Promises." In Vondey, *Routledge Handbook of Pentecostal Theology*, 247–56.

———. "Tongues as a Sign: Toward a Sacramental Understanding of Pentecostal Experience." *Pneuma* 15, no. 1 (1993): 61–76.

———. "Towards Individual and Communal Renewal: Reflections on Luke's Theology of Conversion." *Ex Auditu* 25 (2009): 92–105.

Maddox, Randy L. *Responsible Grace: John Wesley's Practical Theology*. Nashville: Kingswood Books, 1994.

Malpica Padilla, Rafael. "Accompaniment as an Alternative Model for the Practice of Mission." *Trinity Seminary Review* 29, no. 2 (Summer–Fall 2008): 87–98.

Mann, Jeffrey K. "Luther and the Holy Spirit: Why Pneumatology Still Matters." *Currents in Theology and Mission* 34, no. 2 (2007): 111–16.

Mann, Mark H. Review of *Holiness: The Beauty of Perfection*, by Dale M. Coulter. *Pneuma* 27, no. 2 (Fall 2005): 391–92.

Marshall, Bruce D. "Justification as Declaration and Deification." *International Journal of Systematic Theology* 4, no. 1 (March 2002): 3–28.

Marshall, Molly. *Joining the Dance: A Theology of the Spirit*. King of Prussia, PA: Judson, 2003.

Martin, Lee Roy, ed. *A Future for Holiness: Pentecostal Explorations*. Cleveland, TN: CPT, 2013.

Masci, David, and Michael Lipka. "Americans May Be Getting Less Religious, but Feelings of Spirituality on the Rise." Pew Research Center, January 21, 2016. https://www.pewresearch.org/fact-tank/2016/01/21/americans-spirituality.

Mattes, Mark C. "Gerhard Forde on Re-envisioning Theology." *Lutheran Quarterly* 13, no. 4 (1999): 373–93.

———. "A Lutheran Case for Evangelism." *Word & World* 39, no. 4 (Fall 2019): 295–308.

McClung, L. Grant. "Pentecostal/Charismatic Perspectives on Missiology for the Twenty-First Century." *Pneuma* 16, no. 1 (Spring 1994): 11–21.

McNeal, Reggie. *The Present Future: Six Tough Questions for the Church*. San Francisco: Jossey-Bass, 2003.

Menzies, William W. "Non-Wesleyan Pentecostalism: A Tradition the Influence of Fundamentalism." *Asian Journal of Pentecostal Studies* 12, no. 2 (2011): 199–211.

Menzies, William W., and Robert P. Menzies. *Spirit and Power: Foundations of a Pentecostal Experience*. Grand Rapids: Zondervan, 2000.

Mercadante, Linda A. *Belief without Borders: Inside the Minds of the Spiritual but Not Religious*. New York: Oxford University Press, 2014.

———. "Does Alcoholics Anonymous Help Grow the Spiritual but Not Religious Movement?" *Implicit Religion* 22, no. 2 (2019): 184–92.

Mission in Context: Transformation, Reconciliation, Empowerment; An LWF Contribution to the Understanding and Practice of Mission. Geneva: LWF, 2004.

Moe-Lobeda, Cynthia. "The Holy Spirit: Power for Confessing Faith in the Midst of Empire." In *Being the Church in the Midst of Empire: Trinitarian Reflections*, edited by Karen L. Bloomquist, 125–46. Minneapolis: Lutheran University Press, 2010.

———. "The Spirit as Moral-Spiritual Power for Earth-Honoring, Justice-Seeking Ways of Shaping Our Life in Common." In *Planetary Solidarity: Global Women's Voices on Christian Doctrine and Climate Justice*, edited by Grace Ji-Sun Kim and Hilda P. Koster, 249–73. Minneapolis: Fortress, 2017.

Molina, Alejandra. "Black Lives Matter Is 'a Spiritual Movement,' Says Co-founder Patrisse Cullors." Religious News Service, June 15, 2020. https://religionnews.com/2020/06/15/why-black-lives-matter-is-a-spiritual-movement-says-blm-co-founder-patrisse-cullors.

Moltmann, Jürgen. "A Pentecostal Theology of Life." Translated by Frank D. Macchia. *Journal of Pentecostal Theology* 4, no. 9 (October 1996): 3–15.

———. *The Spirit of Life: A Universal Affirmation*. Translated by Margaret Kohl. Minneapolis: Fortress, 1992.

Nessan, Craig L. "Allergic to the Spirit No More: Rethinking Pneumatology." *Currents in Theology and Mission* 21, no. 3 (June 1994): 183–96.

———. *Beyond Maintenance to Mission: A Theology of the Congregation*, 2nd ed. Minneapolis: Fortress, 2010.

———. "Universal Priesthood of All Believers: Unfulfilled Promise of the Reformation." *Currents in Theology and Mission* 46, no. 1 (2019): 8–15.

Neumann, Peter D. "Experience: The Mediated Immediacy of Encounter with the Spirit." In Vondey, *Routledge Handbook of Pentecostal Theology*, 84–94.

———. *Pentecostal Experience: An Ecumenical Encounter*. Eugene, OR: Pickwick, 2012.

Newbigin, Lesslie. *The Household of God: Lectures on the Nature of the Church*. New York: Friendship Press, 1954.

Newport, Frank. "More Than 9 in 10 Americans Continue to Believe in God." Gallup Poll, June 3, 2011. https://news.gallup.com/poll/147887/americans-continue-believe -god.aspx.

Nicol, Todd W. "Lutheran Revivalism: A Request for a Reappraisal." *Lutheran Historical Conference* 12 (1988): 97–117.

Oberdorfer, Bernd. "Embodied Spirit: Outlines of Lutheran Pneumatology." In Rimmer and Peterson, *"We Believe in the Holy Spirit,"* 49–51.

Oberman, Heiko A. "Preaching and the Word in the Reformation." *Theology Today* 18, no. 1 (April 1961): 16–29.

Oliverio, L. William, Jr. *Theological Hermeneutics in the Classical Pentecostal Tradition: A Typological Account*. Leiden: Brill, 2015.

Ortiz, Leila. "A Latina Luthercostal Invitation Into an Ecclesial Estuary." *Dialog* 55, no. 4 (2016): 308–15.

Outler, Albert C., ed. *John Wesley*. New York: Oxford University Press, 1964.

Outler, Albert C., and Richard P. Heitzenrater, eds. *John Wesley's Sermons: An Anthology*. Nashville: Abingdon, 1991.

Pannenberg, Wolfhart. *Christian Spirituality*. Philadelphia: Westminster, 1983.

Perry, David. *Spirit Baptism: The Pentecostal Experience in Theological Focus*. Leiden: Brill, 2017.

Peters, Ted. Review of *The Triune Identity: God according to the Gospel*, by Robert W. Jenson. *Currents in Theology and Mission* 12, no. 4 (August 1985): 244–46.

Peterson, Cheryl M. "The Church Transformed." *Seminary Ridge Review* 17, no. 1 (Autumn 2014): 16–37.

———. "Healing as an Image for the Atonement: A Lutheran Consideration." In *Justification in a Post-Christian Society*, edited by Carl-Henric Grenholm and Göran Gunner, 72–87. Eugene, OR: Pickwick, 2014.

———. "A Lutheran Engagement with Wesley on the Work of the Spirit." In *The Holy Spirit and the Christian Life: Historical, Interdisciplinary, and Renewal Perspectives*, edited by Wolfgang Vondey, 93–108. New York: Palgrave Macmillan, 2014.

———. "A Lutheran Exploration of Spiritual Empowerment, Pentecostal-Style." *Lutheran Forum* 51, no. 2 (Summer 2017): 47–50.

———. "Pneumatology in the Age of #MeToo: An Exploration of the Spirit's Role in Suffering." In *Sisters, Mothers, Daughters: Pentecostal Perspectives on Violence against Women*, edited by Kimberly Irvin Alexander, Melissa L. Archer, Mark J. Cartledge, and Michael D. Palmer, 13–32. Boston: Brill, 2022.

———. "The Question of the Church in North American Lutheranism: Toward an Ecclesiology of the Third Article." PhD diss., Marquette University, 2004. https://www.proquest.com/dissertations-theses/question-church-north-american-lutheranism-toward/docview/305177045/se-2.

———. "Rediscovering Pneumatology in the 'Age of the Spirit': A North American Lutheran Contribution." *Dialog* 58, no. 2 (Summer 2019): 102–8.

———. "Spirit and Body: A Feminist and Lutheran Conversation." In *Transformative Lutheran Theologies: Feminist, Womanist, and Mujerista Perspectives*, edited by Mary J. Streufert, 153–64. Minneapolis: Fortress, 2010.

———. "Theology of the Cross and the Experience of God's Presence: A Lutheran Response to Pentecostal Wondering." *Dialog* 55, no. 4 (Winter 2016): 316–23.

———. *Who Is the Church? An Ecclesiology for the Twenty-First Century*. Minneapolis: Fortress, 2013.

Pew Research Center. "In U.S., Decline of Christianity Continues at Rapid Pace: An Update on America's Changing Religious Landscape." October 17, 2019. https://www.pewforum.org/2019/10/17/in-u-s-decline-of-christianity-continues-at-rapid-pace.

———. "2014 Religious Landscape Study." Accessed January 29, 2023. http://www.pewforum.org/religious-landscape-study/belief-in-god.

Plüss, Jean-Daniel. "Religious Experience in Worship: A Pentecostal Perspective." *PentecoStudies* 2, no. 1 (2003).

———. "Sacrament or Ordinance: A Pentecostal Approach to a Contentious Issue." In *Pentecostals in the Twenty-First Century: Identity, Beliefs, Praxis*, edited by Corneliu Constantineanu and Christopher J. Scobie, 59–75. Eugene, OR: Cascade Books, 2018.

Powers, Janet Evert. "Missionary Tongues?" *Journal of Pentecostal Theology* 17 (2000): 39–55.

Prenter, Regin. "Holiness in the Lutheran Tradition." In *Man's Concern with Holiness*, edited by Marina Chavchavadze, 121–44. London: Hodder & Stoughton, 1970.

———. *Spiritus Creator: Luther's Concept of the Holy Spirit*. Translated by John M. Jensen. Philadelphia: Muhlenberg Press, 1953.

Principe, Walter. "Toward Defining Spirituality." In *Exploring Christian Spirituality: An Ecumenical Reader*, edited by Kenneth J. Collins, 43–60. Grand Rapids: Baker Academic, 2000.

Rambo, Shelly. *Spirit and Trauma: A Theology of Remaining*. Louisville: Westminster John Knox, 2010.

Richmann, Christopher J. *Called: Recovering Lutheran Principles for Ministry and Vocation*. Minneapolis: Fortress, 2022.

———. "Lutheran Charismatics and the 'Chief Article': A Historical Theological Assessment." *Journal of the Lutheran Historical Conference* 3 (2013): 46–73.

Rimmer, Chad M., and Cheryl M. Peterson, eds. *"We Believe in the Holy Spirit": Global Perspectives on Lutheran Identities*. Leipzig: Evangelische Verlangsanstalt, 2021.

Rogers, Eugene F., Jr. *After the Spirit: A Constructive Pneumatology from Resources outside the Modern West*. Grand Rapids: Eerdmans, 2005.

Roof, Wade Clark. "American Spirituality." *Religion and American Culture* 9, no. 2 (Summer 1999): 131–45.

Ruokanen, Miikka. *Trinitarian Grace in Martin Luther's "The Bondage of the Will."* New York: Oxford University Press, 2021.

Sanders, Cheryl J. "Social Justice: Theology as Social Transformation." In Vondey, *Routledge Handbook of Pentecostal Theology*, 432–42.

Scaer, David. "Sanctification in the Lutheran Confessions." *Concordia Theological Quarterly* 53, no. 3 (July 1989): 165–81.

Schaab, Gloria L. *Liberating Pneumatologies: Spirit Set Free*. New York: Crossroad, 2021.

Schaibley, Robert W. "Measuring Spiritual Gifts." *Lutheran Quarterly* 3, no. 4 (Winter 1989): 423–41.

Scherer, James A. "Luther and Mission: A Rich but Untested Potential." *Missio Apostolica* 2, no. 1 (May 1994): 17–24.

Schifferdecker, Kathryn. "Learning from the Global South." *Word & World*, Supplement Series 7 (2017): 174–83.

Schmid, Heinrich, ed. *The Doctrinal Theology of the Evangelical Lutheran Church*. 3rd ed. Translated by Charles A. Hay and Henry E. Jacobs. Minneapolis: Augsburg, 1961.

Schneiders, Sandra M. *Religion and Spirituality: Strangers, Rivals, or Partners?* Santa Clara Lectures 6, no. 2. Santa Clara, CA: Santa Clara University, Dept. of Religious Studies, 2000.

———. "Spirituality in the Academy." *Theological Studies* 50, no. 4 (1989): 676–97.

———. "The Study of Christian Spirituality: Contours and Dynamics of a Discipline." In *Minding the Spirit: The Study of Christian Spirituality*, edited by Elizabeth A. Dreyer and Mark S. Burrows, 38–57. Baltimore: Johns Hopkins University Press, 2005.

Scott, Mark S. M. "God as Person: Karl Barth and Karl Rahner on Divine and Human Personhood." *Religious Studies and Theology* 25, no. 2 (2006): 161–90.

Seilhamer, Frank L. "The New Measure Movement among Lutherans." *Lutheran Quarterly* 12, no. 2 (May 1960): 121–43.

Sepúlveda, Juan. "Reflections on the Pentecostal Contribution to the Church's Mission in Latin America." *Journal of Pentecostal Theology* 1 (1992): 93–108.

Shepherd, William H., Jr. *The Narrative Function of the Holy Spirit as a Character in Luke-Acts*. Atlanta: Scholars Press, 1994.

Shults, F. LeRon. "Spirit and Spirituality: Philosophical Trends in Late Modern Pneumatology." *Pneuma* 30 (2008): 271–87.

Shults, F. LeRon, and Andrea Hollingsworth. *The Holy Spirit: Guides to Theology*. Grand Rapids: Eerdmans, 2008.

Smith, Aaron T. *Theology of the Third Article: Karl Barth and the Spirit of the Word*. Minneapolis: Fortress, 2014.

Sonessa, Wondimu L. "Simul Lutheran et Charismatic in Ethiopia." *Lutheran Forum* 51, no. 4 (Winter 2017): 23–27.

Starkey, Lycurgus M., Jr. *The Work of the Holy Spirit: A Study in Wesleyan Theology*. New York: Abingdon, 1962.

Stephenson, Lisa P. "Pentecostalism and Experience: History, Theology, and Practice." *Journal of Pentecostal Theology* 28 (2019): 186–201.

Stoeffler, F. Ernest. *The Rise of Evangelical Pietism*. Leiden: Brill, 1965.

Streufert, Mary J. *Language for God: A Lutheran Perspective*. Minneapolis: Fortress, 2022.

Studebaker, Steven M. "Baptism among the Pentecostals." In *Baptism: Historical, Theological, and Pastoral Perspectives*, edited by Gordon L. Heath and James D. Dvorak, 201–24. Eugene, OR: Wipf & Stock, 2011.

———. *From Pentecost to the Triune God: A Pentecostal Trinitarian Theology*. Grand Rapids: Eerdmans, 2012.

———. *The Spirit of Atonement: Pentecostal Contributions and Challenges to the Christian Traditions*. New York: T&T Clark, 2021.

Synan, Vinson. *The Holiness-Pentecostal Tradition: Charismatic Movements in the Twentieth Century*. 2nd ed. Grand Rapids: Eerdmans, 1997.

Taves, Ann. *Fits, Trances, & Visions: Experiencing Religion and Explaining Experience from Wesley to James*. Princeton: Princeton University Press, 1999.

———. *Religious Experience Reconsidered: A Building Block to the Study of Religion and Other Special Things*. Princeton: Princeton University Press, 2009.

Taylor, John V. *The Go-Between God: The Holy Spirit and the Christian Mission*. London: SCM, 1972.

Thomas, John Christopher. *Footwashing in John 13 and the Johannine Community*. Sheffield, UK: Sheffield Academic, 1991.

———. "Pentecostal Theology in the Twenty-First Century." *Pneuma* 20, no. 1 (1998): 3–19.

Thompson, W. D. J. Cargill. "The Problems of Luther's 'Tower Experience' and Its Place in His Intellectual Development." In *Religious Motivation: Biographical and Sociological Problems for the Church Historian*, edited by Derek Baker, 187–211. Oxford: Basil Blackwell, 1978.

Tickle, Phyllis. *Emergence Christianity: What It Is, Where It Is Going, and Why It Matters*. Grand Rapids: Baker Books, 2012.

———. *The Great Emergence: How Christianity Is Changing and Why*. Grand Rapids: Baker Books, 2008.

Tickle, Phyllis, with Jon M. Sweeney. *The Age of the Spirit: How the Ghost of an Ancient Controversy Is Shaping the Church*. Grand Rapids: Baker Books, 2014.

Tomberlin, Daniel. *Pentecostal Sacraments: Encountering God at the Altar*. Cleveland, TN: Center for Pentecostal Leadership and Care, 2010.

Vainio, Olli-Pekka. *Justification and Participation in Christ: The Development of the Doctrine of Justification from Luther to the Formula of Concord (1580)*. Boston: Brill, 2008.

———. "Luther and Theosis: A Response to the Critics of Finnish Luther Research." *Pro Ecclesia* 24, no. 4 (Fall 2015): 459–74.

Van Neste, Ray. "The Mangled Narrative of Missions and Evangelism in the Reformation." *Southeastern Theological Review* (2017): 1–7.

Victorin-Vangerud, Nancy. *Raging Hearth: Spirit in the Household of God*. Nashville: Chalice, 2000.

Vondey, Wolfgang. *Pentecostal Theology: Living the Full Gospel, Systematic Pentecostal and Charismatic Theology*. New York: Bloomsbury T&T Clark, 2017.

———. *Pentecostalism: A Guide for the Perplexed*. New York: Bloomsbury T&T Clark, 2013.

———, ed. *The Routledge Handbook of Pentecostal Theology*. New York: Routledge, 2020.

Von Loewenich, Walther. *Luther's Theology of the Cross*. Translated by Hebert Bouman. Minneapolis: Augsburg, 1976.

Wallace, Mark I. *When God Was a Bird: Christianity, Animism, and the Re-enchantment of the World*. New York: Fordham University Press, 2018.

Wariboko, Nimi. "Dialogue: *Fire from Heaven*: Pentecostals in the Secular City." *Pneuma* 33 (2011): 391–408.

Warneck, Gustav. *Outline of the History of Protestant Missions from the Reformation to the Present Time*. New York: Revell, 1901.

Watson, Philip. "Wesley and Luther on Christian Perfection." *Ecumenical Review* 15, no. 3 (1963): 291–302.

Webb, Stephen H. *The Divine Voice: Christian Proclamation and the Theology of Sound*. Grand Rapids: Brazos, 2004.

Webster, John. "The Identity of the Holy Spirit: A Problem in Trinitarian Theology." *Themelios* 9, no. 1 (September 1983): 4–7.

Weissman, Sara. "The Aftershocks of the Asbury Revival." Inside Higher Ed, March 2, 2023. https://www.insidehighered.com/news/2023/03/02/asbury-revival-comes -close#.ZB84ChSOxTo.link.

Welker, Michael. *God the Spirit*. Translated by John F. Hoffmeyer. Minneapolis: Fortress, 1994.

Wengert, Timothy J. *Martin Luther's Catechisms: Forming the Faith*. Minneapolis: Fortress, 2009.

———. *Priesthood, Pastors, Bishops: Public Ministry for the Reformation and Today*. Minneapolis: Fortress, 2008.

Wenk, Matthias. *Community-Forming Power: The Socio-Ethical Role of the Spirit in Luke-Acts*. Sheffield, UK: Sheffield Academic, 2000.

———. "Spiritual Gifts: Manifestations of the Kingdom of God." In Vondey, *Routledge Handbook of Pentecostal Theology*, 301–10.

Wetmore, Robert Kingston. "The Theology of Spiritual Gifts in Luther and Calvin: A Comparison." PhD diss., Concordia Seminary, 1992.

Wicks, Jared. "Holy Spirit—Church—Sanctification: Insights from Luther's Instructions on the Faith." *Pro Ecclesia* 2, no. 2 (1993): 150–72.

Wiles, J. Benjiman. *Becoming Like Jesus: Toward a Pentecostal Theology of Sanctification.* Cleveland, TN: CPT, 2021.

Wilkinson, Michael, and Steven M. Studebaker, eds. *A Liberating Spirit: Pentecostals and Social Action in North America.* Eugene, OR: Pickwick, 2010.

Williams, Anthony Ray. *Washed in the Spirit: Toward a Pentecostal Theology of Water Baptism.* Cleveland, TN: CPT, 2021.

Wilson, Sarah Hinlicky. "Dialogue: Spiritless Lutheranism, Fatherless Pentecostalism, and a Proposed Baptismal-Christological Corrective." *Pneuma* 34 (2012): 415–29.

———. *A Guide to Pentecostal Movements for Lutherans.* Eugene, OR: Wipf & Stock, 2016.

———. "How Is Your Revival Going?" *Lutheran Forum* 50, no. 2 (Summer 2016): 3–6.

Yee, Tham Wan. "Bridging the Gap between Holiness and Morality." *Asian Journal of Pentecostal Studies* 4, no. 2 (2001): 153–80.

Yong, Amos. *Beyond the Impasse: Toward a Pneumatological Theology of Religions.* Grand Rapids: Baker Academic, 2003.

———. *Discerning the Spirit(s): A Pentecostal-Charismatic Contribution to Christian Theology of Religions.* Sheffield, UK: Sheffield Academic, 2000.

———. *Renewing Christian Theology: Systematics for a Global Christianity.* Waco: Baylor University Press, 2014.

———. *Spirit of Love: A Trinitarian Theology of Grace.* Waco: Baylor University Press, 2012.

———. *The Spirit Poured Out on All Flesh: Pentecostalism and the Possibility of Global Theology.* Grand Rapids: Baker Academic, 2005.

Zahl, Simeon. *The Holy Spirit and Christian Experience.* New York: Oxford University Press, 2020.

Zizoulas, John D. *Being as Communion: Studies in Personhood and the Church.* Crestwood, NY: St. Vladimir's Seminary Press, 1997.

Author Index

Subject Index